QUALITATIVE RESEARCH FOR QUANTITATIVE RESEARCHERS

SAGE was founded in 1965 by Sara Miller McCune to support the dissemination of usable knowledge by publishing innovative and high-quality research and teaching content. Today, we publish over 900 journals, including those of more than 400 learned societies, more than 800 new books per year, and a growing range of library products including archives, data, case studies, reports, and video. SAGE remains majority-owned by our founder, and after Sara's lifetime will become owned by a charitable trust that secures our continued independence.

Los Angeles | London | New Delhi | Singapore | Washington DC | Melbourne

HELEN KARA

QUALITATIVE RESEARCH FOR QUANTITATIVE RESEARCHERS

Los Angeles | London | New Delhi
Singapore | Washington DC | Melbourne

SAGE Publications Ltd
1 Oliver's Yard
55 City Road
London EC1Y 1SP

SAGE Publications Inc.
2455 Teller Road
Thousand Oaks, California 91320

SAGE Publications India Pvt Ltd
B 1/I 1 Mohan Cooperative Industrial Area
Mathura Road
New Delhi 110 044

SAGE Publications Asia-Pacific Pte Ltd
3 Church Street
#10-04 Samsung Hub
Singapore 049483

Editor: Alysha Owen
Editorial assistant: Hanna Cavender-Deere
Senior project editor: Chris Marke
Project management: TNQ Technologies
Marketing manager: Ben Sherwood
Cover design: Shaun Mercier
Typeset by: TNQ Technologies
Printed in the UK

Library of Congress Control Number: 2021943003

British Library Cataloguing in Publication data

A catalogue record for this book is available from the British Library

ISBN 978-1-5297-5999-0
ISBN 978-1-5297-5998-3 (pbk)

At SAGE we take sustainability seriously. Most of our products are printed in the UK using FSC papers and boards. When we print overseas we ensure sustainable papers are used as measured by the PREPS grading system. We undertake an annual audit to monitor our sustainability.

To Su Connan, steadfast supporter and very dear friend.

BRIEF CONTENTS

DETAILED CONTENTS

ABOUT THE AUTHOR

Dr Helen Kara, FAcSS, has been an independent researcher since 1999 and an independent scholar since 2011. She writes about research methods and research ethics, and teaches doctoral students and staff at higher education institutions worldwide. Her books include *Creative Research Methods: A Practical Guide* and *Research Ethics in the Real World: Euro-Western and Indigenous Perspectives* for Policy Press, and four books in the SAGE Little Quick Fix series. She also writes comics and fiction. Helen is an Honorary Senior Research Fellow at the University of Manchester, and a Fellow of the Academy of Social Sciences. In 2021, at the age of 56, she was diagnosed autistic. Her neurodiversity explains her lifelong special interest in, and ability to focus on, words, language and writing.

ACKNOWLEDGEMENTS

My first thanks go to the Women in Academia Support Network for the online discussions that inspired me to write this book in particular, and in general for tremendous solidarity.

Six proposal reviewers and two manuscript reviewers helped this book to become much better than it would have been without their excellent interventions. I wish I could credit them for the improvements that resulted from their input. This collective thank-you seems inadequate, but as their anonymity must be maintained, it is the best I can do. If you are one of these reviewers, thank you very much and I hope you feel the published book does justice to your invaluable assistance.

I am grateful to Borja García and Lucas Seuren for helpful clarification of aspects of their work, and to Louise Couceiro for kindly updating me about the progress of her cultural probe methods.

I am thankful to Helen Knowler for alerting me to the knitted graph on Twitter and for putting me in touch with its originator. I am thankful to Abigail Parrish for providing an image of the knitted graph that I could use in this book.

Aly Owen and Charlotte Bush at SAGE were a terrific editorial team: engaged and responsive; I couldn't ask for more.

I am thankful to Policy Press for generously allowing me to reproduce in this book some work that they originally published.

My mother, Julie Miller, died from COVID-19 as I was starting work on this book; her lasting influence and example helped me to get it written during a time of considerable personal difficulty. I would like to thank my lovely family, and my dear friends, for their care during this time. I am particularly grateful to my father, Mark Miller, for funding the index. And I am most grateful of all to Nik Holmes for his unfailing support of my doing and my being.

1

INTRODUCTION

Chapter summary

- Considers the similarities and differences between quantitative and qualitative research
- Explains why I wrote this book
- Gives a brief history of research methods
- Outlines multi-modal research
- Reviews some ethical principles of qualitative research

If you're reading this book, you are probably a quantitative researcher, or a teacher of quantitative research, or both. Maybe you have to learn how to do qualitative research for your work or for your studies. Perhaps you are interested in the idea of qualitative research and the possibilities it offers, and you want to find out more. It could be mixed-methods research you're considering, rather than qualitative research as such, and you need more knowledge of qualitative research to balance your knowledge of quantitative research. Perhaps you are moving into a transdisciplinary field, such as conservation research or supply chain management research, where quantitative and qualitative methods are used. Or maybe you need to expand your teaching into mixed-methods research or qualitative research methods.

Academic disciplines, and the ways in which they approach research, can seem to be static. In fact they move with the times. Take pure mathematics, which has long been thought of as a numerical discipline based on deductive reasoning. Around the turn of the century, the advent of technology enabled the formation of a sub-discipline based on experimental methods (Sørensen, 2016). Experiments in science enable us to develop our understanding of some aspects of the world. In maths, experiments do not produce knowledge in the same way; they often result in a conjecture which then requires the application of conventional mathematical tools for the production of a theorem with a formal proof (Eilers and Johansen, 2017: 1–2). This is done with specialist computer software that enables mathematical insights to be generated, which is 'revolutionizing the way research mathematicians work' (Eilers and Johansen, 2017: ix).

Another example is qualitative physics, which developed in the 1980s to predict and explain the behaviour of mechanisms in qualitative terms (de Kleer and Brown, 1984: 7). The aim was to produce causal accounts of physical mechanisms that were easy to understand, being simpler than classical physics with its maths and equations, while retaining important distinctions such as state, momentum and oscillation. These accounts would provide the foundations for common-sense models for the next generation of expert artificial intelligence systems. Some physicists realised they needed to unpick the nature of intuition, and codify the non-specialist knowledge physicists draw on in solving problems, if they were ever to create artificial intelligence systems that could solve problems as well as human beings (de Kleer, 1993: 107). And the way to do that unpicking and codifying was through qualitative research.

People in other disciplines, too, have realised that quantitative information often provides only partial knowledge, and qualitative information may provide relevant elements to enrich analysis (Condotta et al., 2020: 153). Economists came to qualitative methods in the 1960s (Lancaster, 1965: 395); psychologists, after much debate, in the 1980s (Henwood and Pidgeon, 1992: 99) and engineers in the 2010s (Szajnfarber and Gralla, 2017: 498). Academic journals publishing qualitative research were set up for subject areas formerly thought of as quantitative: *Qualitative Health Research* was founded in 1991, and *Qualitative Psychology* was founded in 2013.

Also, there is currently a wider impulse for researchers of all kinds to have more methods available to use. Among other things, this is leading quantitative researchers to learn about qualitative methods (and vice versa). You may be feeling daunted or excited, resigned or impatient, apprehensive or intrigued at the prospect of learning about qualitative research. It may surprise you to learn that you already know more than you think. There is one research method which is so widespread, so common to all types of researchers, that it is not often thought of as a method. This method is writing. Whether you do laboratory research or field research, whether your discipline is quantum physics or marine biology, you have to write about your findings. You cannot simply provide pages of calculations or equations, graphs or charts without an accompanying narrative.

Writing is a creative process, even scientific writing. Scott Montgomery distinguishes between functional scientific writers who are 'ordinary engineers of the word' (2017: 26) and creative scientific writers who craft their prose more eloquently. I take his point, though I think he does some disservice to engineers who are often highly creative people (Ahearn, 2006: 111) and to functional writers too. Montgomery's implication is that people writing functionally are not creative, and I disagree. However functional or dry someone's writing may be, that person is still putting words together to make sentences that have not been made before, and putting those sentences together to make new paragraphs, and so on. Doing this kind of writing is creative work.

Part of the problem here is that English only has one word for creativity, unlike Polish which has two, *kreatywność* for everyday creativity and *twórczość* for high-level creativity (Nęcka et al., 2006: 272–3). Sternberg (2006) got around this by identifying small c creativity and big C creativity, which equate to the Polish terms. I would argue that the functional scientific writer is displaying small c creativity, while the creative scientific writer is displaying big C creativity. I expect you can think of examples of both types of writer from your own field, and you can probably define yourself as one or the other. So you are already using a creative qualitative method in your own research.

Quantitative and qualitative research are not oppositional but complementary. Each has strengths and limitations (Silverman, 2020: 10–22). Put very simply, quantitative research is generally good at establishing *what* is happening, qualitative research is generally good at establishing *why* and/or *how* that is happening. Quantitative research can tell us which brands of fruit juice people prefer by using sales figures from supermarkets as data. If that is all you need to know, then great; job done. If you need to know why that brand sells so well, qualitative research will enable you to answer questions such as: Is the taste of the juice the most important factor? Or the price? Or the packaging? Or how the juice looks in a glass? Are there other relevant factors such as preferences of people in the household of the person who buys the juice? And so on. Qualitative research is particularly useful in investigating something that is poorly understood, or that cannot be separated from its context (Szajnfarber and Gralla, 2017: 500). Because quantitative and qualitative research are complementary, they can work well together, as shown in Box 1.1.

Box 1.1

Quantitative and qualitative research working well together

A cluster randomised controlled trial (RCT) was conducted of home-based HIV testing uptake in Umzimkhulu, a poor, rural municipality of Kwa-Zulu Natal where HIV status is heavily stigmatised. The RCT used a community survey with 4,154 participants, and found that HIV prevalence was 8% (Doherty et al., 2013: 4), suggesting around 330 people tested positive. Within this RCT, another quantitative project was conducted to track the progress of consenting HIV-positive RCT participants in accessing and using appropriate care. As part of this quantitative project, field notes were made with 196 participants to record any reasons they gave for accessing and using care, or for not doing so. This shows that qualitative data can be of use in

(Continued)

3

quantitative projects. Also within the RCT, a qualitative project was undertaken by Reshma Naik and her colleagues to investigate the factors that influenced partici-pants to seek care. This involved 30 in-depth interviews with participants who sought care quickly, slowly or not at all (Naik et al., 2018: 724). Naik had access to the field notes from the quantitative project and decided to use them as supplementary data for her qualitative project. The qualitative project enabled the researchers to identify various factors influencing HIV-positive people's decisions about whether or not to seek care, and interactions between these factors. This led to the understanding that a holistic, rather than a purely health-oriented, approach to care is needed for people who are HIV-positive.

In summary, this shows how quantitative and qualitative research can play com-plementary parts in helping us to understand and overcome real-world problems.

Why I wrote this book

My first degree was a BSc in Social Psychology at the London School of Economics in the early 1980s when psychology was an entirely quantitative discipline, at least at an undergraduate level. I learned and practised the scientific method. After I graduated, I worked in various jobs that involved little or no research. By the end of the 1990s I was self-employed and some colleagues asked if I could take on a paid research project for them. We decided I could, I enjoyed the work, they appreciated the results, word got around and I was asked to do more. I decided I should upgrade my skills and did an MSc in Social Research Methods – quantitative and qualitative – graduating in 2001. My doctoral studies were qualitative; I remember an argument with my supervisors when I wanted to count and rank some aspects of my data, and they were horrified. I couldn't see a problem.

I wrote this book because I want more people to understand that quantitative and qualitative methods don't need to stand in opposition to one another. We will all be better researchers if we can break away from binary thinking because that inclines us towards conflict, competition and polarisation (Barker and Iantaffi, 2019: 185–7). And indeed we can see this in the history of 20th-century research. Robson and McCartan (2016) describe quantitative and qualitative researchers as 'warring tribes':

> The quantitative camp claimed that their scientific approach was the only way to conduct serious research and cast doubts on the value of qualitative research. Qualitative advocates countered that the dead hand of numbers and statistics was no way to understand anything worthwhile about people and their problems. (18)

Fortunately this is one conflict where the 21st century seems to be bringing peace and reconciliation. In fact the move towards mutual understanding began in the late 20th century, presumably when researchers from each camp decided to find out what the others were doing and whether there was anything useful to learn. This led to the advent of mixed-methods research, which initially meant collecting and analysing both quantitative and qualitative data to provide richer findings. This was later expanded to include mixed methods of reporting research or presenting research findings, the use of different theoretical lenses within the same piece of research and other such inventions of multiplicity. In turn, this led to the realisation that quantitative data could be collected in different ways, or qualitative data could be analysed in different ways – in effect, that research could be purely quantitative or purely qualitative and also usefully mix its methods. Researchers are now using the term 'multi-modal' to reflect this differentiation from the original 'mixed methods' with its implication of quantitative *and* qualitative data. I will say more about this later in the chapter.

A note on terminology: where research terms have been around for some time – clinical trial, survey, questionnaire, interview, focus group – they are reasonably well defined and commonly understood. With more innovative approaches to research methods it often takes a while for the terminology to become clear. This applies to whether those approaches are quantitative, qualitative or somewhere in between. You may well find people using the term 'multi-modal' to talk about what I define as 'mixed-methods', or vice versa. Within this book, though, I will define my terms, and do my best to use them consistently. (There is a useful glossary of research terms on the companion website for my 2017 book *Research and Evaluation for Busy Students and Practitioners* (2nd edn; Policy Press) (see Appendix 1 for URL.)

Essentially, I think we will all do better research if we understand more about methods. That includes quantitative and qualitative methods, as well as methods which may be either or both, such as multi-modal or creative approaches. Some research questions lend themselves towards either the quantitative or the qualitative, but many do not. Then the problem facing researchers is: which method(s) are most likely to help you answer your research question?

One thing I am certainly not doing in this book is arguing that qualitative research is better than quantitative research. Research, by definition, requires us to embrace uncertainty; we are trying to discover new knowledge, and we don't know what that will be, or what implications it will have, until we get there. We may not be sure of the best way to find out what we don't know. The more we know about research methods, the more effectively we can counter that uncertainty.

Qualitative and quantitative research – differences and similarities

One key difference between quantitative and qualitative research is a different way of thinking. There is a classic saying, often wrongly attributed to Albert Einstein, that 'not everything that can be counted counts, and not everything that counts can be counted'

(Cameron, 1963: 13). This points to the desire of many qualitative researchers to investigate the things that count but cannot easily be counted, such as people's experiences, emotions and ideas.

Yet it is a myth that qualitative research involves everything but the numbers. In fact numbers are often present in qualitative research: how many participants, how long it took to collect the data, what proportion of interviewees said X or Y. However, although quantification may be present, the data in qualitative research are not numerical. Then again, the data in quantitative research may not be numerical either; it may be human or animal tissue, collected or cultivated bacteria, people's self-reported attitudes or views, or any other non-numerical phenomena, as long as they can be counted or measured and so converted into numbers for analysis.

Another difference is in the ways quantitative and qualitative research deal with the research context (see Chapter 5 for a more detailed explanation of context). Quantitative researchers try to minimise the impact of the research context in order to isolate and manipulate variables. Qualitative researchers see the research context as a relevant factor and a potential resource. Quantitative researchers value concepts such as representativeness and extrapolation: if a sample is representative of a population, and appropriate analytic methods are used, the findings from the sample can illustrate phenomena in the population as a whole (Moon and Blackman, 2014: 1168). Qualitative researchers, in contrast, value concepts such as relevance and credibility. A community-based researcher would not seek to extrapolate her findings, but she would seek to make them as relevant and credible as possible for the community in its own context, and perhaps also publish them in case they might be of use elsewhere.

US researcher Janet Salmons offers a neat conceptualisation of qualitative researchers' interests at individual, group, community and nation/world levels:

1. Individual – lived experience, such as perceptions, attitudes and feelings
2. Group (or family, or team) – relationships, interpersonal dynamics and interactions
3. Community (or organisation, or institution) – systems, roles, policies, practices and people's experiences with these
4. Nation/world – systems or events that touch many lives (Salmons, 2016: 26, 30)

Also, quantitative and qualitative research are based on different kinds of reasoning. Quantitative research is based on deductive reasoning: formulate a hypothesis and then conduct experiments to test that hypothesis and help you reach (or deduce) conclusions. Qualitative research is based on inductive reasoning, which is more exploratory, drawing on a range of inputs, and open to continual revision (Saldaña, 2015: 26). Of course qualitative researchers also use deductive and other kinds of reasoning, just as quantitative researchers also use inductive and other kinds of reasoning. But the emphasis in quantitative research is on deductive reasoning, and in qualitative research the emphasis is on inductive reasoning.

Identifying these differences is useful up to a point, in helping us to think about the distinctions between quantitative and qualitative research. And these differences underline the fact that qualitative and quantitative research require different perspectives and skills (Szajnfarber and Gralla, 2017: 498). However, it would be misleading to suggest that quantitative and qualitative research are completely separate. In fact there are notable overlaps between them such that the distinction can at times break down (Bryman, 2016: 620–1). Qualitative researchers may need to count aspects of their data and use calculations to present the results. Quantitative researchers may choose to study things that can't be counted, such as emotions or other topics defined by Salmons as of interest to qualitative researchers (above). And there are many other examples, some of which you will find in this book.

Perhaps the difference is not so much between the different types of research as between researchers. Quantitative researchers prefer to work with the countable and measurable aspects of life, and tend to like a high level of certainty. Qualitative researchers prefer to work with the uncountable and unmeasurable aspects of life, and tend to be more comfortable with uncertainty. Some researchers are happy to work in both ways through mixed-methods research. Even so, if you are a quantitative researcher and find yourself needing to do qualitative research (or vice versa), that can be quite bewildering. You know that qualitative researchers collect non-numerical data and analyse it in mostly non-numerical ways. But, you are probably thinking, how do they do that? This book will provide some answers to your question.

Research methods – a brief history

The research methods we are most familiar with today have only been around for a few tens or hundreds of years. The first controlled clinical trial is said to have been conducted in 1747, by British naval surgeon James Lind who worked on the HMS *Salisbury*, a 50-gun ship which patrolled the English Channel. Lind was concerned about scurvy, a common and fatal disease of sailors. He had the idea that acids could arrest the symptoms of the disease, and decided to put this to the test. At the time there were 12 sailors on the ship with scurvy, so he divided them into six pairs, and gave each of them a different experimental treatment. These treatments were: cider, diluted sulphuric acid, a purgative mixture, vinegar, sea water or citrus fruit. The sailors who ate the citrus fruit made a dramatic recovery.

The 'controlled' nature of Lind's trial refers to his control of the variables, which was at the time a radical way to do research. He did not use a control group, nor was his experiment blinded. The first blinded experiment (where information that could influence participants was withheld) is said to have taken place in 1784 at the French

Academy of Sciences to investigate claims of mesmerism. One of the first double-blinded experiments (where both researcher and participants are not privy to information that could influence them) was held in 1835 in Nuremberg to evaluate homeopathy.

Around this time, in the United Kingdom, the social survey was being invented. The Manchester Statistical Society was founded in 1833 and the London Statistical Society (now the Royal Statistical Society) in 1834. The former claims the first house-to-house social survey, and the latter devised the questionnaire in 1838. No doubt the early questionnaires were entirely quantitative, or at least the responses were quantifiable. These days, questionnaires may also include – or even be entirely made up of – qualitative open questions, asking respondents to devise their own written answers.

Over 100 years ago, in the early 20th century, researchers began to adapt the journalistic method of interviewing as a way of gathering more in-depth information. The first focus groups were held in the early 1940s at Columbia University, in market research on radio soap operas.

The history of mixed-methods research is less clear. The current popularity of multi-modal research can make it seem like a new phenomenon, but quantitative researchers were also using qualitative techniques centuries ago in disciplines such as astronomy and geology (Maxwell, 2016). Qualitative researchers came to multi-modal research much later, towards the end of the 19th century (ibid). Possibly the first formalised mixed-methods approach is Q methodology, revealed to the world by its creator, William Stephenson, in the journal *Nature* in 1935 (Ramlo, 2016). Stephenson gained PhDs in physics and then psychology. He became interested in subjectivity, and wanted to find a way to study it systematically. The method he devised has gradually gained popularity among researchers from a variety of disciplines, and is now advocated by the International Society for the Scientific Study of Subjectivity (Robson and McCartan, 2016: 368) and its peer-reviewed journal, *Operant Subjectivity*. Q methodology is outlined in Box 1.2.

Box 1.2

Q methodology

There are three key elements to Q methodology: a concourse, a Q-sort and factor analysis.

A concourse is a complete set of statements that could be made about a phenomenon. Q researchers collect these statements from interviews, mainstream media, academic literature, professional or policy documents, social media, novels, films – anywhere they can gather sources of opinion. Then a set of statements are selected, often using a structured sampling approach, to include the various perspectives represented in the concourse. Each statement in the set is placed onto a separate card.

Q researchers aim to recruit participants with a variety of views on the research topic. In the Q-sort, participants arrange these cards first into piles on a scale from 'agree' to 'disagree'. Then the cards in the 'agree' and 'disagree' piles are ordered into a triangular grid, with the statements people feel strongly about at the edges, and statements they feel ambivalent about in the centre. The cells in the grid are numbered and this enables researchers to record card placement which provides the quantitative data. Q-sorts are usually done face-to-face, and the participant is encouraged to discuss their process with the researcher; this provides qualitative data which can be helpful at the interpretation stage.

While subjectivity is valued at the data gathering stage, the analytic procedure aspires to objectivity. The first step is to calculate a correlation matrix of all the Q-sorts, to show the level of agreement or disagreement between participants' points of view (Robson and McCartan, 2016). Then a version of factor analysis is used with the matrix, to identify clusters of people who think similarly. At the interpretive stage, researchers can go back to the cards and form a composite Q-sort as a visualisation of a cluster.

Q methodology varies in its application. The sorting scale can be of different lengths. Participants may be asked to write down their process, perhaps in response to a set of questions, rather than discussing it with the researcher. Researchers may do the analytic work by hand or using specialist software (see Chapter 8 for more about these options). However it is conducted, Q methodology can enable rich descriptions of what different groups of people think and feel about a topic.

Q methodology also courts controversy. As you read its description, you may have felt intrigued and inclined to investigate further. Or you may have felt repelled, formulating arguments in your head as you read. All methodologies can elicit emotional reactions because each one is based on a philosophical position which may attract some people and repel others. We will explore this in more detail in Chapter 2.

Up to the 1960s research was almost exclusively positivist and conducted by white able-bodied men. Since the 1960s there has been a huge increase in diversity among researchers, methods and approaches, which has both enhanced and complicated the research landscape. No book can offer comprehensive coverage of all the methods and approaches available to qualitative researchers today. My aim here is to familiarise you with the key principles of qualitative research, equip you to use the most common practices and signpost you to further reading and resources in areas where you might want to find out more.

Multi-modal research

The term 'mixed-methods research' was coined at a time when the idea of using both quantitative and qualitative data in one research project was still radical. This is more commonplace now and an example is shown in Box 1.3.

Box 1.3

Mixed-methods research

In 2015 UK researcher Carlie Goldsmith carried out an assessment of the needs of refugees, asylum seekers and migrants for the Royal Borough of Kingston upon Thames in London. She gathered relevant quantitative datasets plus data from interviews and focus groups with refugees, asylum seekers, migrants and staff of organisations working with refugees, asylum seekers and migrants. The datasets enabled Goldsmith to set the context for the research: the proportion of the population of Kingston who were born outside the United Kingdom; the proportion of households with no main-language English speaker; the number, age and gender of immigrants supported by Refugee Action Kingston and their immigration status; and other such relevant contextual factors. The interview and focus group data revealed eight key themes: 'language and communication; benefits and debt; mental health; social isolation; employment; housing and homelessness; health and access to health; and food and nutrition' (Goldsmith, 2015: 6). (Goldsmith also facilitated the completion of photo-diaries by refugees, migrants and asylum-seekers, which are described in more detail in Chapter 7.) The combination of the findings from the quantitative and the qualitative data enabled Goldsmith to assess the needs of refugees, asylum seekers and migrants in the Borough, and to create recommendations for meeting those needs.

These days, researchers are increasingly adopting the term 'multi-modal research' to reflect two more recent developments. First, a research project which is entirely quantitative, or entirely qualitative, may use a range of methods. The term 'mixed-methods', with its connotations of quantitative *and* qualitative, doesn't fit this model. Second, multiple methods can be used beyond data collection and analysis. A researcher could use different theories, or different reporting methods, or different ways of disseminating their findings. In these cases, 'multi-modal' is a more accurate description for the research. An example of multi-modal research is shown in Box 1.4.

Box 1.4

Multi-modal research

Sue Robinson and Andrew Mendelson, communication researchers in America, investigated the ways in which photographs and text interacted for people reading non-fiction magazine articles. They had each already run a project with a different design. Mendelson's project used pre- and post-testing via a survey with open-ended questions, either side of a randomised experimental trial followed by focus group discussions. Narrative and textual analysis was used for the focus group data. Robinson's project used pre- and post-testing either side of a randomised experimental trial, and followed the post-testing with in-depth interviews. She used grounded theory analysis for the interview data. (Grounded theory is covered in Chapter 9 of this book.) The researchers described their approach as a 'qualitative experiment' (2012: 333). In their view, the quantitative work alone would have identified cognitive processing through the difference between pre- and post-test results, but would not have revealed any information about the nature of that processing. The qualitative work alone would have revealed information about the nature of the processing but could not have isolated effects relating to specific variables. Combining them in a 'qualitative experiment' enabled the researchers to form detailed understandings of meanings derived by participants from their readings of the articles, and to compare the ways in which those meanings changed between the different types of media.

Ethics of qualitative and multi-modal research

Quantitative research ethics have, for a long time, been based on the biomedical principle of 'do no harm'. Of course this is an important principle, but more recently researchers have begun to argue that it doesn't go far enough. If you think about it, most researchers are working towards some kind of improvement: market researchers try to find better ways to meet consumer needs, clinical researchers seek to improve health outcomes, evaluators look for ways to improve service provision and so on. Early in the 21st century, researchers began to argue that research ethics needed to be based on wider principles, such as justice (Denzin, 2010; Jolivétte, 2015) or care (Brannelly, 2018).

Research ethics is a huge subject which has spawned many books and academic journals. Here I will offer some of the key points that are relevant to qualitative and multi-modal research.

Research governance, and its implementation through research ethics committees (known as institutional review boards in the United States), is far from the be-all and end-all of ethics in qualitative research. In fact this is a bureaucratic regulatory system, focusing on potential risks during data collection, and designed more to protect institutions than to promote and advance ethical research (Colnerud, 2014; Dingwall, 2016; Stark, 2012). In qualitative and multi-modal research – and, some would argue, in quantitative research too (Kara, 2018) – it is essential for researchers to think and act ethically throughout the research process (Poth, 2021).

There is no agreed definition of 'research ethics'. The term implies something homogeneous, but in fact it refers to a collection of diverse theories and practices (Ball and Janyst, 2008). Also, what is ethical in one context may not be ethical in another. Consider the action of pushing a knife into someone's abdomen. Carried out by one person to injure another: unethical. Carried out by a qualified surgeon in an operating theatre with the aim of saving life: ethical. Same action, different context. So, to think and act ethically, we have to consider the context. And 'context' includes more than location: it may also include intangible factors such as people's agendas, emotions or health conditions.

Let's consider an ethical principle which is widely held by researchers: the need to seek informed consent. It is generally regarded as good practice to give participants information about the research in writing, and to obtain written consent. Yet this is not always appropriate. When working with people from communities where communication is oral, or people who have (or may have) literacy difficulties, or people who are taking a risk by participating and may have no safe place to keep written information, we need to use alternatives such as verbal or audio-recorded consent. And at times there may be good reasons for using more than one approach to seeking consent; an example of this is shown in Box 1.5.

Box 1.5

Multi-modal consent seeking

Andrew Robinson and his colleagues in Australia conducted a wide-ranging multi-modal study of dementia encompassing patients' abilities, carers' stress levels and carers' experiences of dementia services. The researchers used both quantitative and qualitative data because, in their view, quantitative measures of dementia and its impact could only be fully meaningful if they were contextualised with information from carers' lives. They also took a multi-modal approach to seeking consent. The overarching principle was to build strong relationships with participants, with the aim to increase the quality of data they collected. In line with this, the researchers obtained verbal consent from carers on behalf of patients 'with utmost care' (Robinson et al., 2011: 338) in a process taking up to several weeks of liaison, explanation and discussion. Then, when they were sure carers had full understanding of the proposed research, the researchers sought written consent using documents that were 'exceptionally clear and concise' (ibid: 337). This process was informed by their understanding that potential participants were at risk of feeling overburdened, combined with their participant-centred focus which led them to prioritise participants' well-being and interests over researchers' interests and the research aims.

We can see from Box 1.4 that Robinson and his colleagues worked hard to develop and implement an ethical procedure for seeking and obtaining consent. Ethical research is often good quality research, and so it proved here. The researchers achieved a 100% participant retention rate, even though they collected data using several methods over 12 weeks. Also, most participants reported enjoying their involvement in the research. And while there is no control group to enable a full assessment of methodological impact on data quality, the researchers described their data collection as 'successful and rewarding' (Robinson et al., 2011: 342). They seem to have used what Cheryl Poth terms 'ethical reasoning', which she defines as: 'Making a decision in response to a moral dilemma based on a careful and thorough assessment of the different options in light of the facts, circumstances, and ethical issues' (Poth, 2021: 130).

Not all research methods are ethical. Forcing or coercing people to take part in research is a recruitment method that is in use (Cox and McDonald, 2013), including by some national Governments for their census research, though you won't find it in the textbooks because it is deeply unethical. Sadly, there are other unethical methods in use around the world.

Many methods are neutral in themselves, so whether or not their use is ethical depends on the research context. For example, an online questionnaire is, arguably, a reasonably ethical method to use when your participants are college students; it may not be an ethical method to use with people who have severe dyslexia. And a method which may be regarded as ethical in one community or culture may not be regarded as ethical in another (Tuck and Guishard, 2013). Some qualitative researchers argue for methods that give participants more control over the content of the data, then regard it as the researcher's job to find a good way to analyse that data. We can see an example of this in Box 1.6.

Box 1.6

Methods offering participants more power

Dawn Mannay (2010), who describes herself as an Indigenous Welsh researcher, conducted multi-modal qualitative research to find out about the experiences of mothers and daughters on a social housing estate. She asked some participants to draw maps, some to take photographs and some to create collages, to provide visual representations of their homes and surroundings. Then she used each visual output as the basis for an interview with its creator. This gave her participants much more autonomy within the research setting, and enabled Mannay to learn about aspects of her participants and their lives that she might not have thought to ask about if she had used a more conventional interview schedule.

Interestingly, no visual method used by Mannay seemed to have any particular advantage or disadvantage when compared with the others. Mannay's research is creative and innovative, and we will see more details of her research and other examples of such research in Chapter 7.

How to use this book

You may feel tempted to dive straight into one of the data collection or analysis chapters. I would advise against that course of action. This chapter has begun to demonstrate that one of the big differences between quantitative and qualitative research is that they are often based on very different philosophical positions. Without a full and clear understanding of these positions, and the differences between them, the practicalities will make a lot less sense. Worse still, you could end up misinterpreting your results (Moon and Blackman, 2014: 1167). So I would advise you to read Chapters 2 and 3 as a minimum, and to make sure you understand the concepts set out in those chapters. After that, if you like, you can dip in and out of the other chapters to find particular information – and what you find should make sense, which will enable you to use it more effectively.

Summary of the book

This Introduction has introduced and outlined the concepts of qualitative and multi-modal research, and explained why the term 'multi-modal' is more accurate and useful than 'mixed-methods'. It included a brief history of qualitative and multi-modal research methods, and introduced the ethical dimensions of qualitative and multi-modal research. It also outlined the rationale for the book, explaining that it is an overview text which signposts readers to more detailed information on methods of interest.

Chapter 2 defines and explains the important concepts of ontology and epistemology. It discusses methodology and outlines the differences between methodology, methods and approaches to research. The chapter also covers asset-based research and explores the relationship between research and activism.

Chapter 3 covers the role of theory in qualitative research. It explains what theory is and what it is for. Classifications of theories are discussed, and the chapter offers illustrative examples of some ways theory can be used in research.

Chapter 4 focuses on research design. It considers the formulation of research questions and sampling strategies for qualitative research. It demonstrates the importance of planning each stage of the research process carefully at the outset. The chapter also introduces the impact of colonialism, and considers collaboration, in research design.

Chapter 5 looks at the need to set qualitative research in context, whether through an academic literature review, a document analysis or some other means. The chapter considers the potential role of field notes in contextualisation and outlines some of the key issues in writing that arise when contextualising research.

Chapter 6 discusses the mainstream methods of gathering qualitative data: questionnaires, interviews, focus groups and observation. It explores the role of the case study in qualitative research, outlines the options for using field notes as data and discusses some of the ways technology can help in gathering qualitative data.

Chapter 7 considers alternative methods of gathering qualitative data. This chapter covers some ways to enhance interviews and focus groups and some techniques for gathering arts-based data. It looks at embodied data gathering and multi-modal data gathering and outlines some debates around gathering qualitative data using video and other digital methods.

Chapter 8 introduces the main points to consider when working with qualitative data. These include how to manage, store, prepare and code your data, and whether to do your analysis by hand or with the help of specialist computer software. The chapter also discusses the pros and cons of collaborating on qualitative data analysis.

Chapter 9 begins by reviewing debiasing strategies that can be used during analytic work, and looking at the role of theory in qualitative data analysis. Then it outlines the main types of qualitative data analysis and considers innovation in qualitative data analysis.

Chapter 10 outlines the similarities and differences between reporting on quantitative, qualitative and multi-modal research. It discusses good practice in research reporting and outlines the potential for research reporting of a range of creative techniques and formats. The chapter also distinguishes multi-modal reporting from multi-modal research.

Chapter 11 covers good practice in presenting and disseminating qualitative research findings. It looks at performative, complex, multi-modal, collaborative and arts-based presentation methods, and at arts-based and multi-modal methods of dissemination. It considers how dissemination can be linked with other aspects of research and looks at how dissemination may be carried out by people other than researchers.

Reflective questions

1. Why do you want or need to learn about qualitative research?
2. Which aspects of qualitative research do you particularly like or dislike?
3. What are the implications of this for your learning practices?
4. How could you work with your emotional response to qualitative research to enhance your learning?
5. What are the ethical implications of your emotional response to qualitative research?

2

WAYS OF KNOWING

Chapter summary

- Introduces the concepts of ontology and epistemology, positivism and post-positivism
- Distinguishes between methodologies and methods
- Outlines realist methodologies and gives an example
- Outlines constructivist methodologies and gives an example
- Outlines interpretivist methodologies, introduces the concept of reflexivity and gives examples of both
- Introduces transformative methodologies and gives an example
- Introduces asset-based research
- Discusses research and activism

Introduction

This chapter introduces some important concepts which, though complex, are not difficult to understand. Many are as relevant to quantitative as to qualitative research. However, it is possible to do much quantitative research without attending to these concepts, whereas with qualitative research they often have a higher profile.

If these concepts are not strictly necessary for the doing of research, you might ask: why are we attending to them? The answer is: because they can help us gain a fuller understanding of our reality and how we relate to that reality (Dahlberg and Dahlberg, 2020: 891). This in turn helps us to create better quality research.

Qualitative researchers (and, increasingly, quantitative and multi-modal researchers) view reality as something we are part of, not something that exists independently of us. How we view reality, and what we do with our views of reality, has a profound influence on our research. This applies whether or not we attend to the relevant concepts. However, if we do not, we are to some extent working in the dark. If we take a little time to understand what we believe and how we think we know what we know, our research activities will be more fully informed.

One caveat: thinking on these topics is still evolving, and in some respects contested. This means you may find this material presented in slightly different ways in other books on qualitative research, such as those by Creswell and Poth (2018) and Denzin and Lincoln (2018). Methodology is where research methods intersect most closely with philosophy, and philosophy is full of disagreement (Plant, 2012), so it is not surprising that this extends into people's thinking about research methodologies.

Ontology and epistemology

These long words sound like very complicated concepts, but really they are quite straightforward. They are important because all research methodologies are aligned with ontological and epistemological positions.

If you have a background in computer science, information science or related topics, you may understand ontology as a way of naming and defining properties and categories of a subject area, and showing how they are related. In qualitative research, ontology, or ontological position, has a different meaning: essentially, it means someone's worldview. Everyone has a worldview formed by their upbringing, society, culture, religion or belief, political views, and other such factors, combined with their personality. Your worldview can change, but usually quite slowly and in response to major life events, so it should not be too hard to figure out your ontological position at a particular point in time. And it is worth that small effort because your ontological position will influence the way you do research (Bryman, 2016: 30).

Epistemology, or epistemological position, means how we understand things to be learned or known. Again we all have an epistemological position, or a theory of knowledge: the principles and rules we use to decide what can be known and how, and how that knowledge can be validated and shown (Mason, 2016: 7). Our epistemological position can change more quickly than our ontological position, on the basis of new evidence – though it is by no means a given that evidence contradicting someone's epistemological position will cause that position to change (Barger et al., 2016: 1). Ontology and epistemology are intimately linked (Moon and Blackman, 2014: 1170), so someone's epistemological position is likely to be closely aligned with their ontological position. I will explain this in more detail in relation to some philosophical frameworks, or methodologies, that are relevant to research.

From positivism to post-positivism

All research exists within philosophical frameworks, whether stated or unstated, and that includes quantitative research. Quantitative research was historically allied with positivism which, like all human thought systems, is not homogenous but includes a range of views and perspectives. However, in general, positivism claimed to be objective, fact-based and value-free.

The rapid rise of positivist thought in Euro-Western civilisation is remarkable: from invention to dominance in well under a century. Positivism was developed by French philosopher Auguste Comte in the 1830s and 1840s, and his influential work was translated into English in the 1860s. By the start of the 20th century positivism had become aligned with the dominant 'scientific method' (Kaboub, 2008: 343) in the Euro-Western world.

The 'scientific method' involves empirical observation, i.e. observation which is experimental, verifiable and replicable, because potentially confounding factors or variables have been controlled. 'Observation' here does not simply mean looking at things, but also counting, weighing, measuring and so on. The aim is to investigate reality, which is viewed as singular and separate from people, and to establish facts and, ideally, universal laws. Scientists, who did this work, were required – and believed – to be impartial and objective, and the whole project was held to be value-free.

Ontological positions associated with positivism include: the world is external to and separate from people, and there is a single objective reality which is unaffected by other factors and has the capacity to be fully understood. Epistemological positions associated with positivism include: learning comes from actions such as observation and measurement.

The scientific method developed alongside positivist philosophy, and for much of the 20th century they seemed to go hand in hand. However, positivism and the scientific method were not as secure and homogeneous as they appeared, and philosophers of science provided debating points which helped to widen the field of thought. In the 1930s, the Austrian philosopher of science Karl Popper put forward his idea of falsifiability (also known as refutability) which means that a statement or a hypothesis can be contradicted by evidence. This is important because it is not always possible to observe all of the available evidence. For example, to prove that all cats have four legs, you would need to check the physical manifestation of every cat in the world. However, to disprove this statement, you only need to see one three-legged cat. Popper claimed that falsifiability, alongside empirical observation, was key to the scientific method.

Then in the 1960s, the American philosopher of science Thomas Kuhn suggested that as knowledge develops, scientific fields do not develop in a linear way. Instead, they experience 'paradigm shifts', or changes in what is known and how, as new understandings unfold. No paradigm is commensurate with its predecessor or its successor; their assumptions and methods will diverge (Bryman, 2016: 637). Kuhn's view was that ideas change – even ideas about fundamental concepts like truth – such that these cannot be established by an objective method, but require the consensus of a community. Kuhn called for science to acknowledge and incorporate subjectivity, claiming that any 'objective' research is in fact heavily influenced by the researchers' worldviews and biases.

In the 1970s, the German philosopher of science Paul Feyerabend challenged the scientific method by proclaiming that there are no universal rules for scientists to follow in their work. He valued innovation, creativity and opportunism in research. The work of Feyerabend, Kuhn and Popper was highly influential in Euro-Western thought. As a result, classical positivism, with its emphasis on empirical observation combined with objectivity, has been replaced by post-positivism. Post-positivists value quantitative research and a scientific approach, and regard reality as separate from people, but they have a more flexible outlook than positivists. They still aspire to objectivity, but recognise that researchers have limitations such as bias, and so agree that reality can only be partially known or understood (Robson and McCartan, 2016: 22). They also understand the belief that research can be theory-free is in itself a theoretical position (Collins and Stockton, 2018: 2) (theory is covered in more detail in Chapter 3).

Ontological positions associated with post-positivism include: the world is external to and separate from people, and there is a single objective reality which is unaffected by other factors, though this can only be partially understood. Epistemological positions associated with post-positivism include: learning comes from actions such as observation and measurement.

Methodologies and methods

In research, positivism and post-positivism are both methodologies. We will consider some other methodologies later in the chapter. First, let's take a look at the difference between methodologies, methods and approaches to research. We will also discuss the relationship of these to each other and to research topics and questions.

A methodology is a philosophical framework for research which is based on beliefs and values. Positivism is a methodology which, as we have seen, is based on the belief that reality is singular and separate from people, and which values objectivity, neutrality and facts. Post-positivism is a methodology which is based on the belief that reality is separate from people, though it can only be known partially because of people's limitations, and which also values objectivity. It is not essential to conduct research within a methodological framework, but it can be helpful for logical coherence.

There are also approaches to research which are neither methodologies nor methods. These include evaluation, ethnography and fieldwork. Evaluation is a type of applied research which is intended to assess the effectiveness of a service, intervention or policy. There are different philosophies of evaluation, such as realist evaluation (Pawson and Tilley, 1997) and utilisation-focused evaluation (Patton, 2008), which are based on different beliefs and values. Ethnography originates from anthropology and is now used in a wide range of disciplines. The word is drawn from Greek terms for 'people' and 'writing', and the approach is most widely used to study the culture of a group or community. Fieldwork is most often associated with geography and involves gathering data outside standard research settings such as laboratories or libraries. Evaluation, ethnography and fieldwork can be used within different methodological frameworks and can in turn incorporate different methods; quantitative as well as qualitative.

Methods are the tools we use to conduct research, such as questionnaires, polls and statistics. There is no direct relationship between methodologies and methods; most methods can be used with most methodologies. However, methodologies and methods are inextricably linked with a research topic and question(s) (Mason, 2016). There are no prescribed relationships, but your research topic and question, plus the context for your research work, should guide your choice of methodology and methods. This is discussed in more detail in Chapter 4.

Realist methodologies

Realist methodologies are explicit about their use of theory. Theory is covered in more detail in Chapter 3 but, in brief, realist methodologies may use 'grand' or 'middle-range' theories (Merton, 2012[1949]; Mills, 1959). Grand theories include Marx's theory of social class, Foucault's theory of power and Butler's theory that gender is performed. This type of theory is most often used as a lens through which researchers can bring a specific focus to their work and their findings. Middle-range theories are the theories of people involved in the topic being investigated, which 'can be tested and refined through research' (Kara, 2017: 44).

Realist methodology views facts as always questionable and laden with theory. Knowledge is seen as socially and historically produced. Reality is thought to be complex and stratified into different levels such as individual, group, institutional and social realities (Robson and McCartan, 2016: 31). Also, realists acknowledge the importance of context. Gunpowder is often used as an example (Robson and McCartan, 2016: 33). Under laboratory conditions, it is easy to prove that gunpowder ignites when brought into contact with a flame. This is known as successionist or sequential causation: thing 1 (flame), when applied to gunpowder, causes thing 2 (explosion). However, realist researchers point out that the context for the test is an essential factor. Gunpowder will not ignite if no oxygen is present, or if the powder is damp, or if the flame is not applied for long enough (Robson and McCartan, 2016: 33). This is called generative causation: the context enables thing 1 (flame) to cause thing 2 (explosion).

The principle of generative causation, with its recognition of the importance of context, means that realist methodologies can be applied to real-world research such as evaluation. Realist methodologies incorporate the assumption that we can find out why something in society works, or doesn't work, by uncovering its hidden mechanisms (Stame, 2013: 362) and identifying the influence of contextual factors. This diverges from the positivists' emphasis on empirical observation as the only means of discovery (which still underpins some evaluation research work) and enables researchers to find out not only what happens but also how and why (Kara, 2017: 44). However, realists do expect research to be replicable if the context can be replicated.

Ontological positions associated with realism include: the world and its inhabitants and things are entwined within contexts. Epistemological positions associated with realism include: learning comes from assessment of phenomena in context.

Box 2.1 shows an example of realist research in practice.

Box 2.1

Realist research in practice

Supply chain management research is transdisciplinary, encompassing disciplines such as engineering, organisation studies and geography (New, 1997: 15). A 'supply chain' is a complex concept with a variety of meanings. It most commonly refers to the supply chain of an individual organisation such as a retailer or manufacturer, or the supply chain of a specific product such as gold or wine, or is used as a catch-all term for the management of purchasing, materials and distribution (New, 1997: 16). Supply chain management researchers Neil Towers, Ismail Abushaikha, James Ritchie and Andreas Holter conducted three case studies of supply chain management, one of which used a realist methodology. The aim of this research was to identify scope for improvements in transport purchasing for a medium-sized UK industrial manufacturer with a multi-national supply chain (Towers et al., 2020: 450). The researchers used action research, a participatory and practical method, and conducted ten cycles of action research over a six-year period. (See Chapter 6 for more details of action research.) This enabled an iterative approach to making and testing improvements, which ultimately improved the profitability of the company by over £6m (Towers et al., 2020: 452).

In summary, the use of realist methodology enabled Towers and his colleagues to include context as a key factor, which helped them to link evidence to conclusions based on that context and so make causal explanations (Towers et al., 2020: 450). Also, the action research method supported participants to generate, test and develop their own middle-range theories during the research process.

Constructionist methodologies

Constructionist methodologies are explicit about being subjective and value-based. They include phenomenology and symbolic interactionism. The constructionist view is that reality does not exist independently of people, but is constructed by social actors. Therefore reality cannot be objectively observed and measured because it is being constructed by the same social actors who would be doing the observing and measuring – indeed, the actions of observing and measuring would contribute to the construction of those people's realities. As this suggests, constructionists do not regard reality as singular; they think there are multiple realities (Robson and McCartan, 2016: 24–5). Furthermore, this goes beyond the realist view of stratified realities; for constructionists, there is potentially a different reality for each person on the planet.

Constructionists argue that various social phenomena, such as money and institutions, are constructed rather than real. If you think about it, money only works because everyone agrees to the rules about how money operates in society – and those rules were constructed by people. Similarly with institutions. Monarchy can be defined as an institution; you can probably think of monarchies around the world which people have constructed, and others that people have destroyed.

Researchers using a constructionist methodology and doing primary research with people would be likely to view those people not as research participants, but as co-constructors of knowledge through research (Robson and McCartan, 2016: 25). Most constructionist researchers use qualitative methods to enable them to include multiple perspectives. One of the exciting things about constructionist methodologies is that they support research into less tangible topics such as emotion and culture.

Ontological positions associated with constructionism include: people construct or co-construct facts and phenomena. Epistemological positions associated with constructionism include: learning comes from creating or co-creating meaning out of experience. Box 2.2 shows an example of constructivist research in practice.

Box 2.2

Constructivist research in practice

Towers and his colleagues, whose work we saw first in Box 2.1, conducted a second case study, of the supply chain in the fashion industry in the Middle East, using a constructivist methodology alongside resource-based theory (RBT). The aim was to assess the level of integration of the supply chain, i.e. the extent to which everyone involved worked within the same system. RBT focuses on resources that can help organisations construct unique strategies to maximise opportunities and minimise threats, and so increase their competitive advantage (Grant, 1991: 130). An integrated supply chain could be viewed as such a resource. The research was an

(Continued)

exploratory study of seven organisations, over three years, using semi-structured interviews with supply chain managers plus documentary data. RBT was used to look at three areas: suppliers, customers and the internal functions of organisations. This combination of theory and methodology helped the researchers to understand that supply chain integration enabled more information to be visible, and that this helped companies understand how to increase their competitive advantage (Towers et al., 2020: 450).

In summary, the constructionist methodology allowed for the different perspectives of manufacturers, suppliers and customers, and took into account the complexity of the business world (Towers et al., 2020: 449).

If the role of theory in this case study doesn't quite make sense to you, don't worry; we will be discussing theory in more detail in Chapter 3.

Interpretivist methodologies

Like constructionist methodologies, interpretivist methodologies are explicitly subjective and value-based. Also, interpretivists would certainly subscribe to the notion that there are as many realities as there are people. However, where constructionists view reality as something we construct, interpretivists view reality as something we interpret. Like realist methodologies, interpretivist methodologies acknowledge the importance of context. Where they differ, though, is that interpretivists regard each context as unique, and so would not expect research to be replicable.

An interpretivist would say that as you read this chapter, you are interpreting the material I have written in accordance with your own subjectivity, biases, prejudices and experience – i.e. your reality. And this is not a simple matter of I write – you read. As I write, I am interpreting the work of others from books, journal articles, websites and so on, which I pick up and put down, or click around in, to stimulate my own thought processes. Then there are further interpretations of my work by peer reviewers, based on the intersection between my draft and their reality, and those interpretations lead to their input which I then interpret for use as I complete the manuscript. So your reading is based on layers of interpretive work by a variety of scholars in a range of contexts, as well as being influenced by your own reality.

One example of interpretivist methodology is hermeneutic methodology. Also, both phenomenology and symbolic interactionism can be used by interpretivist as well as constructionist researchers. Interpretivist researchers privilege reflexivity, or 'a form of critical thinking which aims to articulate the contexts that shape the processes of doing research and subsequently the knowledge produced' (Lazard and McAvoy, 2020: 160). Reflexivity requires critical self-examination in an attempt to help researchers prevent their work being dominated by their preferences, prejudices and biases (Finlay, 2011: 114). And of course reflexivity is itself an interpretive process (Dean, 2017: 10).

Quantitative researchers from a range of disciplines and fields have argued for the usefulness of reflexivity in quantitative as well as qualitative and multi-modal research. These include (but are not limited to) quantitative researchers working in midwifery (Kingdon, 2005: 622), behavioural science (Shimp, 2007: 154), evidence-based social work (Cluver et al., 2014: 53) and sociology and Native studies (Walter and Andersen, 2016: 50). However, it is acknowledged that reflexivity may be a challenging approach for quantitative researchers who are used to dealing with the scientific method, facts, P values and algorithms (Kara, 2018: 118; Lazard and McAvoy, 2020: 160). Nevertheless, it is clear that the use of reflexivity has a positive impact on research quality (Johnson et al., 2020: 145) (see Chapter 4 for more on research quality).

Box 2.3 offers some guidance on how to practice reflexivity.

Box 2.3

Reflexivity in practice

There are no set rules or guidelines for how to practise reflexivity, though there are some clues in the literature. First and perhaps most importantly, there is no 'right way' to do reflexivity – and, indeed, the process involves facing up to the imperfections of ourselves, our research and the world around us. 'We may be hypocritical, inconsistent, messy, or unsure, but the important thing is to try' (Dean, 2017: 147).

However, there is a 'wrong way' to do reflexivity, which involves falling into one or more of the traps of narcissism, self-indulgence or meaningless regression (Dean, 2017: 141; Lazard and McAvoy, 2020: 167). Reflexivity must not become your main focus; it should always be used to serve your research purpose, not the other way around.

Lazard and McAvoy (2020) recommend using an epistemological focus to help your reflexive work serve your research purpose by expanding beyond the personal and into the realms of the 'nature, scope and limitations of knowledge' (167) as well as creating scope for making insightful links between personal and epistemological elements. They also offer some questions (168–73) which can be used as a starting point in practising reflexivity:

1. Why have you chosen your research topic rather than another?
2. Why are your research questions important to you?
3. What are the rationales for your ontological and epistemological positions?
4. Why are you working with theory in the way that you are?
5. How will your choices and assumptions about the methods you plan to use affect the knowledge you produce?
6. How does your relationship with your participants contribute to this process?

(Continued)

7. What effect do your last two answers have on your analytic work with your data?
8. How do you position yourself in your research?
9. How will you make that explicit for your audiences?
10. What will you need to disclose about yourself in this process?
11. Are there aspects of yourself or your life that would be useful to disclose but which you are not willing to reveal?
12. If so, what will the impact of that concealment be on your research?

Much of this work can be accomplished through internal dialogue, though it is always worth writing down your thoughts and conclusions at some point (see the section on field notes in Chapter 5 for different ways to do this). However, it does not have to be a wholly solo endeavour. Seeking and including the perspectives of colleagues, participants and others may add richness to your reflexive practice (Lazard and McAvoy, 2020: 167).

Although I have introduced reflexivity in connection with interpretivist research, I actually think it is relevant for all methodologies. It is also relevant at all stages of the research process. This is demonstrated by the reflective questions at the end of each chapter in this book.

Ontological positions associated with interpretivism include: people interpret facts and phenomena. Epistemological positions associated with interpretivism include: learning comes from identifying and interpreting multiple realities. Box 2.4 shows an example of interpretivist research in practice, again from the researchers whose work we have seen in Boxes 2.1 and 2.2.

Box 2.4

Interpretivist research in practice

Towers and his colleagues conducted a third case study, to investigate relationships between customers and production processes in four medium-sized UK manufacturers of fashion products, and the consequences of those relationships. They used 64 in-depth semi-structured interviews with key informants from the manufacturers, observational assessments and process mapping of production operations, over a two-year period, supplemented by documentary data (Towers et al., 2020: 447). This process of continual interpretation led to three important insights into the relationships and their consequences.

In summary, the researchers were able to understand their participants' perspectives. Altogether the method and data offered 'a rich source of hermeneutic information through the continual interpretation of observations and objects enabling a greater understanding and meaning of the production activity control and trading relationships phenomena in a dynamic and constantly changing small business environment' (Towers et al., 2020: 447).

The work of Towers et al. in Boxes 2.1, 2.2 and 2.4 also shows that different methodologies can be used to good effect within the same field and/or research area.

Transformative methodologies

Transformative methodologies are explicit about research causing – as well as, sometimes, studying – change. These methodologies include feminist research, activist or emancipatory research, participatory research, community-based research, queer research and asset-based research. Many transformative methodologies were devised by people experiencing oppression or marginalisation: women, people with disabilities, people from the LGBTIQA+ communities, people of colour. Some of the oppression these people experienced was at the hands of researchers, as a result of which various groups of oppressed and marginalised people around the world decided that if they were to be the subjects of research, they would do that research themselves. This removes the conventional quantitative researcher's aspiration of distance between researcher and researched, but now we know from experience that being close to a topic, while not offering a guarantee, does have the potential to enable, rather than act as a barrier to, high quality research. (See Chapter 4 for more on research quality.)

One thing all transformative methodologies have in common is the desire to reduce power imbalances and redress inequalities. This strong ethical focus allies transformative methodologies with aspirations to social justice (Kara, 2020: 27). Box 2.5 shows an example of transformative research in practice: **emancipatory research** from the UK in the early 21st century.

Box 2.5

Transformative research in mental health

Diana Rose is a mental health service user and activist. She worked with other researchers who had experience of mental illness and mental health services, and with clinician researchers, as part of a user-led research group at the UK's Institute of Psychiatry. This group was commissioned by the UK Government to investigate the effectiveness of electro-convulsive therapy (ECT). ECT is a treatment which involves applying electric shocks to a patient's brain to induce seizures (Rose et al., 2002). It was controversial because it led to persistent memory loss in around one-third of its

(Continued)

recipients. Rose and her colleagues collected 26 academic reports of research into ECT, nine of which were produced in collaboration with researchers who had experience of mental illness and mental health services. Rose et al. also collected 139 individual accounts of receiving ECT from email forums and other internet sources. These sources were analysed using quantitative and qualitative techniques including a combination of content analysis (themes decided before close reading of data) and discourse analysis (content and detail of those themes emerging from data, and online interactions attended to). (See Chapter 9 for more on content and discourse analysis.) The researchers found that the 17 purely academic research reports identified much higher levels of satisfaction with ECT than the collaborative academic research or the accounts collected online. The highest levels of satisfaction were recorded from information patients gave to their doctors immediately after treatment. Rose et al. concluded that patients were expressing more satisfaction than they felt, in the hope of avoiding further treatments (Thornicroft and Tansella, 2005: 2). Later and online, or in discussion with researchers who were also users of mental health services, people felt able to be more honest about their views. These conclusions were widely disseminated, and influenced both change to the national UK guidelines on ECT and a Royal College of Psychiatrists review of training and information (SCIE, 2007: 9–11).

In summary, Rose combined her insider knowledge with good research practice to gather evidence which transformed psychiatric services in the United Kingdom.

Ontological positions associated with transformative methodologies include: people, facts and other phenomena can combine to create change. Epistemological positions associated with transformative methodologies include: learning comes from relationships with people and the environment.

A more recent development is **asset-based research**, which was prompted by people noticing that research was inclined to focus only on problems and deficits. These critiques have come from single disciplines, transdisciplinary work and oppressed and marginalised groups.

The single disciplines making these critiques include organisation studies and psychology. Organisation studies tended to focus on problems, with the aim of finding out how they could be solved. Appreciative Inquiry was an approach devised by David Cooperider and Suresh Srivastva in the late 1980s in the United States. This approach is 'the study of what gives life to human systems when they focus at their best' (Whitney and Trosten-Bloom, 2010: 1). Research in organisations, using this approach, began by identifying the strengths and aspirations of the organisation before considering any problems that might exist. Similarly, psychology tended to focus on problems such as mental illness, trauma and criminality. Around the turn of the century, a positive psychology movement began to develop, to study phenomena such as well-being, happiness and resilience (Seligman and Csikzentmihalyi, 2000: 5).

An example of asset-based transdisciplinary thinking comes from the Indian philosopher and economist Amartya Sen. He argues that it is too reductive to focus on people's needs and rights alone, without taking into account their capabilities (Sen, 1979: 218). So a person in fear of their life from a repressive regime in their country needs, and has the right to seek, asylum overseas – but if they don't have the capability to get to another country, their needs and rights are irrelevant. Sen's capabilities approach could be seen as a refinement of realist methodology.

Indigenous peoples may be defined as the native peoples of lands that have been colonised by settlers from other nations (Cram et al., 2013: 16; Lambert, 2014: 1). Indigenous peoples have been, and are, systematically oppressed and marginalised by colonisers – and research has been, and is, a tool in this process (Dunbar-Ortiz, 2014: 231; Moodie, 2010: 818; Rix et al., 2018: 5, 7). Euro-Western researchers who study Indigenous peoples often start from a deficit model, focusing on problems with health, education, housing and so on, rather than looking at Indigenous people's strengths and the positive contributions they can make to society (Ball and Janyst, 2008: 37; Chilisa, 2020: 239; García et al., 2013: 368; Sherwood, 2013: 204). Indigenous researchers Maggie Walter (from Tasmania) and Chris Andersen (from Canada) use national censuses as a case study. The national censuses of many powerful countries claim objectivity and impartiality, though census questions are set or approved by government ministers for political reasons (Kara, 2018: 28). Walter and Andersen (2013), who are quantitative researchers themselves, argue that quantitative research is shaped by the researcher's ontological and epistemological positions (56). They say, of the Australian census: 'While the overt intention is to disseminate a neutral statistical reflection of the Australian Indigenous social and economic reality, this perception fails to acknowledge that it is a particular view of reality being reflected' (37). This argument is built on a range of examples, from national census questions being set with no involvement from Indigenous people, through statistical calculations being used for comparisons in ways that distort the picture, to data being collected about aspects of Indigenous peoples' lives such as 'risky health behaviours' (AIHW, 2011a: 36, cited in Walter and Andersen, 2013: 39) when there are no parallel data being collected in respect of non-Indigenous peoples.

It is interesting to note that census research undergoes no ethical scrutiny. In some countries, such as Australia and the United Kingdom, the ethical principle of informed consent is abandoned in favour of coercion in census research (Kara, 2018: 28).

Summary of methodologies, ontologies, epistemologies and methods

I hope it is clear by now that every methodology has value. It is also fair to say that every methodology also has weaknesses. This is why it is important to understand the different qualitative methodologies, so you can make use of whichever one is most likely to help with your own research.

Table 2.1 sums up the different methodologies, ontologies, epistemologies and methods described above.

Table 2.1 Methodologies, ontologies, epistemologies and methods

Methodology type:	Positivist	Realist	Constructionist	Interpretivist	Transformative
Sub-divisions include:	Post-positivist	Critical realist	Postmodernist Grounded theory	Phenomenologist Symbolic interactionist Hermeneutic	Participatory Feminist Emancipatory/activist User-led Decolonising
Ontology (how the world is known)	Facts and phenomena exist independently of people	Facts and phenomena are entwined in complex contexts	People construct facts and phenomena	People interpret facts and phenomena	People, facts and phenomena can combine to create change
Epistemology (how that knowledge of the world is learned)	Through observation and measurement	Through assessment of complexity in context	By creating meaning from experience	By identifying and interpreting multiple realities	Through relationships with people and the environment
Methods likely to be used	Randomised controlled trials, surveys, technology-based methods	Mixed methods	Interviews, arts-based methods, discourse analysis	Interviews, focus groups, participant observation	Arts-based methods, interviews, community-based research

Originally published in Kara (2017, p 48). Republished with permission of Policy Press (an imprint of Bristol University Press, UK).

Research and activism

We have seen that transformative methodologies grew from oppressed and marginalised people deciding that if their lives were going to be studied through research, they would do that research themselves. This is one reason why activists become researchers. Another reason is to find evidence in support of their chosen cause. Also, researchers may themselves be activists, in which case their activism and their research may be separate (such as an engineering researcher who campaigns for better animal welfare) or linked (such as a prison researcher who campaigns for better conditions for inmates) (Livesey, 2014: 189).

The relationship between research and activism can be uneasy and uncomfortable. Activism can influence activists' research questions and design and affect their interpretations of their findings (Kende, 2016: 408). If activists find evidence which challenges their goals in relation to their chosen cause, they are likely to disbelieve that evidence (Dreger, 2015: 27). Some researchers have little or no choice about becoming activists, particularly academics from marginalised groups such as Indigenous academics (Coombes, 2013: 81; Kovach, 2009: 164), women, academics of colour and women of colour in academia (Harris and González, 2012: 2–3) as well as those with disabilities (Oliver, 2019: 1028). We have seen an example of disability activist research in Box 2.4.

One line of argument suggests all researchers are activists by definition. It is certainly true that researchers working on topics that interest them are, in general, happier and more productive than those slogging away at a project which bores them. This is why I would argue that reflexivity is important for all researchers, not only those working with interpretive methodologies. Among other things:

- Post-positivist researchers need to 'critically reflect on the limits of their objectivity' (Kende, 2016: 407)
- Realist researchers need to reflect on their own context and how it interacts with and influences (and is influenced by) their research context
- Those using constructionist methodologies need to reflect on their own reality and how it interacts with and influences (and is influenced by) the realities of others
- Those using transformative methodologies need to reflect on their own power and how they use it, as well as the shifting balances and imbalances of power within and beyond the research team.

Conclusion

Whether or not you use a methodology in your research work will depend in part on your own beliefs and values. Some people have strong beliefs and values which lead them to work exclusively with one or two methodologies. Others take a more flexible approach, starting with a research question and then selecting the methodology they think is most likely to help them answer that question. We have seen examples of this in the case studies from Towers et al. (2020) in Boxes 2.1, 2.2 and 2.4, and it is discussed further in Chapter 4. However, whichever methodology you choose – or even if you choose to work without a specific methodology – I would recommend that you practise reflexivity, to help ensure the quality of your research.

Even if you have strong beliefs and values which draw you to one particular methodology, it is worth considering alternatives because in some research contexts a different methodology may be more useful. No methodology is intrinsically 'better' than any other; they all have different principles and assumptions, and support different interpretations, and they are all legitimate (Moon and Blackman, 2014: 1168). Understanding and accepting these different approaches to research can be particularly helpful in transdisciplinary work.

Reflective questions

1. What are your ontological and epistemological positions?
2. What, in your view, is the relationship between methodology and ethics in qualitative research?
3. Which methodology do you feel most drawn to (or least repelled by)? What are the implications of that for your reflexive work?
4. How do you feel about working reflexively? What are the implications of that for your qualitative research work?
5. Are you an activist? If so, what impact could this have on your research?

3

THINKING WITH THEORY

Chapter summary

- Introduces the concept of theory in qualitative research
- Considers classifications of theory
- Outlines ways in which theory is, and can be, used in qualitative research
- Discusses the theory building approach
- Sets out some links between colonialism and theory use
- Reviews some ethical considerations for working with theory in qualitative research

Introduction

As a quantitative researcher, you have probably been taught that 'a theory is a set of interrelated concepts and propositions that explains or predicts events or situations' (Pickler, 2018: 61). Conversely, in qualitative research, a theory is 'a big idea that organises many other ideas with a high degree of explanatory power' (Collins and Stockton, 2018: 2). We saw this in practice in Box 2.2, where supply chain management researchers Neil Towers and his colleagues used resource-based theory to help them understand the level of integration of supply chains in the fashion industry in the Middle East.

Theory and research cannot be separated, any more than reading and writing. Theory permeates research, whether or not the researcher understands or acknowledges this (Collins and Stockton, 2018: 1). In qualitative research, theory is for thinking with (Jackson and Mazzei, 2012: vii). Reading, using and thinking with theory is hard intellectual work. Language is slippery and concepts amorphous, and this is a hindrance, though it can also, in some contexts, be a help by allowing useful flexibility.

I know from the students I work with that people coming to theory in qualitative research for the first time often reach conclusions such as:

- Qualitative research is stupid,
- I am stupid, or
- Although I am not stupid, I can't do qualitative research.

Qualitative research is intellectually challenging – as, of course, is quantitative research. If you were stupid, you would not be reading this book. And yes, you can do qualitative research – or you will be able to soon. This chapter deals with some complex concepts and we will work through them step by step.

As always, using a single word as a category label makes it seem as though the contents of that category are homogenous. As usual, with theory, this is not the case. Theory in qualitative research operates differently from theory in quantitative research. Broadly, in quantitative research, theories exist to be tested and then, based on the test results, either verified, modified or rejected. Equally broadly, in qualitative research, theories exist to increase our understanding by offering different ways to look at, think about and organise data and findings.

Although theory sounds like an abstract cerebral phenomenon, it can also be surprisingly practical (Lewin, 1944: 27). Using theory effectively can help research to be more considered and thorough, in part by 'making implicit assumptions explicit' (Collins and Stockton, 2018: 4), and thereby increasing the explanatory power of research. Working with theory can be as practical as conducting experiments; indeed, it can be argued that all experimental work involves theory and all theorising involves experiments (Barad, 2007: 55). And theory is not only applicable to research but also to practice, particularly in some situations. Queer theory is helpful in moving us beyond binary thinking along axes such as male-female, gay-straight or normal-abnormal (Barker and Scheele, 2016: 102–14), and so can help us to understand complexity. Social identity theory is useful for understanding situations involving individuals and groups of people such as organisations and events. Some Indigenous scholars 'recognise the importance of theory in developing critical consciousness as people cooperatively work to build another world' (Simpson and Smith, 2014: 9). And this is not a one-way relationship because, while theory can have practical uses, practice also informs theory (Darder, 2019: 12).

Classifying theories

There are many types of theory that qualitative researchers can use. Here are some examples (not an exhaustive list):

Grand theories – aiming to explain a lot about society (e.g. Karl Marx, Sigmund Freud, Emile Durkheim)

Critical theories – aiming to reveal and challenge social power structures and cultural assumptions of power (e.g. Theodor Adorno, Jürgen Habermas, Paulo Freire)

Feminist theories – aiming to reveal and challenge gender-based inequality (e.g. bell hooks, Aileen Moreton-Robinson, Catherine Obianuju Acholonu)

Queer theories – aiming to reveal and challenge heteronormativity and identity politics (e.g. Adrienne Rich, David Halperin, José Esteban Muñoz)

Post-colonial and subaltern theories – formulated by colonised or other marginalised people, who have little power, and aiming to reveal and challenge colonial or other oppressive thought and action (e.g. Gayatri Spivak, Homi Bhabha, Dipesh Chakrabarty)

Euro-Western theories – formulated by Euro-Western people

Indigenous theories – formulated by Indigenous researchers and other Indigenous people

Transdisciplinary theories – formulated by people working across two or more academic disciplines

Middle-range theories – formulated by research participants and other interested people

Grounded theories – formulated from work with research data

Some theorists work in single disciplines, such as Freud in psychology, Freire in education and Bhabha in literature, while others work across disciplines. Also, I should note here that these types of theories are not necessarily mutually exclusive. Adrienne Rich was a feminist, Aileen Moreton-Robinson does post-colonial work and so did José Esteban Muñoz. Even so, the distinctions are useful in helping us think about different topics and perspectives.

Theories can be classified in different ways, such as by dividing them into micro, meso and macro (Pickler, 2018: 61); formal and informal; or remote and engaged. Micro theories are individual or very specific; meso theories include middle-range theories; macro theories include grand theories. Formal theories also include grand theories; informal theories include middle-range and micro theories. Remote theories are those conceived in a rarefied atmosphere far from everyday life, and include knowledge that seeks to be accepted. Engaged theories are conceived in the boat or the tractor, the slum or the barrio, and include knowledge designed to be questioned.

These are some illustrative examples of the many classifications of myriad theories that exist in disciplines from anthropology to economics (Kaufman, 2010: 153). A complete list of theories or even classification options would be impossible to produce (and even if it were possible, it would be very boring to read). I offer these examples here to show the kinds of theories and classifications that exist in qualitative research, and to prepare you for meeting these concepts again.

Using theory in qualitative research

There are a number of ways to use theory in qualitative research. We have already seen that theory can be used as a lens through which to view data and findings for increased understanding. Theory can also be used as an organising framework or 'coat closet' to help arrange and connect data (Collins and Stockton, 2018: 4), or as a navigational aid to help you steer a course from research questions to results (Evans et al., 2011: 289). Theory can be used for generating ideas, comparing perspectives or doing analytic work. An example of theory in use is in Box 3.1. This is followed by a more detailed explanation of two contrasting theorists first encountered in Box 3.1, Barad and Foucault, showing how their work could yield different kinds of findings within the same research project.

Box 3.1

Theory in use

Alecia Jackson and Lisa Mazzei (2012) provide a useful case study in their book *Thinking with Theory in Qualitative Research*. They took two interview transcripts from a project they were working on about first-generation academic women who became professors, and used them as data for analytic readings from different theoretical perspectives. Jackson and Mazzei chose the perspectives of six individual theorists, each of whose work includes a concept that seemed key to their research:

Jacques Derrida – deconstruction
Gayatri Spivak – postcolonial marginality
Michel Foucault – power/knowledge
Judith Butler – performativity
Gilles Deleuze – desire
Karen Barad – material intra-activity

Using their knowledge of each theorist's work around the selected key concept as a prompt, Jackson and Mazzei formulated an analytic question for each reading. Then they worked with their transcripts to investigate each analytic question in the light of the relevant theorist's work, and wrote about what they found. Their writing is not intended as definitive; rather, it is joyfully exploratory. What it shows, clearly and usefully, is how different theories can be used for thinking with data.

Theorists, and people working with theory, tend to write a lot – and therefore also read a lot. Karen Barad's seminal book, *Meeting The Universe Halfway*, runs to over 500 pages. Her work is particularly relevant for consideration here because she did her PhD in physics and then worked as an academic physicist for some years, gaining tenure, before she broadened out into transdisciplinary work. Her theoretical work, inevitably, draws on her expertise in physics, and she calls her theory 'agential realism'. Like many theorists, the concepts she uses are complex, so I will try to simplify some of them here:

Entanglements – everything is linked such that no existence is independent or self-contained (2007: ix)

Phenomena – material entanglements such as things, words, events; 'specific material configurations of the world's becoming' (2007: 91)

Intra-action – because everything is linked, interaction of separate entities is impossible; instead, intra-action represents the connection between two phenomena that are both within and part of a wider entanglement such as 'society' or 'institution'. 'It is through specific intra-actions that phenomena come to matter – in both senses of the word' (2007: 140). This 'constitutes a reworking of the traditional notion of causality' (2007: 140)

Reconfiguration – a result of every intra-action

Agential cut – enactment, not individually owned or created, though an individual person may contribute to an enactment

Onto-epistem-ology – for Barad, ontology and epistemology cannot be separated; they are 'mutually implicated' (2007: 185)

Ethico-onto-epistem-ology – ethics cannot be separated from onto-epistem-ology

Diffraction – a term from physics which describes the ways in which waves change when they encounter obstacles or each other. Barad talks of 'diffraction patterns': imagine a pebble dropped into a pond, then another pebble dropped into the ripples and the resulting effect of criss-crossing ripples would be a diffraction pattern. For Barad, this is a helpful metaphor for agential cuts within entanglements.

Barad (2007) sees matter as 'a dynamic intra-active becoming that never sits still' (170) and considers that everything is in constant flux through the 'ongoing dynamics of agential intra-activity' (149). I find her theory useful for work in complex domains where Cartesian causality – X caused Y – is unhelpful. Cate Watson writes of a schoolboy being diagnosed with attention-deficit hyperactivity disorder (ADHD). She uses a narrative approach, identifying two narratives in particular: the narrative of the professionals (educational, medical and psychiatric) which positioned the family as deviant and the narrative of the child's mother who saw the diagnosis as resulting from a sequence of trivial events (Watson, 2011: 402). We can see from Watson's narrative theorising that there is a question here about causality – what caused the diagnosis? Was it the family's alleged deviance, or the trivial events, or something else? In this complex situation, we can detect entanglements of phenomena: home and school are linked through the child, his teachers and his mother; the educational, medical and psychiatric professions are linked through this case. The diagnosis is a phenomenon involving the intra-actions of adults, professions and institutions. Superficially, the diagnosis reconfigures the child from a child with no ADHD diagnosis to a child with an ADHD diagnosis. Looking more deeply, we can suggest that the diagnosis would have been created from a range of enactments or 'agential cuts' and would have reconfigured people, relationships, phenomena and entanglements in various ways. The process of diagnosis could be seen as a pattern of diffraction, with different 'pebbles' of enactment dropping into the situation to create ripples that criss-crossed other ripples in an ongoing process of reconfiguration.

If we look at this case again using Foucault's theorising, we see it from a different angle. Concepts used by Foucault include:

Power – there are various types of power, but the key points here are that power exists in all relationships, and it may be productive as well as repressive (Portschy, 2020: 401–2)

Knowledge – something that is produced due to facilitatory conditions in a particular time and place, not something already in existence and waiting to be discovered

Discipline – a strategic exercise of power to regulate individual or group behaviour (Portschy, 2020: 406–7)

Resistance – ways in which the use of power and knowledge can be resisted (Portschy, 2020: 396)

Although these words are in more common usage than most of Barad's terms, Foucault uses the concepts in quite specific ways. Using these concepts with Watson's case would lead us to interrogate the power relations between different groups of professionals, professionals and the mother, professionals and the child and perhaps even mother and child. It would enable us to ask questions about the kinds of knowledge needed for, and created by, a diagnosis. It would help us to perceive and understand links between diagnosis and discipline. We could question the circumstances in which diagnosis should perhaps be resisted, or could itself be a form of resistance.

I hope you can see from this brief discussion how each theory could help to reveal different aspects of the case set out by Watson. Broadly, Barad could help to identify and highlight the complexity of the case; Foucault could help to identify and highlight power relations, power imbalances and their effects. Other theorists could help to identify and highlight other aspects. Antonio Gramsci's work would assist with a focus on institutional power; the work of José Esteban Muñoz would bring a focus on minority identities; Nancy Chodorow's work would offer a psychoanalytically informed focus on gender roles. And there are many more.

This kind of applied theoretical work is not easy. Perhaps it should not be easy. Theory cannot be rigidly or dogmatically applied (Collins and Stockton, 2018: 9). In qualitative research, even choosing which theory or theories to work with can be a difficult process. Some qualitative researchers ally their ontological and epistemological positions with a theoretical position; they may describe themselves as 'a Bourdieusian' or 'a Foucauldian'. I can see the appeal of sticking with a theory that you understand and that is aligned with your own philosophical standpoint. However, I do not think this necessarily leads to the best research, as it limits your options. In my view, it makes more sense to choose a theory or theories which will help you to use concepts and ask questions that are relevant to the research you are doing. However, it is perhaps inevitable that your epistemological position will influence your choice (Collins and Stockton, 2018: 6). Also, if you are working with more than one theory, they probably need to be complementary, at least to some extent. Some theories are philosophically opposed to one another in which case it may not be easy or fruitful to try to use them together.

Theory needs to be balanced with methods. Over-reliance on theory can be as detrimental to research as ignoring or dismissing theory. Too much emphasis on theory can reduce scope for exploration, obscure important features of the data and support confirmation bias (Collins and Stockton, 2018: 9). As a result, some researchers wait until they have analysed their data before they begin applying theoretical concepts, with the aim of letting 'the data speak for itself' and the findings 'inform the choice of theoretical framework' rather than the other way around (Mackieson et al., 2018: 973). Conversely, when theory and methods are balanced with each other well, they can 'become mutually reinforcing in the greater pursuit of knowledge' (Collins and Stockton, 2018: 7).

Building theory in qualitative research

Another role for theory in qualitative research is that it can be built from data or findings. Grounded theory was developed within health-care research by Barney Glaser and Anselm Strauss in the 1960s, and is now widely used across disciplines from engineering to sociology (Belgrave and Seide, 2019: 300). It is not the only method for building theory from data, but it is probably the best known. It can be used within various methodologies including post-positivist, constructivist and interpretive frameworks (Belgrave and Seide, 2019: 304).

Grounded theory is a systematic method based on inductive reasoning to build theory as data are being collected and analysed. There is no prescription about how data should be collected; interviews are common, and documents, observations and other forms of data may also be gathered. Data, rather than literature, are the starting point for grounded theory, though literature may be used as data (Corbin and Strauss, 2015). Analysis begins as soon as any data are available, and the results are used to inform ongoing data collection, and so on, in an iterative process (Belgrave and Seide,

2019: 302). Data are coded; that is to say, sections of data are labelled to indicate what they are about (see Chapters 8 and 9 for more on data coding and analysis). Data and codes are constantly compared with each other, and short memos are written to capture analytic thoughts as data are coded and recoded. This process of constant comparison is the foundation of grounded theory (Belgrave and Seide, 2019: 305). When possible, codes are combined into categories, and these are integrated into a theoretical framework. Again, there is constant comparison between the more abstract theorising and categorisation, and the more concrete data and coding (Belgrave and Seide, 2019: 314). Data collection stops when 'saturation' is reached; that is, when no new information is being gathered (Strauss and Corbin, 2015: 134).

Within this broad outline, there are a range of approaches to grounded theory: different ways of coding, different theoretical lenses and so on. Grounded theory can be used alone or as part of a multi-modal research project. However, using grounded theory in different disciplines can present new challenges (Box 3.2).

Box 3.2

Grounded theory in computer science

The discipline of computer science has used grounded theory quite extensively for research in software engineering. In this field, there are many data sources in a range of formats, such as computer code, online discussions and software design diagrams and documents. This means researchers need to be able to manage large amounts of heterogeneous data, devise ways to code different types of data and find ways to constantly compare within this complex research environment (Stol et al., 2016: 129). Nevertheless, researchers have generated useful theories around topics such as how the software development process is managed, how software processes form and evolve and how self-organising 'agile teams' actually self-organise (Stol et al., 2016: 126).

An alternative method of theory building, rather than using the inductive approach of grounded theory, is to use an abductive analytic method. Abductive thinking involves considering multiple possibilities – essentially, all the available options and choices – before reaching a conclusion (Saldaña, 2015: 25). Of course these distinctions between types of thinking are not absolute; grounded theorists use abductive thinking (Charmaz, 2014: 200) and abductive analysts use inductive thinking (Timmermans and Tavory, 2012: 180). But the point here is that inductive thinking is primary to grounded theory, and there are other options.

Abductive thinking is 'an inferential creative process of producing new hypotheses and theories based on surprising research evidence' leading to 'new theoretical insights'

(Timmermans and Tavory, 2012: 170). The way abductive thinking is used depends on the researcher's ontological and epistemological frameworks plus their existing knowledge of the topic at hand (Timmermans and Tavory, 2012: 173). One big difference between abductive and inductive theory building is that abductive work requires a good knowledge of existing theories and literature. Beyond that, similar methods of collecting and coding data, creating categories and building theories and constant comparison can be used. Abductive theory builders look for anomalies, or unexpected elements, and try to connect them with existing theories. If they are able to make such a connection, then the existing theory is verified. If they cannot make a connection, they need to develop a tentative new theory (Timmermans and Tavory, 2012: 179). Abductive researchers recognise that theory is not only built at the researcher's desk or bench but also within collaborative relationships, during seminar or conference presentations, while giving or working with received feedback on written outputs and so on (Timmermans and Tavory, 2012: 179). So instead of theory being viewed as emerging from data, new concepts are devised to account for empirical evidence that is not already accounted for by existing theories (Timmermans and Tavory, 2012: 180).

One problem with grounded theory is that the method doesn't always lead to any actual theory (Stol et al., 2016: 126; Timmermans and Tavory, 2012: 168). This also applies with abductive approaches. Perhaps in time researchers will become able to identify how and when to use inductive or abductive thinking, or indeed how to combine and balance them both in theory building; but we're not there yet.

Colonialism in theory development and use

As the examples in this and the previous chapter suggest, theory is not neutral or value-free. I first learned about theory in 2000 when studying at a university in England for an MSc in Social Research Methods which included a ten-lecture module on theory. Nine of those lectures focused on the work of white European men who were old or dead. The tenth included the work of living, working American women Donna Haraway and Sandra Harding. So as well as learning about specific theorists, I also learned that theory came from the Euro-Western world and was mostly created by men. Names like Marx, Weber, Durkheim, Bourdieu and Foucault seemed quite godly, with their theories being received like commandments, lofty and unquestionable. It would be another 15 years before I learned that important work on theory development and use had been, and was being, done outside the Euro-Western world.

We saw earlier in the chapter that theory has practical uses. The examples given would be viewed by most people as positive. Theory can be, and has been, used in negative ways as well. For example, grand theories served to support the colonial project by erasing the experience of most of the world's peoples from the centre of scholarly thought (Connell, 2007: 46). Subaltern, post-colonial and Indigenous theories are gaining ground due to the increasing realisation that the views of marginalised peoples can provide unique insights into our world.

In many African countries, *Ubuntu* is a philosophy, a knowledge system, a theory and a way of life. (In some countries, this is known by different names, such as *Maaya* or *Bantu* (Mugumbate and Chereni, 2019: 28) but *Ubuntu* is perhaps the best-known term outside Africa.) *Ubuntu* means 'I am we, I am because we are, we are because I am, I am in you, you are in me' (Chilisa, 2020: 98). It exists at individual, family, community, environmental and spiritual levels, and incorporates relationships between these levels (Mugumbate and Chereni, 2019: 30–1).

Oral history shows that *Ubuntu* has existed in African culture 'since time immemorial' (Mugumbate and Chereni, 2019: 29). This is radically different from the Euro-Western theory of 'I think therefore I am' which was put forward by the French philosopher and scientist René Descartes in the 17th century (Chilisa, 2020: 99). *Ubuntu* is a relational perspective which emphasises the interdependence of people and values collectiveness, communality and consensus. It operates very differently from theory in the Euro-Western world where, in general, theories are only understood and used by scholars. *Ubuntu* is used by many African peoples as part of their lived experience (Mugumbate and Chereni, 2019: 29).

Ubuntu is also used by African researchers; indeed, it seems that, for many African researchers, it would not be possible to operate without this theory which is also an ontological position. There is a debate around the extent to which *Ubuntu* can, or should, be used by researchers who are not African. Its use would certainly have big implications, requiring 'researchers from all worlds to see themselves first as related and connected by the same goals of commitment to build harmony among communities they study; to reciprocate by giving back to communities for what they take; and to strive for truth, justice, fairness, and inclusiveness in the construction of knowledge' (Chilisa, 2020: 236).

This is just one example of a theory from beyond the Euro-Western world. There are many other such theories, some of which may be as old as *Ubuntu*, while others have been developed more recently (Connell, 2007: viii). As with Euro-Western theories, it would probably be impossible to create an exhaustive list. The point here is to understand that theory is not the sole province of Euro-Western intellectuals nor are the shapes of Euro-Western theories the only possible shapes for such concepts and processes.

Ethical work with theory

The need for awareness of theory beyond our Euro-Western purview is one ethical imperative around the use of theory. Of course there are also theories of ethics (Kara,

2018: 34–5), though reviewing those is beyond the scope of this book. Here we are focusing on how and why to work ethically with theory.

Some theorists say little or nothing about ethics, though this doesn't mean their work is necessarily unethical, or cannot be used ethically in research. Other theorists see ethics as relevant, important or inseparable from their work. Barad gives her theory a strong ethical framing. 'The yearning for justice, a yearning larger than any individual or sets of individuals, is the driving force behind this work, which is therefore necessarily about our connections and responsibilities to one another – that is, entanglements' (Barad, 2007: xi). And some theories, such as *Ubuntu*, can also act as ethical frameworks in themselves (Chilisa, 2020: 235).

Some researchers argue that theory and research cannot be separated, and therefore regard working explicitly with theory as an ethical imperative in itself (Childers, 2012: 752). Ethical work with theory will include choosing your theory or theories carefully, and aiming for a good balance of theory and method. Using a theory which doesn't fit with your research may distort your data and findings (Evans et al., 2011: 289). Another ethical imperative is to be explicit about which theory or theories you are working with (Pickler, 2018: 62) and how you are doing that work. This enables your readers or other audiences to judge your work more fully.

Conclusion

It is interesting to see the links between some of the theories outlined here. Barad's concept of entanglement in particular, and her theorising in general, has a lot in common with *Ubuntu* – though I can find no evidence that Barad was influenced by, or even knows of, the African theory. Some theories used by qualitative researchers address a few specific dimensions of life, such as feminist or queer theories, while others, such as *Ubuntu* and Barad's work, are quite comprehensive theories. Finding a 'theory of everything' is one of the major unsolved problems in quantitative research. Perhaps qualitative research could offer some useful insights.

Reflective questions

1. What are your intellectual and emotional reactions to this chapter?
2. What does that tell you about how you might work with theory, and about any support you might need in doing so?
3. Which of the theoretical perspectives or approaches outlined in this chapter do you feel most drawn to?
4. What are the ethical implications of your answer to question 3?
5. How could using theory in qualitative research affect researcher bias?

DESIGNING QUALITATIVE RESEARCH

─Chapter summary─

- Explains the importance of designing qualitative research carefully and ethically
- Discusses criteria for assessing the quality of qualitative research
- Outlines the need to allow for flexibility, with examples from practice
- Considers the formulation of research questions and sampling strategies
- Shows the importance of planning research contextualisation, data gathering, data analysis, research reporting, presenting and disseminating findings, aftercare and researcher well-being
- Introduces the impact of colonialism in research design
- Considers collaboration in research design
- Advises on how to finalise your research design

Introduction

Designing research involves thinking through and planning for the entire research process, from contextualising the research questions to disseminating the findings and aftercare. You need to think about who your audience or audiences will be, from the very start of the process, because this will affect your planning (Flick, 2018: 37). Of course, these points apply to quantitative as well as qualitative and multi-modal research, but some of the considerations are different. The aim is to produce good-quality research, while leaving scope for flexibility when needed.

When you are designing your research, it is vital to consider the ethical issues that may arise at each stage. Of course, you can't predict every possible ethical question that may arise, but creating a good research design is an ethical act in itself because it can help to prevent ethical problems arising during the project (Kara, 2018: 71). Some overarching ethical questions include the following:

- How can you make sure your design will lead to good-quality research?
- How will you guard against bias?
- What will you do to ensure you include any existing research that contradicts your own convictions?
- What skills, qualities and cultural competences do you need for your research? (Kara, 2018: 74) Are there any gaps between those you need and those you have? If so, how could you fill those gaps? and
- Would involving participants, or potential participants, in designing your research help to make it more ethical? If so, how can you do this?

In most qualitative or multi-modal research, the design should be heavily influenced by the research question or questions. It should include the methodology (if used), theoretical stance and methods deemed most likely to help answer the question(s) in the specific location of the research. 'Location' here has a wide definition including place, time, type or types of participants, policy context and so on. There are exceptions, such as exploratory research, which may be useful when a topic is too new or not well enough understood for research questions to be constructed. In this case, research should be designed in the way that seems likely to yield most information about the topic.

Quality

Perhaps the most important aspect of designing research is to do what you can to ensure your research will be of good quality. Creating an appropriate and workable research design is a vital component of good-quality research. Every researcher should be able to make sound judgements about research quality (Hammersley, 2009: 15). You are likely to be familiar with the quantitative researcher's quality criteria of objectivity, reliability and validity, and with the different kinds of validity such as internal and external validity. Initially, qualitative researchers tried to create parallels to these, and came up with four quality criteria for qualitative research (Lincoln and Guba, 1985, cited in Bryman, 2016: 44):

- Confirmability, or the extent to which the researcher's own values have influenced the research (parallel to objectivity)
- Dependability, or the extent to which the findings could apply at other times (parallel to reliability)

- Transferability, or the extent to which the findings could apply in other contexts (parallel to external validity) and
- Credibility, or how believable the findings are (parallel to internal validity)

Some qualitative and multi-modal researchers resisted the use of quality criteria, seeing them as too regulatory and inflexible (Tracy, 2010: 838). Others continued the debate and put forward other criteria. In 2010, US researcher Sarah Tracy analysed and considered the debates on quality in the research literature, and designed eight quality criteria, with the aim of ensuring that qualitative research would be comprehensible, flexible, universal and supportive of dialogue and learning (Tracy, 2010: 839). These criteria can also be useful in assessing the quality of multi-modal research. They are the following:

1. Topic is worthy – relevant, topical and interesting
2. Research is rigorous – suitable theoretical basis, critical and rigorous methodology, appropriate methods and enough data
3. Research is sincere – making good use of reflexivity and transparency
4. Research is credible – enough detail and explanation, includes different perspectives and trustworthy
5. Research is resonant – transferable findings and presented using aesthetic and evocative methods that have an affective impact on audiences
6. Research is significant – makes a contribution to different forms of knowledge, such as theoretical, methodological, ethical and/or practical
7. Research is ethical – in the holistic sense
8. Research is coherent – does what it claims to do, using suitable methods and making meaningful connections between literature, research topics, findings and interpretations (Tracy, 2010: 840).

These are not rules to be followed so much as guidelines to consider. In fact, they may conflict in real research contexts. Transparency could conflict with promises of anonymity to participants. In some contexts, gathering primary data is unethical, but using secondary data can compromise rigour. Where these kinds of conflicts arise, Tracy's view is that the primary obligation of researchers is to be truthful with themselves and their audiences (Tracy, 2010: 849).

In the same year, that Tracy's article was published, the Office of Behavioral and Social Sciences Research of the National Institutes of Health in the US commissioned some work from experienced mixed-methods researchers to begin defining quality for mixed-methods research (Klassen et al., 2012: 378). This led to the publication of guidelines which suggest that good-quality mixed-methods or multi-modal research will do the following:

- Be used when a quantitative or a qualitative method alone cannot fully address the research question

- Intentionally combine or integrate qualitative and quantitative methods so as to maximise their strengths and minimise their weaknesses
- Be underpinned by one or more theories
- Be clear about where 'mixing' occurs – whether in data gathering, analysis, interpretation or elsewhere
- Have enough time and resources allocated to manage all the methodological and logistical issues that arise when multiple forms of data are gathered and analysed by a team of people from different disciplinary backgrounds and
- Be explained concisely and clearly for audiences including, but not limited to, funders and participants (Klassen et al., 2012: 378–80).

None of these guidelines for assessing the quality of qualitative and multi-modal research are presented here as definitive. There are other ways to think about research quality, depending on the perspective of the researcher and the context for the research (Fàbregues and Molina-Azorín, 2017). A researcher conducting an interpretivist participatory investigation of the role of childcare in community settings will have a very different idea of quality from a post-positivist clinical researcher adding a qualitative component to a randomised double-blind controlled trial.

Fortunately, the guidelines offer scope for flexibility. In their review of literature on the quality of multi-modal research, Fàbregues and Molina-Azorín (2017) suggest researchers agree on a set of core criteria that they can then build on to create the optimum quality criteria for each research project. Then those defined criteria can be used for benchmarking, as you design and conduct the research, to make sure you are preparing and carrying out a high-quality project. The two sets of guidelines above can serve as a starting point.

Flexibility

It is important to build in some scope for flexibility, particularly in longer-term projects, to enable changes to be made if necessary. This flexibility may be proactive, such as by using an iterative design and allowing for changes in the light of initial and/or mid-stage findings, or reactive, such as by changes in response to new legislation or unforeseen events that affect the research. However, the need for flexibility does not negate the point of creating a good research design. Qualitative and multi-modal research generally goes more or less to plan, and the better the design, the better the research will be.

That said, even excellent plans can lead to unexpected outcomes. This too can require flexibility, whether your outcomes are much more positive than you expected, or much more negative. Of course, this applies to quantitative research too: we have all seen stories in the media of randomised controlled drug trials being halted early because the drug under test was found to be so effective that it had clearly become unethical to continue withholding it from the control group. That is a positive outcome, but even failure of some aspect of your qualitative research can be overcome with a flexible approach. There are examples of flexibility in qualitative research in practice in Boxes 4.1 and 4.2.

Box 4.1

A flexible approach to recruitment

UK researchers Mark McCormack, Adrian Adams and Eric Anderson investigated ways in which the lives of bisexual men were influenced by decreasing levels of homophobia. They were particularly interested in the effects of age and location, so they chose to interview men in three age groups (18–22, 28–32 and 40–50) and in three cities: Los Angeles, New York and London. They received ethical approval to recruit participants online, through LGBT social networking and dating sites, for face-to–face interviews to be held in a café or bar. However, their chosen recruitment method turned out to be time-consuming and ineffective. They only had one week in each city, and after half of the time allotted for data collection in Los Angeles, they had only secured two interviews. As their time was running out, they decided to try a more personal approach. They went to Venice Beach, a crowded bohemian area of the city, and shouted to people in the street that they were looking for bisexual men to interview. Using this method, they secured 14 interviews in just five hours. They treated this as a pilot, and repeated the experiment in several other crowded places in each of the three cities. They wore cowboy hats, carried clipboards with brightly coloured fliers and shouted, 'Bisexual men, we're paying forty dollars for academic research' every 20 seconds (McCormack et al., 2013: 233). They took turns to do the shouting and the interviews, with two of them shouting and the third in a nearby café or on a bench ready and waiting to conduct the next interview. This recruitment strategy was very successful, yielding around three interviews in each hour, from a very diverse group of bisexual men.

These researchers did not have time to check their revised recruitment strategy with their ethics committee. They took care to keep everything else consistent with their initial plans, discussing the aims of their project with potential participants before seeking written consent, and guaranteeing confidentiality and anonymity. And they argue that there are times when qualitative researchers will need to adapt their methods as they conduct research, and that ethics committees should grant experienced researchers the autonomy to do this when necessary (McCormack et al., 2013: 237).

McCormack and his colleagues employed flexibility to respond to the negative situation of a carefully planned but failing recruitment strategy. Conversely, Dariusz Galasiński and Olga Kozłowska, in Poland, employed flexibility to respond to a positive situation.

Box 4.2

A flexible approach to gathering data

Polish researchers Dariusz Galasiński and Olga Kozłowska investigated people's experiences of unemployment in post-communist Poland. They planned to compare answers to the same questions collected first during interviews and then using questionnaires. They recruited 20 unemployed people at an urban job centre. The first participant, when completing the questionnaire and without being asked to do so, commented on his response choices all the way through the task. The interviewers found this so fascinating that they asked all the other participants to 'think aloud' as they completed their questionnaires (Galasiński and Kozłowska, 2013: 3511). For the researchers, 'thinking aloud' is a normal social and discursive practice because in everyday life, people sometimes speak to themselves and/or others while undertaking a task (Galasiński and Kozłowska, 2013: 3512). They learnt that research participants view questionnaire completion as a form of communication between themselves and the researchers who devised the questionnaire and will read and analyse their responses. The researchers were surprised to discover that all participants displayed high levels of uncertainty about which questionnaire responses to choose. They concluded that people conduct complex internal 'negotiations about what it actually means to put a mark on a questionnaire' (Galasiński and Kozłowska, 2013: 3518).

The qualitative findings of Galasiński and Kozłowska have implications for the quantitative instrument and its analysis. A change of researcher could lead to different results, because the participant would be communicating with someone different. Also, the high levels of uncertainty displayed undermine the idea that participants ultimately choosing the same response are in fact equivalent. Galasiński and Kozłowska are not trying to work against or diminish the usefulness of questionnaires in research. They are demonstrating that interactivity exists in the completion of a research instrument which is intended to be non-interactive, and that acknowledging the relational aspects of this type of research work leads to more nuanced and richer findings.

Research questions and sampling

Much research is designed to solve, or help to solve, a problem. Researchers all over the world are working on big problems such as how to prevent or treat disease, how to improve air and water quality, how to give everyone access to clean water and good food. Evidently this kind of research is important. Recently, though, as we saw in Chapter 2, some researchers have become interested in investigating assets as well as deficits. What causes some people to be healthy, happy and resilient? How can we extend those qualities to others? What are the strengths of marginalised people? How can we recognise and honour those strengths?

This applies to quantitative as well as qualitative research. The questions we ask, as researchers, shape the realities of our world. Let's look at an example: the Australian census, and particularly the questions it asks about Australian Indigenous peoples. These questions seek to measure the social, health and economic inequalities which Indigenous peoples in Australia suffer from (Walter and Andersen, 2013: 35). This constitutes 'reality' in the form of what Indigenous peoples lack, and the findings contribute to social and economic policies which somehow always fail to remedy the problem. Now imagine that instead, the census sought to measure the social, health and economic privileges of Australian settlers, and the findings contributed to policies of equality and redistribution of resources. This would constitute 'reality' in the form of power imbalances and redress to Indigenous peoples. Or perhaps the census could try measuring the strengths and knowledge of Indigenous peoples, and the findings could contribute to policies of education and governance. This would constitute 'reality' in the form of valuing and including Indigenous peoples.

These points also apply to qualitative research. As responsible researchers, we need to consider the realities we are constituting with our research questions. Ethical considerations begin as soon as we have thought of a research topic or question (Leavy, 2017: 24; Walter and Andersen, 2013: 50). Could research in that area lead to improvements in society, the economy or the environment? Could findings be misused by people with different agendas? It is essential that we ask these kinds of questions at the outset. We should be passionate about the subject we plan to investigate, because that passion will carry us over unexpected hurdles and through boring patches. However, we must also be alert to the possibility of our passion making it difficult for us to achieve the necessary distance to consider these questions (Kara, 2018: 73).

Formulating research questions is a tricky business, often starting with a question or even a topic that is too broad to be useful, and part of the point of careful research design is to help focus this down to a more manageable question or questions (Flick, 2018: 38). Imagine you are interested in long-term intimate couple relationships. You might think, OK, I could look at the difference between married and unmarried couples who have been together for 20 years or more. That sounds quite straightforward until you start delving further into the subject, and find there are different kinds of marriage: love marriage, arranged marriage, forced marriage, marriages of convenience, religious marriage, humanist marriage – and to complicate things further, none of these are homogeneous categories. Some people are happily married and choose not to live together because, for them, that works best; some have and/or adopt children and some don't, for a variety of reasons. Also, long-term intimate relationships do not only exist between couples; there are long-term polygamous relationships of three, four or more people. And the notion of 'marriage' varies between different cultures. As Facebook might say, it's complicated.

Researchers' time and resources are always limited (Flick, 2018: 35). This can feel like a nuisance but in one way it helps because it makes us focus. Deadlines and budgets are often set externally, and we can supplement those by making decisions on sampling. You might decide that, although you're interested in everything to do with long-term intimate couple relationships of at least 20 years' duration, you will focus on love-based commitments and include religious marriage, humanist marriage and no marriage, with children and no children in each, making six categories of potential participants. So, your research question might be the following: how does the type of commitment, and the presence or absence of children, affect long-term love-based couple relationships?

The location or locations of potential participants is another consideration, whether geographical or virtual or both. If you plan to do face-to-face work, your potential participants will need to be close at hand unless you have a generous travel allowance in your budget. If you can work with participants remotely, you can recruit from anywhere. You may wish to recruit online, via social media, groups, or forums, in which case you may need to limit the number in your sample – though as we saw in Box 4.1 above, online recruitment is not always successful. You would also need to consider the other limitations of online recruitment: excluding people who do not or cannot use the internet, and excluding internet users who do not or cannot use the virtual platform or arena where your recruitment is taking place. There may be an argument for recruiting both online and offline.

A sample in quantitative research is usually required to be representative of its population so that statistical tests can be used to enable generalisation from the subset in the sample to the population as a whole (Flick, 2018: 48). This generalisation is achieved using statistical calculations which work on the basis of probabilities. There are several ways of deriving a representative sample from a population, such as random sampling, systematic sampling, stratified random sampling and cluster sampling (Robson and McCartan, 2016: 277–8).

In qualitative research, samples are not based on the logic of probability but on different logics. A type or types of sampling will be selected to suit the research project, its methodology and its likely participants or other data sources. Options include (Cooksey and McDonald, 2019: 857–82; Robson and McCartan, 2016: 280–1; Suri, 2011) but are not limited to the following:

> *Quota sampling* – This involves aiming to include data from different elements of a
> population, usually in equivalent proportions to their proportions in the
> population as a whole. So if you were doing organisational research into the

quality of communication in a company with 20 administrators, 100 sales executives and 10 managers, you might decide to include four administrators, 20 sales executives and two managers in your sample, i.e. 20% of each category. Quota sampling is also used in quantitative research as it can yield a representative sample. However, that sample is not random, so data gathered from quota sampling cannot be subjected to statistical tests designed for use with random samples to make inferences about the population. In qualitative research, quota sampling is often used with post-positivist or constructivist methodologies.

Purposeful sampling – this sampling is to meet specific needs. For example, if your organisational research question was about the effectiveness of managerial strategies, you might purposefully include all 10 managers in your sample (to ensure that you captured all the strategies in use), plus two administrators and 10 sales executives (to find out how well these strategies worked in practice). Purposeful sampling is often used with constructivist or interpretivist methodologies.

Theoretical sampling – this is used in grounded theory research (which was covered in Chapter 3). Some data are gathered from a small preliminary sample, then those data are analysed, and in the process, theoretical ideas and interpretations begin to form. These are then used to guide the next round of sampling, and so on, with the aim of building, testing and refining theories from the research.

Snowball sampling – this may include as few as one person recruited by the researcher, who then goes on to recruit others from the group in which the researcher is interested. This is useful for working with groups of people that may be stigmatised or harder to reach, such as people who break the law, nomadic people or members of secret societies. Snowball sampling is often used with constructivist or interpretivist methodologies.

Convenience sampling – This involves including the people you can reach most easily and who are willing to participate in your research. This is not a well-regarded sampling method for full-scale qualitative research, but it can be useful when you are learning to do qualitative research, piloting data collection methods or for initial exploratory work.

When necessary, more than one type of sampling can be used within a single research project. An example of this is shown in Box 4.3 below.

The list above includes the most common forms of sample. There are many others, such as maximum variation sampling and criterion sampling. Also, as so often with qualitative research, the terminology is not entirely fixed. For example, purposeful sampling is also known as purposive sampling.

Box 4.3

Euro-Western research methods in an African context

Nomazulu Ngozwana investigated rural and urban people's understanding of democracy and citizenship, and their implications for civic education, in Lesotho. She conducted narrative research within an interpretivist methodology, and aimed to carry out in-depth interviews and focus groups with community leaders, civic education providers and members of the public. Ngozwana used purposive sampling to recruit community leaders and civic education providers for in-depth interviews, and snowball sampling to recruit members of the public, mostly for focus groups with a few in-depth interviews for people who were too busy to take part in a focus group. In the main, Ngozwana was able to implement her research design, though she encountered some difficulties when interviewing chiefs in both rural and urban areas. An African chief is 'a public figure who serves all people openly, meaning that, what is discussed at a chief's place is not a secret, but open and accessible for public consumption' (Ngozwana, 2018: 27). When Ngozwana was interviewing chiefs, there were constant interruptions from people coming to the chief for help; witnesses were present throughout the interviews; and chiefs invited others present, or the researcher herself, to answer the research questions in their stead. 'It is standard in an African society for people to seek witnesses when they are engaged in discussions' (Ngozwana, 2018: 27) and the chiefs' behaviour was entirely in line with the African ontological position of *Ubuntu* (discussed in Chapter 3). This shows that the Euro-Western research concept of seeking confidential and anonymous views from experts can come into conflict with African research which involves social interaction and interconnection, such as through action learning or performing an activity (Ngozwana, 2018: 19).

In qualitative research, smaller sample sizes are much more acceptable than in quantitative research. Yet qualitative researchers usually collect more data, and/or data which are more complex, than quantitative researchers. There are still big debates about what is 'enough' data, and many writers on research methods avoid the question. Ideally you would collect just enough data to enable you to answer your research question (Kara, 2018: 96) though how much this is can be very difficult to figure out. Some methods give guidance: as we saw in Chapter 3, grounded theory research suggests that data should be collected until 'saturation' is reached, i.e. no new information is being gathered (Cooksey and McDonald, 2019: 885). There are a couple of ethical points to be made about this. First, with primary data collection, participants can be over-researched and experience 'research fatigue' which can have a significant negative impact on their well-being (Ashley, 2021). It is not ethical to over-burden participants, or to collect data that researchers don't go on to use. Second, with secondary data collection, gathering too much data burdens the researcher, and researcher well-being is also important. On the plus side, in qualitative research, a flexible approach to data collection and to sampling is sensible and often encouraged. Flick (2018: 56) suggests that 'you should be ready to adapt to conditions in the field and to new insights resulting from data collection, which might suggest changes in the original sampling plan'. Also there is a role for common sense here. I would argue that with the above project on couple relationships, probably 4–6 couples in each category would be sufficient as long as rich data are gathered from each couple.

Planning research contextualisation

This involves working out what information you need to set the context for your research. Qualitative researchers in academia usually do this by reviewing relevant academic literature, and sometimes other literature too. Practice-based researchers may use a literature review, or a document analysis, or take a multi-modal approach such as by using literature, documents and statistics.

Whatever method you intend to use, the planning stage will involve some initial searching to scope the material you want to draw on and to plan the strategy or strategies you will use to search for that material. In qualitative research, it is good practice to think widely and aim to find sources from beyond your discipline, field and/or research arena. It is important to include any relevant work you dislike or disagree with (Kara, 2018: 75), and to treat that work with the respect it deserves.

You also need to plan how to record contextual information in the form of field notes. There is no set way to do this, but it is sensible to take a systematic approach, and to decide which of your field notes you are willing to make public if you find, at a later stage, that it would be useful to do so. See Chapter 5 for more detailed information about field notes.

Planning data gathering

We have seen that primary data collection is a burden for both participants and researchers. Therefore, a key ethical consideration here is to gather secondary data first, and only include primary data if it is absolutely necessary. Working with secondary data raises other ethical considerations, and these are covered in Chapter 6.

Whatever kind or kinds of data you collect, only gather as much as you need to answer your research question. People who are new to qualitative research often believe that more data lead to better research, but this is not the case. We have seen that gathering too much data causes unnecessary extra work for the researcher, in both gathering and analysing data, and if those data are primary, they also increase the burden on participants.

Whether you are working with secondary or primary data – or both – you need to plan where you will gather those data from, and the methods you will use. This can often involve a piloting stage, where you may scope out a search strategy for secondary data to ensure the results will be manageable, or test some interview questions or arts-based activities with volunteers to get feedback on how well they work.

During this planning phase, you need to look in two directions: You need to look back at the research questions, to ensure the methods you choose have a good chance of helping you answer those questions. You also need to look ahead to the probable audiences for your research, to assess whether their reception of your work could be affected by the methods you choose.

Planning data analysis

The nature and amount of data you plan to collect has implications for your analytic work. Therefore, when you are designing your research, it is essential to plan your analytic approach as well as your data collection. Analytic work with qualitative data includes data management, storage, preparation and coding, as well as the core inter-pretative work of the actual analysis. Each element needs careful planning to ensure that your work is manageable and will fit with any constraints such as budget or timescale.

Then there is the question of whether to work manually or digitally. Generally, analysis by hand is easier with smaller datasets; the larger your dataset, the more likely you are to need to use computer software in your analytic work (see Chapter 8 for more information about qualitative analysis software). If you prefer, you can work digitally with a small dataset. However, no matter how strong your preference, I cannot recommend manual analysis for a large qualitative or multi-modal dataset because the time required would be prohibitive.

You also need to plan how you will use theory, in your research in general and particularly for the analytic stage. You can either use one or more theories as a guide for your analytic work, or you can use your analytic work to help build a theory. Within this broad distinction, there are a plethora of options so considered planning is important. (See Chapter 3 for more information about theory in qualitative research.)

Another thing to plan is the strategies you will deploy to mitigate your own biases, and perhaps also the biases of team members or others who may be part of your work, during the analytic process. Whether you are working alone or not, this merits dis-cussion with others, as it can be very difficult to detect our own biases, and input from other people can be helpful.

Planning research reporting

The first step here is to think about who will need and/or want to know about your findings. Identify your audience(s) and then work out how to meet their needs. So far, so similar to quantitative research – but reporting on qualitative and multi-modal research is different because there is usually more to report.

There are many ways to report on qualitative research, from a standard written report or journal article to comics and performance. You may choose more than one method to meet the needs of different audiences. If your research concerns young children and their families, you might share your findings through a short animation for the children and a longer video for their parents and carers. If your research is cross-cultural, you may need to report in different languages which could require the help of translators.

Reporting can also be multi-modal, whether or not the research being reported is multi-modal itself. This occurs when different methods of communication are used within a single output, such as text, photographs and poems. Any kind of research may be reported multi-modally, and multi-modal research can be reported using a single reporting method.

Planning research presentation and dissemination

With presentation and dissemination, again, your planning starts with identifying your audiences. Academics at a conference? Participants in a community? Funders, managers, colleagues? The general public? When you have figured out who they are then, again, you can work out how best to meet their needs.

Presenting your findings in person, whether at an actual or virtual event, is often important. Dissemination is always important because it enables your findings to reach many more people. Your dissemination strategy should be planned at the outset, partly to ensure you can allocate enough resources, and partly to help guard against findings that prove unpopular being withheld from publication – although this cannot be completely guaranteed (Morris, 2008: 21).

Planning aftercare

Depending on the nature of your research project, it may be necessary to plan aftercare for data, participants and their communities, findings and/or researchers ourselves (Thomas, 2013: 96). It is not always clear when a research project ends (Matebeni, 2014: 122). Does it end when the money is all spent, or when the last output is published, or at some other time? Whenever the end point is, beyond that data should be preserved for re-use, participants should be able to contact the researcher or their representative, findings should be accessible and put to use and researcher well-being should be supported and maintained.

Planning for researcher well-being

Advance preparation helps to ensure researcher well-being (Moncur, 2013: 1885). Think about the project you are planning. Is the researcher likely to encounter physical, emotional, mental, spiritual or relational risks? If so, how can you design the research to mitigate, minimise or avoid those risks? Risk is not reserved for qualititative researchers; quantitative researchers, too, may research conflicts and disasters which involve physical risks, experience relational risks as a result of discrimination from colleagues or managers or encounter mental or spiritual risks as they struggle to reconcile their personal and professional ethics. However, the literature suggests that qualitative researchers may be more likely than quantitative researchers to face emotional risks (Qwul'sih'yah'maht, 2015: 193–4; Velardo and Elliott, 2018: 312–3).

Colonialism in research design

We saw in Chapter 3 that Euro-Western theories have limited applicability outside Euro-Western contexts. The same applies to Euro-Western research methods. Euro-Western researchers are inclined to reify their main methods – the controlled trial, questionnaire, interview and focus group – although, as we saw in Chapter 1, these methods are comparatively new. Researchers in other parts of the world have found these methods do not always work effectively in different cultural contexts. An example of this is shown in Box 4.3.

Ngozwana identifies and discusses 'the effects of imperialism on African people' (Ngozwana, 2018: 19). However, she does not consider that her own use of Euro-Western research methods, rather than Indigenous methods, may be one of those effects.

Collaboration in research design

Collaboration can be very helpful in designing qualitative research because there are so many options to choose from. I have been designing qualitative and multi-modal research projects for over 20 years and I always value others' input at the design stage. This input can come in many forms, from a 'second opinion' where someone casts an eye over your design to see if they can think of anything you've missed, to a full-scale research team collaboration. Useful collaborators include other researchers, doctoral supervisors, research managers, funders, potential participants – anyone with an interest or a stake in your research.

If you are using a participatory methodology, then you will want to co-design your research with some or all of your participants. (See Chapter 2 for more on transformative methodologies which include participatory methodologies.) This can be problematic if you need formal ethical approval from a research ethics committee or institutional review board, as these bodies usually require researchers to gain their approval before contacting any potential participants. Experienced participatory researchers have called for a change from this kind of 'top-down' approach to research ethics to a more 'bottom-up' approach aligned with the values of participatory research (Banks and Brydon-Miller, 2018: 8).

Finalising your research design

When you have a complete draft design for your research project, I recommend that you return to the core quality criteria you have decided to use, and check your design against those criteria. All of the criteria are important to meet, though at this stage, coherence and ethical quality are perhaps the most important. Your design should be coherent, with clear alignment between your research questions, methodology, theoretical stance and methods (Johnson et al., 2020: 138). Also, your design should include explicit ethical considerations for each stage of the process. If your design does not meet these standards, then revise it as needed until you are confident you have a good-quality design that is likely to result in good-quality research. This will help you to minimise potential risks and maximise the potential benefits of your research (Poth, 2021: 27).

Conclusion

All of this planning may seem like a lot of work – and indeed it is. It can be very tempting to just get going on context-setting or data gathering. However, putting in time at the planning phase will save both time and stress later in the process. It will also help to ensure that your research is of good quality, with robust findings that inspire confidence.

Reflective questions

Think about a qualitative project you would like to undertake – or, if relevant, one you will undertake in the near future.

1. What would be the main ethical considerations to take into account in designing that project?
2. Who would be useful for collaborative working on the research design?
3. Which quality criteria would you propose to use, and why?
4. Who would make up the audience or audiences for the research outputs? What kind of outputs would best meet their needs?
5. How do you think reflexivity (discussed in Chapter 3) could contribute to the research design process?

5

CONTEXTUALISING QUALITATIVE RESEARCH

Chapter summary

- Introduces the importance of context to qualitative research
- Considers the potential role of field notes
- Discusses the academic literature review
- Outlines the alternative option of the document analysis
- Covers some of the key issues in writing at the context-setting stage
- Reviews some of the ethical aspects of context-setting

Introduction

Context is crucial to qualitative research (Kara et al., 2021: 32). When you are doing qualitative or multi-modal research, you will need to be aware of the context, and communicate it to your audience or audiences through your research reporting and the presentation and dissemination of your findings. The concept of context in qualitative research is quite complex, including elements such as prevailing social policy and legislation, the physical and temporal locations of your research, all those with an interest in your research (funders, managers, colleagues, peers, participants and the groups or communities they represent, and so on), and your own ontological and epistemological positions (Kara et al., 2021: 32) (see Chapter 2 for more on ontology and epistemology).

Different types of qualitative and multi-modal research are contextualised in different ways. Academic research is usually contextualised through a review of literature, primarily academic literature though increasingly now including other kinds of literature. Indigenous researchers take a very broad view of literature as including stories, legends, artifacts, songs, rituals, poems, dances and tattoos, among other things (Chilisa, 2020: 62). Evaluation research is often contextualised using sources such as documents and statistical data. Contextualisation for arts-based research may include poems or a comic strip. Participatory research may be contextualised primarily through conversations. However you do it, you need to describe the research situation, justify your choice to work in that situation, outline the relevant history and background, and explain the key issues (Bloomberg and Volpe, 2012: 8).

Quantitative data and research findings can play a useful role in contextualising some qualitative research. If you were investigating people's lived experience of cancer, you might contextualise your research with local and national data about cancer prevalence. If you were studying audience reactions to an art exhibition, you might use existing information about audience numbers and durations of visits to help contextualise your research. If you were doing research in a school, you might include pupil numbers, class sizes and pupil–staff ratios as part of your contextualisation. And so on. There is no reason for qualitative research to exclude quantitative elements that can help people to understand the context you need to communicate.

Field notes

Field notes are used by qualitative researchers to record information about context during the research process. This helps to ensure that important contextual details are remembered for use during analysis and reporting (Phillippi and Lauderdale, 2018: 381). There is no set way to make field notes: researchers use a variety of methods, from jotting down odd thoughts on scraps of paper or as text or voice notes in a smartphone app, to more formalised approaches such as research journals, diaries and logs. Barbara Bassot suggests that logs are for recording facts such as what you did and what you found and when, diaries are calendar-driven and useful for planning, and journals are for researchers to write in as they please (Bassot, 2020: 12–13).

In recent years it has become evident that this need not be limited to writing alone. Giorgia Lupi and Stefanie Posavec devised and tested a method of making field notes based on drawing, and Clare Danek created a stitch journal using textile art (URLs for both of these are in Appendix 1). No doubt there are other creative methods in use and others still will be devised in future.

From my own experience and observation, I would assert that individual preference and skills have often influenced the way qualitative researchers make field notes. However, as usual in research practice, a more systematic approach leads to better results, and may render qualitative research more rigorous, transparent and replicable (Mackieson et al., 2018: 967). Phillippi and Lauderdale (2018: 383) have offered qualitative researchers some signposts to the creation and use of good quality field notes:

- Plan how you will make, use, disseminate and archive your field notes
- Ensure your plans are aligned with your ontological and epistemological positions, theoretical framework and methodology (see Chapter 2 and Table 2.1 for more on this)
- Document your plans in your research design
- Include details of your plans in any application for ethical approval, and in participant consent forms
- Digitize and organise your field notes so they can be easily searched and reorganised during data analysis
- Include relevant excerpts from your field notes in your reports and presentations
- Archive your field notes with your data for future use

Some researchers regard their field notes as entirely personal and private; some regard them entirely as data; and some regard them as a combination of the two. Therefore, as part of your planning process, it may be useful to consider where you want to place the boundary between public and private. Might your research include stressful or distressing elements that you would prefer to write about privately to help you process your experience? Do you want to structure your field notes in such a way that they can all be used as data, and use other methods to deal with any emotional processing you may need? Would you like to run two journals in parallel, one for private reflections and the other for public records? Is it more sensible to keep your field note system simple, to minimise your workload, or to use a more complex system which will increase the quality and rigour of your research? Such a system is shown in Box 5.1.

Box 5.1

A complex system of field notes

Penny Mackieson and her colleagues in Australia analysed official records of parliamentary debates (the analytic process they used is described in Box 9.5). The researchers created a Codebook to record 'the key elements and step-by-step process of the research' (Mackieson et al., 2018: 973). This Codebook was structured as follows:

Purpose – why the research was being undertaken
Analytic objectives – what the researchers wanted to achieve

(Continued)

Data in scope – a description of the data included in the project and the rationale for that inclusion

Definitions – of research terms used such as data, theme, and code

Rules for applying codes – to the data

Rules for counting code frequencies – how many times a code occurred in the data

Coding reliability – how this would be established

Data reduction – the techniques to be used to identify and extract relevant data

Quantification – the quantitative and other analytic techniques to be used in formulating results

Output – the research outputs

Code map – showing the relationships between the codes

Code definitions – the definition of each code (this took up over half of the Codebook)

References

The researchers used their Codebook to record every decision they made and the reason or reasons for making that decision. Their view is that the Codebook 'enables an outside reader to both review the conduct of the research and to replicate it' (Mackieson et al., 2018: 973).

As you can see, there are many options for how to make field notes. This may seem daunting, but the plus side is that you can choose a system which is likely to work well for you and for your research. Also, once you have a system in place and become familiar with using it, making field notes becomes much easier (Phillippi and Lauderdale, 2018: 383).

Literature review

Some quantitative researchers conduct literature reviews, and there are some quantitative methods of reviewing research literature such as meta-analyses which bring together quantitative results from a range of studies. So this may be a familiar concept. However, there are many different types of literature review that are used by qualitative and multi-modal researchers. Some commentators have attempted to devise taxonomies for these literature reviews, such as scholastic (for academic purposes) and interventionist (for practice or policy purposes) (Hart, 2018: 93) or systematic (to synthesise and compare evidence), semi-systematic (to track research development over time) and integrative (to critique and synthesise) (Snyder, 2019: 339). I don't find these taxonomies particularly convincing because there are so many different kinds of literature review in use in qualitative and multi-modal research, with new varieties frequently being devised. Here are some examples (Ferrari, 2015; Fleischmann, 2009; Grant and Booth, 2009; Jesson et al., 2011; Kaniki, 2006; Snyder, 2019; Tight, 2019).

- Summary review, also known as an overview. This enables you to describe the literature and its characteristics.
- Scoping review, to identify the amount and nature of existing literature. This is useful at an early stage to help decide what other type or types of review to carry out.
- Rapid review, also known as a rapid evidence assessment. This is designed to find out what is already known about an aspect of practice or policy.
- Methodological review, focusing on a particular method or methodology. This helps to understand the strengths and weaknesses of that method or methodology.
- Expert review, conducted by an acknowledged expert on the subject. This benefits from the reviewer's expertise but may be limited by their ontological and epistemological positions.
- Historical review, which traces the development of a body of literature through time. This can be useful for assessing the progress of a subject or field.
- Theoretical review, to identify theoretical developments, usually in a particular subject area, sometimes linking the developments with empirical evidence. This can be useful for assessing the progress and influence of a theory or concept.
- Empirical review, to assess the empirical findings of research on a particular subject. This can establish what is known through research evidence, and perhaps what still needs to be investigated through future research.
- Narrative review, to identify and summarise what has been published on a particular subject. This helps researchers to avoid duplicating work and to find gaps that could be filled by future research.
- Thematic review, looking at different perspectives, themes or debates in the literature. This is useful for subjects that have been investigated by researchers in different fields and disciplines. An example of a thematic review is given in Box 5.2 below.
- Critical review, in which the literature is both reviewed and critically evaluated. The critical evaluation is intended to add an element of quality control to the review.
- Systematic review, to include everything that has been published on a particular subject, or (where there is too much to include it all) everything that has been published on a particular subject which also fits pre-determined inclusion criteria such as size of sample or type of participant. This aims to provide a comprehensive picture.
- Semi-systematic review, for use when there is too much literature from too many disciplines to review it all. This may focus on how research within one field has progressed over time, or on how a topic has developed across disciplines.
- Knowledge review, which includes academic literature alongside other forms of evidence such as policy documents and documented testimonial evidence. This is intended to summarise what is known about a particular subject.

- Integrative review, combining literature and findings from different fields and disciplines. The intention here is to generate new theories or conceptual frameworks.
- Multi-modal review, using two or more review methods.

As usual, this is not an exhaustive list. Also, as so often with qualitative research methods, the terminology is labile, and you are likely to find other definitions for at least some of these terms than those I have given here. In fact there is not even an accepted definition of 'literature'. Historically this meant academic literature, published in academic journals, books and conference proceedings. Now it can include 'grey' literature, which is research-related but not formally published and so can be difficult to find; work published online such as blogs; ephemera, such as leaflets; and even creative outputs such as videos, novels and poems.

The above list suggests a taxonomy which may form a more useful way of thinking about qualitative research reviews:

1. Overview reviews (summary review, scoping review)
2. Descriptive reviews (rapid review, methodological review, expert review)
3. Progress tracker reviews (historical review, theoretical review, empirical review)
4. Analytic reviews (narrative review, thematic review, critical review)
5. Comprehensive reviews (systematic review, semi-systematic review, knowledge review)
6. Research project in review form (integrative review)

As with many taxonomies in qualitative research, the categories here are not mutually exclusive. The integrative review can form a full research project in its own right, being designed to generate findings in the form of new theories or conceptual frameworks. However, a narrative review or a critical review could also form a full research project. An expert review is more likely to be a descriptive review, but could be an analytic review – and so on. What this taxonomy is useful for, though, is to help you think through the kind of review that will be most appropriate for your research.

Whatever kind of qualitative literature review you undertake, there are some good practice points to bear in mind (Snyder, 2019: 336). These include the following:

1. Select the type of review which best fits your research purpose.
2. Work out how you will search for the literature to include.
3. Document your search strategy, including where you will search (databases, libraries, archives etc.), the search terms you will use, and any criteria for including items you find in, or excluding them from, your review.
4. Decide how you will extract the information you want from the literature you find, and how you will use that information.
5. Document your plans for extracting and using information.

6. Test your search strategy to check whether it is having the desired effect, and make any necessary revisions.
7. Keep records of your search process and results as you conduct your search.
8. Test your extraction method to check whether it is working as you want, and make any necessary revisions.

I would add another suggestion to this: assess and record the status of each piece of literature you include. This involves recording information such as follows:

Author
Date
Publisher
Funder(s)
Any likely funding bias?
Clarity of method
Overall quality
Potentially useful for:

These are examples; there may be other aspects of the literature you collect that you choose to include. This is sometimes known as a 'literature grid' (Kara, 2017: 103–4). A spreadsheet is a useful format for setting up your literature grid, because it can be searched and sorted quickly and easily.

Once you have set up and implemented the systems for your research, you can work on extracting and using the information you want from the literature you have found.

Box 5.2 contains an example of a thematic multi-modal review, showing how the researchers worked across disciplines to investigate a worldwide problem.

Box 5.2

A thematic multi-modal literature review

Janice Du Mont and Deborah White wanted to find out why the medico-legal findings generated by standardised rape kits were rarely related to rapists being brought to justice. Rape kits are sealed boxes containing the instructions, documents, and implements for health workers or specially trained legal professionals to collect evidence from victims. The evidence is then handed on to other legal personnel to be passed to scientists for analysis. Therefore this needed to be a transdisciplinary literature review, including health, legal, and scientific disciplines. Also it needed to be a worldwide review.

Du Mont and White searched for academic and 'grey' literature from the disciplines of psychology, sociology, medicine and law. They looked for peer-reviewed academic literature via internet search engines and databases such as Web of Science and Medline. They searched for 'grey' literature on the websites of

(Continued)

international organisations, national governments, non-governmental organisations and research centres. Also, in 16 countries around the world, they 'consulted academics, policy makers, and service providers with expertise in the area for leads on published and unpublished materials' (Du Mont and White, 2013: 1230). Some of the people they consulted asked other colleagues in a further nine countries. The researchers also posted requests for information on two online mailing lists. This multi-modal search strategy yielded over 400 documents for review.

Document analysis

There is no agreed definition of 'document'. Aimee Grant offers a helpful definition of a document as something that includes 'written, graphical or pictorial matter, or a combination of these types of content, in order to transmit or store information or meaning' (Grant, 2019: 11). There are many types of document: reports, letters, emails, social media posts, forms, meeting minutes, web pages, lists, articles, leaflets and so on. As Grant's definition suggests, documents have different purposes. They are rarely simple containers of information, more often created by a person or people who would like something to happen or to change as a result, and sometimes used by others to achieve their ends. If a customer receives poor service from a business, they could look on their supplier's website for its customer service standards, then use that document to hold the supplier to account (Kara, 2017: 146). Legal judgements and Government legislation are written to have an impact on society. A child's birthday present wish-list, or an adult's last will and testament, are written to affect the lives of specific individuals.

Qualitative researchers working outside academia, such as community researchers, agency researchers or practitioner-researchers, may contextualise their research with a document analysis rather than a literature review. Academics may also use document analysis for context, though this is likely to be in addition to a literature review.

Documents can also be used as data, and this is covered in Chapters 7 (collection of documents for use as data) and 9 (analysing documentary data). Collecting and analysing documents for context-setting is a different process from collecting and analysing documents as data. First, you need to decide what kinds of documents can help to provide context for your research. Some types of documents you might consider including are as follows:

- Legal documents (national law such as Acts of Parliament or Acts of Congress, regional and local laws and regulations, case law)
- Policy documents, stating the objectives of a government or institution
- Organisational documents (annual reports, accounts, meeting minutes, project plans, funding bids)
- Historical documents, usually found in archives
- Relevant reports in the mainstream media

- Web pages
- Videos

Once again, this is not an exhaustive list; it is intended as a stimulus for your own thoughts. Also, while it is of course sensible to plan the collection and analysis of documents for your context-setting, it is also worth taking a flexible approach to document collection. Documents exist in relation to other documents, a phenomenon named 'intertextuality' by the critical theorist Julia Kristeva in 1966. Sometimes it is useful to track those relationships and so find more relevant documents. I was doing some work for a hospice once and, while searching their archives for specific material, I stumbled on the wills of people who had left legacies to the organisation. The information in those wills gave a strong sense of the value placed on the hospice by members of the local community, which was really useful for context-setting, and which I doubt could have been assessed as effectively in any other way. Box 5.3 shows another example of a document analysis being used to help set research into context.

Box 5.3

Document analysis for context

Jan Lauren Boyles, from Iowa State University in the United States, studied the ways in which news production can help to strengthen the symbolic bonds between urban residents and their city. She focused on New Orleans in its recovery from the devastation caused by Hurricane Katrina in 2005. Boyles carried out in-depth interviews with 49 print, digital, radio and television journalists, plus ethnographic observation of the city's news environment over three months in 2013. She also interviewed 11 community leaders, and did observational research in 'places where news was produced and consumed (i.e. libraries, coffeehouses and community centers) throughout the city' (Boyles, 2017: 951). For context, she did a small-scale document analysis of public records of the city's history before and after the hurricane, including 'archival documents, news accounts, and oral histories from The Louisiana and Lower Mississippi Valley Collections at Louisiana State University' (Boyles, 2017: 951). The findings from the document analysis and the observational research gave a sharper focus to the insights from the interviews.

When you are analysing documents for context-setting, you are looking only for information that is relevant to your purpose of setting your research into context. It is helpful to categorise your documents in an overview by recording aspects of metadata such as follows:

- Type of document
- Date of document

- Author(s) of document
- Purpose of document
- Audience(s) for document

Then, during analysis, it is usually sensible to use both quantitative and qualitative approaches (Tight, 2019: 136). For example, if you were analysing meeting minutes, you might record the number and frequency of meetings; the number of attendees at each meeting; the number of meetings each individual attended; the number of discussion points at each meeting. Unless you only have a few documents, you can use descriptive statistical calculations to provide an overview of the meetings. Then you can read the text of the meeting minutes and extract any information that could help you set your research into context.

When you are recording metadata, it may also be useful to include a brief qualitative summary of the document's content and purpose. This only needs to be a sentence or two long. It is useful as an aide-memoire and also enables you to get a quick qualitative overview of your documents and see whether there are any gaps or overlaps.

Writing the context

A literature review, document analysis, or other context-setting process is also a product: it is something you do *and* something you create (Leavy, 2017: 56). So far this chapter has focused on the doing, and now we will consider the creative process of writing the context for your research.

Part of the creativity lies in selecting what you will use in your write-up, and how. You are unlikely to need to use everything that is relevant. Often you will have far more information than you can use. Occasionally you may have the opposite problem, when the body of available literature or other documents is so small that you need to think laterally and search more widely before you can understand the context well enough yourself to convey it to others. But mostly the task is to go through the information you have extracted from your literature and documents, and narrow that down to its most applicable parts.

Writing is a key skill in all types of research, but qualitative research uses writing more than, and differently from, quantitative research. First, and perhaps most importantly, the first person is becoming increasingly acceptable in qualitative research writing – and, it should be acknowledged, in quantitative research too, albeit more slowly. Some high-profile science journals such as *Nature* now request that writers use the first person, though this is still unusual in STEM subjects in general and some other predominantly quantitative academic disciplines such as psychology still use the third person as standard (Lazard and McAvoy, 2020: 162). The first person is particularly helpful when writing about reflexivity, which was introduced in Chapter 2 of this book, because the first person offers a good way to express 'the specific personal, social, theoretical, and/or political influences that shape the research' (Lazard and McAvoy, 2020: 163).

I argued in Chapter 1 that all writing is more or less creative. In qualitative research there is more scope for writing creatively, though some quantitative researchers are also finding space for this (Davis et al., 2008; Harron, 2016). In qualitative research writing, the creativity may be on a large scale, such as by presenting research in graphic novel format (Sousanis, 2015; Sou and Cei Douglas, 2019). Or it may be on a small scale, perhaps by using fiction writers' techniques such as strong sensory language or metaphor – or somewhere between the two. These options are discussed in more detail in Chapter 10.

Research itself is fundamentally a creative, imaginative endeavour. It has long been understood that imagination is a central plank of any kind of research (Mills, 1959: 211–12; Rapport, 2004: 102). Indeed, without imagination, research could not exist, because a researcher has to be able to imagine a project before they can design and carry out the research (Kara, 2020: 92–3). And all research is to some extent creative: projects are created by researchers, and these projects create new knowledge for those researchers and others to use. We saw in Chapter 1 that the most familiar research methods were invented a comparatively short time ago – and we know that new methods are being devised and tested around the world right now. So any perception of research methods as prescribed or mechanistic is incorrect, and this includes methods for writing up a literature review or document analysis.

We also saw in Chapter 1 that writing is a creative qualitative method which is used by all researchers. Writing up a literature review or a document analysis is, as the latter term suggests, also an analytic process – and qualitative analysis is a creative endeavour. Your write-up should not be simply a list of who said what or which points were made where (Thomson and Kamler, 2016: 76). That is, your first draft might be, or include, such a list – but then, or ideally before that point, you should be looking for patterns and links, disjunctures and interstices, exploring what they tell you, and writing that down. You may also wish to review your field notes to see what they can contribute to your context-setting. This is where the creativity lies in writing at this stage: how you build a rich and detailed picture of the context for your research, to inform your audience or audiences.

In qualitative research this may also be where your analytical work begins because of the complex relationship between reading, thinking, writing and producing knowledge (Murray, 2011: 127). You need to assess the quality of the documents or literature you are using, and give more weight to those of higher quality. Critical thinking is useful here – that's critical as in 'critique', i.e. making considered assess-ments, not critical as in criticising everything in sight. In creating the context for your work, you are evaluating the work of others; not only its quality but also the links and gaps between different ideas and practices (Murray, 2011: 127). Then at a later stage, when you have analysed your own data, information from your context-setting work may help to confirm or contradict your findings (Bloomberg and Volpe, 2012: 150).

Quoting from literature or documents can be useful, but should be kept to a minimum rather than being over-used. It is essential to 'frame' any quote you use: to introduce the quote, explain why you are using it, and connect it with your narrative (Thomson and Kamler, 2016: 80–1).

The ethics of context-setting

Working to contextualise qualitative or multi-modal research can feel like a stand-alone project, but it is not. Also, few – if any – of the documents a researcher will draw on in that process will be stand-alone documents. As we have seen, most documents exist in relation to other documents, such as through referencing. Also, remember that qualitative researchers use a wide definition of documents that includes web pages, leaflets, social media posts and so on. Being aware of the links between documents is an ethical way to proceed, giving you a wider view of the relationships within your material as well as the material itself, and enabling you to make links explicit when relevant. Doing this will also help you to understand how the writing you produce, to contextualise your research, exists in relation to all the documents it references and to all the documents that may reference it in the future.

When you are contextualising research, there is a fine line between explaining the background to and justifying the need for your research, and becoming persuasive. There is always some rhetoric in writing (Becker, 2007: 15; Montgomery, 2017: 24) but I would recommend keeping it to a minimum. As far as possible, report the facts as you understand them from your sources.

Another ethical element in context-setting is to do your searching thoroughly, in accordance with your planned strategy. And another is to treat all your sources respectfully and fairly: read them properly and use them well. When you are busy, as most of us are, it is tempting to skim-read, but this is not ethical other than to assess a document for inclusion or exclusion. The ethical approach is to read carefully and make sure you understand both the specific arguments being put forward and where those arguments are located in the wider conversation (Kara, 2018: 90). Think about how much work you are putting into your context-setting, then treat others' work with the respect you would like for your own.

Conclusion

Good work in context setting accomplishes several things. It explains what led to the current situation of your research, describes that situation, and demonstrates why your research is needed (Bloomberg and Volpe, 2012: 65). This sets the stage for your readers and helps them to understand your work more fully. It also provides a useful resource for you, at the analytic stage, to set your own findings in context.

Your context-setting section may be quite brief; even just a page or two, though sometimes more is needed. However, this short section often represents a lot of work in searching, reading, thinking and drafting. Skimping on this work will not serve you well; I recommend thoroughness and diligence.

Reflective questions

1. Which method(s) of making field notes appeal to you?
2. What are the ethical implications of your answer to question 1?
3. This chapter introduced wide definitions of 'literature' and 'documents'. Can either or both of these definitions help you to think more widely about sources that might be useful for your research?
4. How can you mitigate against your own biases when you are contextualising your research?
5. Are you naturally meticulous? If not, what steps could you take to improve your attention to detail?

6

GATHERING QUALITATIVE DATA: MAINSTREAM METHODS

Chapter summary

- Introduces the debate about collecting or constructing primary qualitative data
- Considers the ethical and practical importance and relevance of secondary qualitative data
- Outlines the main methods of gathering qualitative data: questionnaires, interviews, focus groups and observation
- Explores the role of the case study in qualitative research
- Describes action research
- Explains the options for using field notes as data
- Discusses some of the ways technology can help us to gather qualitative data
- Covers some key ethical issues in qualitative data gathering

Introduction

There is a debate in qualitative research about whether primary data are collected, as in effectively being harvested from people, or constructed, that is created in conjunction with participants. This is linked with different ontological and epistemological perspectives as discussed in Chapter 2. It seems to me that some primary qualitative data are collected, such as observational data where participants are unaware of the researcher's presence, and some are constructed, such as artistic or crafted items co-created by researcher and participant during an enhanced interview (enhanced interviews are discussed in detail in Chapter 7). I also think there are grey areas, where data are both collected and constructed, such as observational data where some participants are aware of the researcher's presence and some are not. An example of this could be observational data collected in a care home for people with advanced dementia, where staff and some residents are aware of the researcher's presence while other residents are unaware. I use the term 'gathering data' to encompass all points of this debate.

This chapter begins by considering the role of secondary data in qualitative research. Then it covers the most used and most long-standing methods of gathering qualitative primary data: the questionnaire, the interview, the focus group and observation. We will also discuss the qualitative case study method, and some of the ways technology can aid us in gathering qualitative data. The next chapter will cover some of the newer and more creative methods of gathering data. You may feel drawn to one or more of the methods in these two chapters, but remember, the methods you use in your research should be the ones most likely to help you answer your research question, not the ones you most fancy trying out.

Secondary data

Secondary data are data that have been collected, compiled, collated or created for any purpose other than your research. 'Data' is the word researchers use to define information they want to analyse. So secondary data may come in many forms: archival data, media data, other researchers' data and so on.

Defining information as 'data' creates scope for abuse. This may be large-scale, such as in the United States where museums, universities and other institutions hold the remains and burial offerings of around two million Indigenous people. Indigenous peoples in the United States want these items back so they can give their ancestors the proper respect and ceremonies. Legislation was passed to enable this over 30 years ago, but because Euro-Western researchers have labelled the human remains and burial offerings as 'data', they have been able to avoid returning them to their communities (Dunbar-Ortiz, 2014: 231). Or abuse may be small-scale, such as a single researcher harvesting personal blog posts that are publicly available online without seeking consent from the writers to use the posts as data. This is currently legal in most countries but – in the view of many researchers – not ethical (Lomborg, 2013: 25). Qualitative researchers need to be aware of the potential risks of abuse that secondary data present, and take care to avoid these risks.

Using secondary data requires a lot of ethical re-thinking. The principle of informed consent is built around primary data gathering and is profoundly challenged by the use of secondary data (Hughes and Tarrant, 2020b: 43). Unless 'enduring consent' (Neale, 2013: 14) for the reuse of the data has been obtained, researchers may need retrospective consent. This can be difficult to obtain, and if researchers are able to contact participants and their representatives, those people may become irritated or even traumatised by repeated requests for consent (Grinyer, 2009: 2). Similarly, the principles of anonymity and confidentiality are profoundly challenged by the use of secondary data from social media (Nguyen, 2021: 195). And it is not safe to assume that people will suffer no ill-effects from working with secondary data. There is evidence showing the risk of emotional harm from transcribing others' qualitative data on distressing topics such as domestic violence and child abuse (Kiyimba and O'Reilly, 2016: 473).

However, there are also strong ethical arguments for using secondary data, not least that it reduces 'research fatigue' (Ashley, 2021). Enormous amounts of data are produced and published online for public use by governments, health authorities, national and global organisations. A great deal of historical data is available through archives, libraries and museums. Research funders in many countries are now routinely requiring researchers to make their data available for others to use. It is arguable that most researchers should use secondary data first, to see if they can answer their research question or questions that way, and only turn to primary data gathering if there are still gaps in knowledge that cannot be filled using secondary data.

Also, secondary data have some considerable advantages (Bryman, 2016: 312–4). Much secondary data are quick and easy to collect, reducing researchers' workloads or freeing up more time for other parts of the research process. International or global data can be gathered from your desk. Reanalysis of qualitative data can offer new insights, particularly if different analytical methods and/or theoretical lenses are used. And secondary data can be set more clearly in its historical context than primary data (Coltart et al., 2013: 16).

There are a number of online sources of secondary qualitative data (Edwards et al., 2020: 80–1; Kara, 2017: 125–6) and more are being created all the time. (Of course there are many more online sources of quantitative data, and these can be useful too if you are conducting multi-modal research.) The UK Data Service has identified five ways of re-using qualitative data for research[1]:

1. Description – of the attributes, attitudes and behaviour of individuals, communities, groups or organisations at the time of the original project.
2. Comparison – such as over time, or between social groups or geographic locations.
3. Re-analysis – using different methods, or applying different topics of investigation, to ask new questions of the data.
4. Research design – to assess the design used in the light of the quality of the data and findings it yielded, and draw conclusions to inform future research designs.

---

[1] https://ukdataservice.ac.uk/use-data/guides/methods-software/qualitative-reuse.aspx (accessed 25 June 2021).

5. Methodological advancement – to assess the methods used in the light of the quality of the research findings, and identify ways in which existing methods can be improved and new methods devised.

An example of secondary data used for re-analysis is in Box 6.1.

Box 6.1

Secondary data used for re-analysis

Wanda Martin, Joan Wharf-Higgins and two colleagues in Canada wanted to assess the evidence literacy of public health practitioners in British Columbia. To do this they re-analysed data from two previous research projects. The first was a healthy living study exploring how practitioners used evidence in deciding how to implement a public health programme. This involved 29 interviews with organisational representatives and public health managers and staff from urban and rural areas in two health authorities. The second was a knowledge-to-action study focusing on knowledge translation strategies supporting the use of evidence in public health programme development and implementation. This involved 49 interviews and three focus groups with organisational representatives, food safety staff and managers, and injury prevention staff and managers, in three health authorities (including the two covered in the first project). Each of the two projects had been worked on by one of the named authors. The first had obtained ethical approval for secondary analysis; for the second, ethical approval for secondary analysis had to be obtained before that analysis could take place. These data proved useful in answering the new research question: To what extent are public health practitioners who work in these three health authorities evidence-literate? (Martin et al., 2017: 2–3). The analytic method used with the evidence-related data in the first project was reviewed and considered appropriate for re-use with the data from the second project. The re-analysis was rigorous, thorough and collaborative, and yielded findings that could help to strengthen evidence literacy in public health.

Questionnaires

The questionnaire is an instrument often used in survey research. It can be entirely quantitative or entirely qualitative, or – probably most often – a combination of the two. In the 19th and 20th centuries, a questionnaire was a paper form to fill in by hand, but these days most questionnaires are presented online or on digital devices. This has led to the questionnaire being arguably the most over-used research method in existence, with everything you buy online and many goods or services bought in person coming with a link to a 'survey' or a 'feedback form' or a 'chance to review' which is often, in fact, a questionnaire.

As with all methods, questionnaires have advantages and disadvantages (Gillham, 2008a: 5–8; Kara, 2017: 139). The advantages include the following:

- Low cost
- Easy to administer
- Can be completely anonymous
- People can respond when it suits them, and take as much time as they need to think about their answers
- Researcher not present so can't influence responses
- Range of question types offers flexibility
- Consistent instrument maximising comparability of responses
- Analysis of closed questions is quick and easy

Disadvantages include the following:

- It is difficult to design a good questionnaire
- How the questions are worded and presented can have a big effect on the answers
- People with digital or other literacy problems may not be able to respond
- Response rates are often low
- Responses may be incomplete, inaccurate or dishonest
- Respondents may feel frustrated if their knowledge or experience doesn't fit into the predetermined categories
- Data are often superficial
- Not useful for researching sensitive or intimate topics

Some questionnaire designers try to minimise inaccuracy or dishonesty by including questions such as 'If you are paying attention, please select the answer "orange" in response to this question' and then discarding any responses where a different answer is selected. So this is an option you could consider, though I am not sure how well it works, and I have been unable to find any evidence for or against its efficacy.

Questionnaires are often most useful in the early stages of a research project, or used in conjunction with other methods of gathering data.

Questionnaires are, as the name suggests, made up of questions. These may be closed, with predetermined answers, or open, where the respondent can write the answer in their own words. There are five main kinds of closed question:

- Binary question
- Choose one option from a list
- Choose more than one option from a list

- Rank responses in a list
- Choose one option from a scale

Binary questions have two answer options to choose from such as yes or no, hot or cold. They can be useful for dividing people's responses into categories. You may then direct respondents to different parts of the questionnaire, like this:

1. Do you use public transport? yes/no

   If 'no', please go straight to question 6.

Choosing one option from a list is useful for asking 'most' or 'least' questions, such as:

2. Which form of public transport do you use most often? Please tick one.

   - □ Taxi
   - □ Bus
   - □ Overground train
   - □ Underground train
   - □ Tram
   - □ Ferry
   - □ Cable car
   - □ Other – please specify

Choosing more than one option from a list is useful for gathering more detailed information, such as:

3. Which forms of public transport have you used in the last year? Please tick as many as apply.

   - □ Taxi
   - □ Bus
   - □ Overground train
   - □ Underground train
   - □ Tram
   - □ Ferry
   - □ Cable car
   - □ Other – please specify

Ranking responses in a list is useful for finding out about preferences and behaviours. Here's an example:

4. Please rank these forms of public transport from 1 to 8, with 1 being the one you like best to 8 being the one you like least.

  □ Taxi
  □ Bus
  □ Overground train
  □ Underground train
  □ Tram
  □ Ferry
  □ Cable car
  □ Other – please specify

Choosing an option from a scale enables you to gather more nuanced information about a topic, like this:

5. Please circle the number that best represents how satisfied you are with the form of public transport you use most often.

  Very satisfied 1   2   3   4   5   6   7   Very unsatisfied

The scale you choose can be of any length. Also, shorter scales can be given in words rather than numbers, such as:

6. Please tick one to show how satisfied you are with the form of public transport you use most often.

  □ Very satisfied
  □ Quite satisfied
  □ Neither satisfied nor unsatisfied
  □ Quite unsatisfied
  □ Very unsatisfied

There is a debate about whether it is better for a scale to be odd-numbered or even-numbered. An odd-numbered scale allows the respondent to choose a neither-nor or neutral midpoint, but this can be unhelpful for analysis. An even-numbered scale forces the respondent to choose a side, which is more useful for analysis, but may be frustrating for respondents whose actual response would be a midpoint. Also, it could be regarded as unethical to force such a choice. One compromise is to use a long even-numbered scale. Some questionnaires use a 'thermometer' scale with 100 'degrees' to seek highly nuanced information. This is only likely to be useful if you have a large number of respondents, and if those respondents are willing and able to, in effect, represent their views or feelings as percentages.

Open questions can have short answers, as for the 'Other – please specify' options in the questions above, which might have answers such as rickshaw or tuk tuk. Or they can have long answers, or at least the scope for long answers. A common formulation is along the lines of 'Is there anything else you would like to tell us about [topic]?' with a text box that may or may not be set to allow a maximum number of words or characters. If you really want respondents to have free rein, you would not put a limit on the length of their response; if you want to make your own life easier at the analytic stage, you would, in which case it is good practice to make this clear to the respondent.

It is easy to understand the types of questions that are used in questionnaires. It is much more difficult to write good questions – and answers, because for any closed questions you need to write the answers too (Gillham, 2008a: 23). That can make it tempting to use more open questions, but too many open questions can be off-putting for respondents, as many people don't like to write too much. Also closed questions are easier to analyse because, as the sharp-witted reader will have realised, they yield quantitative data while open questions yield qualitative data. (For this reason, some qualitative researchers regard the questionnaire as a quantitative instrument, while some quantitative researchers regard it as a qualitative instrument because it is mostly made from words. Me? I don't care how it's labelled; it is a useful research method in some quantitative, qualitative and multi-modal contexts.)

Questionnaires can be long and complex, but this is not generally a good idea because the longer and more complicated a questionnaire is, the fewer responses you are likely to get. Having said that, online questionnaire design enables you to conceal questions people don't need to answer. So question 1 above wouldn't need to specify 'If no, please go straight to question 6', because the questionnaire can be set up in such a way that anyone who answers 'no' to question 1 is automatically routed straight to question 6. This means there is more scope for complexity online with less impact on response rate.

Another advantage of digital questionnaires is that they can vary the order of the answers in lists, and the direction of scales, from respondent to respondent. This is helpful because the order of the answers you provide can influence responses (Bryman, 2016: 208), so varying the order in a randomised or systematic way can help to reduce this answer order effect.

With some groups of participants, such as older people or those living in rural, coastal, desert or forested areas where internet connectivity is limited, you may need to use old-style paper questionnaires. These have several disadvantages over digital questionnaires: they cost more to produce and send to potential respondents; if you need to chase responses, you have to send another letter; people can (and do) choose points between numbers in scales, or circle two numbers together or write in the margins of paper questionnaires; and you need to enter the data into a computer for analysis, which is time-consuming and tedious. But if they are the only way to reach people you want to reach, then they are what you need to use.

When your questions are all written and you have a fully designed questionnaire in draft, it is essential that you test your questionnaire. You should not test it on people who might be your actual respondents, but on people as similar to those people as possible. This is not always easy and sometimes you have to settle for the best option you can manage. If possible, sit with each of your pilot respondents and ask them to give a commentary or 'think aloud' while they complete your draft questionnaire. This can be very enlightening and you will quickly learn about any ambiguities that may have crept in or any lack of clarity in the writing of your questions and answers. Also, check their responses to see whether your questionnaire is actually yielding the kind of data you want. Use the feedback from your pilot respondents and their responses to revise your questionnaire, then pilot it again until it is as good as you can get it.

Interviews

The research interview is the most common, most familiar method for gathering data in qualitative research. Most people have taken part in a research interview at some time or another. It is sometimes known as a 'conversation with a purpose'. Interviews may be conducted face-to-face, by telephone or online.

Interviews have advantages and disadvantages (Kara, 2017: 143). The advantages include the following:

- Interviewers can ask supplementary questions to follow up interesting points made by the interviewee
- Face-to-face and online interviews allow the researcher to observe as well as listen
- Telephone and online interviews are cheap and can enable more anonymity
- Interviews can enable comparison of data from different individuals, groups, communities, institutions and so on
- Recording data enables exact reproduction of someone's words, plus information about non-verbal sounds such as laughter, and about pauses

Disadvantages include the following:

- It can be difficult to design interview questions that will elicit the information you want
- Interviews are time-consuming
- Talking about sensitive subjects with a stranger is unusual
- Interviewers' manner and input can influence interviewees' answers
- Interviewees' manner and input can influence interviewers' interpretation of the resulting data
- It can be difficult to keep an interview on track as it may mimic an everyday social interaction
- Transcribing interview data is time-consuming or costly

The word 'interview' can be off-putting to some potential participants because it has formal and quite negative associations: job interview, disciplinary interview, police interview, immigration interview. For this reason, researchers may choose not to use the word with participants, instead using a more informal term such as asking for a chat for their research (Nguyen, 2021: 191). However, 'interview' is the professional research term, so I will continue to use it here.

Interviews can be structured, unstructured or semi-structured. In a structured interview, predetermined questions are asked in the same order of each respondent. Unlike questionnaires, though, the researcher does not predetermine any of the answers. Respondents have more freedom in interviews, and they can – and do – answer questions you have not asked. Even so, the data they provide are likely to be valuable, and there should be enough flexibility in your analytical methods to make use of most, if not all, of that data. Structured interviews are useful when you want to try to compare different participants' responses.

An unstructured interview may have just one initial question, and then proceed through discussion rather than question-and-answer. This can be useful when you want to explore a topic about which little is known. It can also be useful when you want your participants to decide how and what to share without undue influence from your questions.

A semi-structured interview is the most common type of interview. This usually involves a set of predetermined questions, with more freedom for the researcher to follow up points of interest than in most structured interviews. There is often a final question along the lines of, 'Is there anything else you would like to say about [topic] that we haven't already covered?' This allows the participant to set part of the research agenda. Sometimes this is the most useful question of all (Box 6.2).

Box 6.2

Biographic narrative interpretive method in practice

Denise Turner and Marie Price, researchers at two universities in the south-east of England, used the BNIM in a pilot study exploring the impact of bereavement on the well-being of social work students. They describe the BNIM as 'a free association narrative method, which allows research participants an uninterrupted narrative flow. Underlying this is the theory that participants will choose whatever is important to them and select the order for this, thereby reducing researcher intervention and helping to diminish bias' (Turner and Price, 2020: 5–6). They recruited from their universities 11 social work students who had recent experience of bereavement, and held the interviews in quiet rooms away from the teaching areas. They formulated a standard 'question' – actually a short statement – as follows:

Please tell me about your experience of bereavement, during your social work training. This should include all the events and experiences that were important to you personally no matter how insignificant they might seem. Begin wherever you like. I'll just listen. I won't interrupt. I might jot down some notes for afterwards (Turner and Price, 2020: 7).

This enabled participants to speak in an open and self-directed way, which led to the researchers discovering that the dominant western Christian paradigm disenfranchises bereaved students in the United Kingdom, particularly those from black and minority ethnic backgrounds, and that there is a need for greater understanding of power differentials relating to culture (Turner and Price, 2020: 15).

There are variations on these three main types of interview. For example, the biographic narrative interpretive method (BNIM) involves the interviewer asking each participant just one key question (Bolton et al., 2005). This combines the structured and unstructured approaches. An example of this in practice is shown in Box 6.1.

Doing research interviews is part of the work of many qualitative researchers. Each interview is a unique human encounter. Many participants are quite open and forthcoming, and hearing what they have to say can feel like a great privilege. It is important, though, to listen sensitively, with awareness that something you might regard as quite innocuous could be upsetting for someone else. If an interviewee becomes upset, whatever the reason, you have a duty of care for that person. Stop the interview and do what you can to support your interviewee in their distress. Make it clear that they don't need to continue if they don't want to. Be a human (Ross and Call-Cummings, 2020: 507).

You can interview two people at once, known as couple, pair, joint or dyadic interviews. Sometimes this is simply a useful time-saving measure, and sometimes it is indicated by the research topic and question. It has often been used by researchers studying shared experiences such as marriage or co-habitation, illness and disability (Zarhin, 2018: 844). This method enables researchers to observe interpersonal dynamics and interactions within relationships, providing richer data than interviews with one individual. However, relationships are not always equal, and one interviewee may dominate the encounter and silence the other in a form of 'symbolic violence' which can be uncomfortable for researchers to witness, particularly if they feel they are 'unwilling abettors' (Zarhin, 2018: 846).

Focus groups

An interview with more than two people is known as a focus group, and these have advantages and disadvantages (Kara, 2017: 145). Advantages include the following:

- You can get views from several people at once
- Interactions between focus group members can enrich data
- Some people find it easier to speak in a group than one-to-one
- Researchers can ask supplementary questions
- You can compare data from different groups

Disadvantages include the following:

- Focus groups can be difficult to arrange
- Focus groups may need two researchers, one to facilitate the group and one to take notes, which increases costs
- Some people find it difficult to speak in a group
- Groups can be difficult to facilitate and may become unruly
- Transcribing focus group data is time-consuming or costly

The best size for a focus group is probably six to eight people. You can run a focus group with as few as three people, or more than eight – though if there are too many people in the group, they may spontaneously divide into two or three smaller groups, each having a separate discussion (Nyumba et al., 2018: 23). The difficulty in arranging focus groups is because most people have more interesting things to do than come and talk in a group to a researcher about a topic the researcher is more interested in than they are. The best option, when possible, is to gain access to an existing group. Sometimes research topics facilitate this, such as research into different kinds of support groups or sports clubs. If this is not the case, think about where your potential participants might get together, and whether you could reach a group of them in that place.

The optimum length for a focus group meeting is probably between one and two hours (Nyumba et al., 2018: 23). The discussion may be shorter, if people are pushed for time or don't have much to say, or longer, if people are willing and have a lot to say.

Focus groups can be conducted online as well as offline. This could be in a dedicated online space, if you have the skills and facilities to make that happen, or via an online service such as Skype, Zoom or Google Hangouts. Online focus groups may be easier for people to attend, and provide an opportunity to bring people together in ways that would be impossible in person, such as when they live in different countries. However, online focus groups depend on technology, which is inaccessible for some people and, even when it is accessible, can break down. Also interacting online is more stilted than in person, and people are not always willing or able to have visual as well as audio contact, so there is much less scope for researchers to include observational data. On the plus side, the data generated are not noticeably different between online and off-line focus groups (Woodyatt et al., 2016: 741). Box 6.3 shows an example of focus groups being used in research practice.

Box 6.3

Focus groups in practice

Victoria Wibeck and eight colleagues used focus groups to study lay people's sense-making about climate engineering in Japan, New Zealand, the United States and Sweden. The researchers regard 'sense-making' as 'an interactive process by which people understand, describe and relate to their surroundings' (Wibeck et al., 2017: 3). The interactive element of this concept led to the decision to use focus groups, with the hope of witnessing sense-making in action. Participants were recruited with no mention of climate engineering, to make sure discussions would be spontaneous rather than including prepared responses. Twenty-three focus groups were held in regional university towns in the United States, New Zealand and Sweden, and in a large metropolitan city in Japan. These included a total of 136 participants with diverse characteristics across age, gender, socio-economic status and cultural backgrounds. Each focus group was semi-structured, led by a moderator and lasted for one to two hours. Discussions started with open-ended questions, avoiding pre-determined frames, and information about climate engineering was gradually introduced to allow participant reactions to common aspects of the scientific discourse such as 'the climate emergency' (Wibeck et al., 2017: 4). The focus group data were transcribed and analysed within and between countries to look for commonalities and variations.

Observation

Observation sounds like a simple method for qualitative researchers: you just go and watch people at a sports match, or an organisation's annual general meeting or an airport. However, if you try it, you will soon realise that there is so much going on that it can be overwhelming (Robson and McCartan, 2016: 322). Facial expressions, speech, body language, interactions, physical contact, movement – what is relevant for your research? There is no way you could record it all, so you have to be selective, and plan what you will record and how.

Gillham distinguishes between structured and unstructured observation. He sees structured observation as non-participatory research in which the researcher uses 'structured observation schedules which involve the recording and counting of pre-determined categories of behaviour' yielding mostly quantitative data (Gillham, 2008b: 4). And he regards unstructured observation as participant observation, where the researcher spends an extended period of time with their participants in a social context, gathering mostly qualitative data.

These are visual observation methods. Another option is mechanical observation, using technology for observational purposes (Bogomolova, 2017: 127). This is used in quantitative market research with data from supermarket checkouts, retail websites, loyalty cards and so on. There are also options for qualitative researchers to include data from cameras such as CCTV, vehicle dashboard cameras and personal photo and video cameras.

As is so often the case, the distinctions between structured and unstructured, visual and mechanical observational research are not hard and fast. Box 6.4 gives an example of observational research in practice which bears out this point.

Box 6.4

Observational research in practice

Clive Pope conducted an ethnographic study of the Maadi Cup, a major rowing competition in New Zealand which takes place over one week and includes hundreds of races and dozens of finals. Pope spent 10 days at the competition site, to observe the preparations and aftermath as well as the competition itself, and to learn about rowers and rowing culture. Ethnography usually involves spending an extended period of time in the field, but this was not an option in this case, so Pope conducted a 'compressed ethnography' (Pope, 2010: 134, drawing on Jeffrey and Troman, 2004) using photography and video to record and revisit actions and interactions between people and sport. This meant he could continue his observational work after the event – which was essential because the event itself was so busy and brief that he could not fully appreciate what was happening and why. He used the photos and videos to 'rewind, revisit and reframe the setting, repeatedly seeking new learnings and understandings' (Pope, 2010: 135). This 'replaced the inductive and emerging discoveries that often evolve in situ during prolonged conventional ethnographies' (Pope, 2010: 135).

As always, observation as a research method has advantages and disadvantages. Advantages include the following:

- Observation is a direct technique which can be useful in situations where other methods are hard to use, such as airport check-in areas or school gates.
- Researchers are free to observe people in public places such as streets, courts and cemeteries, without needing to go through a gatekeeper or ask for anyone's consent.
- Video can be used to record observational data for closer examination at a later date.

Disadvantages include the following:

- Observational data may be patchy as even with a plan it can be difficult to record everything you want to record.

- The presence of the observer may affect the behaviour of the people being observed (and there is no way to know for sure whether it does or not).
- Observation raises difficult ethical issues. How detached or involved should, or can, the researcher be? How can participants give their consent? Is it ethically acceptable to observe people who have not given consent, even in public places?

Observation is rarely used as the sole method in a research project. It is more often used as one of the methods in multi-modal research, or at an early exploratory stage of a research project (Gillham, 2008b: 6–7). Even ethnographers often combine their central method of participant observation with other methods such as surveys, interviews and archival research (Cohen, 2015: 44).

Because of the richness and variety of observational data in any given situation, it may be useful to have two or more researchers. Either they can be assigned different tasks and so collect more data, or they can be assigned the same task so that their data can be compared.

Case study research

Case study research is not only related to data gathering, it can be a whole method in itself. Robert Yin usefully distinguishes between case study research (the mode of enquiry), case studies (the method of enquiry) and a case (the unit of enquiry in a case study) (Yin, 2018: xx). So case studies can be used as a method within other forms of research, and case study research can include other methods than case studies.

Let's say the unit of enquiry is a small business, located in and serving a specific geographical community. You want to use this small business as a case study – your unit of enquiry – to help you understand how local businesses and local communities interact. So you conduct case study research, collecting documents and conducting interviews with staff, customers and suppliers of the business, as well as local residents who are not connected with the business.

There is another example of case study research in Box 6.5, this time including case studies as one of the methods of enquiry.

Box 6.5

Case study research in practice

In the late 20th century the ethnomusicologist Roland Bannister studied the Kapooka Band of Wagga Wagga, New South Wales, Australia. Wagga Wagga is the largest inland city in New South Wales and is an important agricultural, economic and transport hub for its region. The Kapooka Band is the only military band in the area,

(Continued)

and formed a useful case for considering the relationship between music and war. So the Kapooka Band was the unit of enquiry in Bannister's case study research – and he used case studies as one of his methods too, within his case study research, such as the case study of Captain Ian, the band's Commanding Officer, taking a band rehearsal (Bannister, 1995: 147–8). Other methods and approaches Bannister used within his case study research included fieldwork and participant observation, and he gathered data in the form of field notes and interview transcripts (Bannister, 1995: 4).

Spending months or years doing fieldwork and participant observation is not the only way to conduct case study research. The methods you use will depend on the case(s) you are studying, and can include a selection of most methods – even quantitative and experimental methods if applicable. The point is to produce a holistic, 360-degree, complete view of the case(s) in all its, or their, uniqueness (Thomas, 2016: 5). The aim is to increase knowledge and/or develop theory, rather than to generalise (Yin, 2018: 21).

It will not surprise you to learn that case study research has advantages and disadvantages. Advantages include the following:

• Useful for investigating real-world phenomena in context
• Flexible – can be used with most ontological and epistemological positions, theoretical perspectives and methods
• Relevant for applied research, such as evaluation, as well as academic research

Disadvantages include the following:

• Case study research can turn out to be longer and more arduous than it might at first appear
• Some people confuse case studies in research with case studies used in other professions such as teaching or media

In qualitative research, $n = 1$ is not regarded as a disadvantage, though it does require some justification.

Case studies in the more journalistic sense are also used in reporting research of many kinds, and this will be covered in Chapter 10.

Action research

Action research was devised in the 1940s by social psychologist Kurt Lewin. It is a collaborative method, enabling groups of people to research a problem they are facing, either by themselves or with support from a professional researcher (Kara, 2017: 49). There are various types of action research such as organisational action research, critical action research and empirical action research (Cohen et al., 2018: 441). However, in all of these, people will 'collaborate in the diagnosis of a problem and in the development of a solution based on the diagnosis' (Bryman, 2016: 387).

Action research is characterised by a cycle of 'plan, act, observe, reflect' which repeats as often as necessary. We saw in Box 2.1 that Towers and his colleagues conducted ten cycles of action research over a six-year period. This suggests that each cycle lasted around seven months, though in some action research projects a cycle might be completed in a much shorter time, or in other cases it might take longer. Also, in some action research, only a couple of cycles might be needed, where other projects could need many cycles to complete. So, in essence, action research is 'an iterative process of reflection and problem solving in groups and communities' (Kara, 2017: 49).

There are no prescribed methods for use in action research. It is a holistic approach, embedded in its context, which relies on the creativity, ingenuity and knowledge of its practitioners (Banks, 2016: 29, 27). However, it must be collaborative, and is sometimes called participatory action research. It is a flexible approach, easy to learn and use and there are some helpful resources online (see Appendix 1 for the URL).

Field notes

You can decide in advance that you will construct some field notes to use as data, or you can decide in retrospect that some or all of your field notes would form useful data. We saw in Chapter 5 that there are many options for how to create field notes. If you are going to use field notes as data, it would be useful to take a systematic approach, such as recording your impressions and feelings immediately after each interpersonal encounter, or noting specific observations or attributes of participants or settings.

Box 6.6 shows an example of systematic field notes that the researcher decided in retrospect to use as data.

Box 6.6
_____

Field notes as data

As we saw in Box 1.1, Reshma Naik and her colleagues studied the factors influencing people to seek appropriate care after a home-based positive HIV test in South Africa. This qualitative research was situated within a cluster randomised controlled trial (RCT) of home-based HIV testing uptake in Umzimkhulu, a poor, rural municipality of Kwa-Zulu Natal. Tandazile Cagwe conducted 30 in-depth semi-structured

(Continued)

interviews with consenting RCT participants who tested HIV positive to investigate what influenced them to seek care. At the same time, another quantitative study situated within the RCT tracked the progress of consenting HIV-positive RCT participants in accessing and using appropriate care. As part of this quantitative study, Celiwe Ngidi wrote field notes about 196 participants to record any information they shared about their reasons for accessing and using care, or for not doing so. When Naik reviewed Ngidi's field notes, she 'felt strongly that the content was informative and complemented the in-depth interviews' (Naik et al., 2018: 724) and so decided to include them as data for the study.

The role of technology in data gathering

Qualitative researchers are increasingly using technology, in all sorts of different ways, to help them gather data. Questionnaires can be administered via SMS or an app on a smartphone. Qualitative researchers can study families on Facebook, dating on Tinder, political awareness on Reddit and any number of other topics on a wide range of social media platforms. Entire computer games are designed with a double function: to be fun to play, and also as vehicles for researchers to gather data.

Digital storytelling is the process of creating a 'first-person mini-movie' (Willox et al., 2013: 312) using images (photos, video, artworks) and sound (voice-over narrative, music, sounds from the world). This method has been used widely in education research (Phillips and Kara, 2021: 133), mental health research (De Vecchi et al., 2016: 188) and with marginalised groups such as Indigenous people (Willox et al., 2013) and refugees (Lenette, 2019). Researchers using digital storytelling commonly give participants control over how they shape their narrative in response to a simple prompt. Willox and her colleagues used digital storytelling to find out about the impact of climate change on the people of Rigolet, a remote coastal community in northern Labrador, Canada; their digital stories can be viewed on YouTube (see Appendix 1 for the URL). The level of control given to participants in digital storytelling is more characteristic of alternative methods than mainstream methods. Digital storytelling would once have been considered an alternative method – but it is now so widely used that it could be seen as mainstream.

The opportunities offered by technology for qualitative data gathering are many, various and increasing all the time. Box 6.7 shows an example of qualitative data gathering using technology.

Box 6.7

Qualitative data gathering using technology

Borja García and his colleagues in the United Kingdom studied the role that football plays in the daily lives of football fans. They decided to ask participants to take pictures of their involvement in football, and to keep an audio-visual diary of four football-related events in an eight-week period. Then each participant would be interviewed during which they would be asked to explain and interpret their photos. Early in the design process it occurred to the researchers that an app would simplify the process for participants, make participation more fun and interactive and encourage participants to capture their lives in real time (Garcia et al., 2016: 511). The researchers worked with a local software company with experience in designing apps for research, and found that app design involves a number of decisions that can affect the type, quality and amount of data gathered. They decided to structure the app into four sections, aligned with the planned methods. First, an introductory task to help users become familiar with the app, ensure there were no technical problems and enable the collection of demographic data and information about participants' football support activities. Then the photos, the audio-visual diary and an optional 'anytime' task to provide an open and flexible upload option for participants. The photography task was structured with six pre-determined tags such as 'football traditions' and 'what football means to me'. Five of these tags were generated by a review of relevant academic literature, and the sixth was 'no category' to offer flexibility for participants if they felt none of the other five would fit. The audio-visual diary offered participants the option to make audio or video diary entries, and for each event they were asked to make an entry the day before, the day of and the day after each event. The app automatically tagged each entry with the date and time of recording. It was piloted to ensure usability, and feedback was helpful in finalising the design and operation of the app. The researchers thought long and hard about whether to make smartphone ownership a condition of participation, and decided not to do this, but to make the app optional. They recruited 37 participants, mostly through an online call, and 14 opted to use the app. The others were provided with cameras and voice recorders, though some participants chose to use their own camera or other device to take photos. This helped to make the research inclusive, but led to some concerns about consistency (Garcia et al., 2016: 518). The researchers met with each participant before data gathering began, either face-to-face or via Skype, which also allowed for a brief demonstration of a test version of the app for those who had elected to use it. The app was expensive, particularly as it was only used by 14 people, but it saved researchers' time in various ways. First, it was easy and quick to monitor partic-ipants' activity and progress automatically, rather than having to contact them to check. Second, researchers had instant access to data uploaded through the app, via the web portal where it was stored, while non-app users provided data by email or through a file sharing website which was much more time-consuming to receive and store. Another advantage was that the app provided reminder notifications to participants, which non-app users did not receive.

Other options provided by technology include gathering video data and gathering data via social media. These will be discussed in Chapter 7.

Ethics of gathering qualitative data using mainstream methods

Data gathering is the element of research where ethical difficulties come into sharpest focus. As researchers we have a duty of care to our participants and to others who we may encounter during the data gathering process such as gatekeepers. We are responsible for doing all we can to maintain the well-being of these people, and of ourselves. Ethical guidance for doing this cannot be formed from hard-and-fast rules because context is always a factor. For example, in much Euro-Western research, participant anonymity is a central ethical principle, yet in some contexts this can do more harm than good. American educational researcher Kristen Perry worked with Sudanese refugees, and to her surprise they became upset when she said she would use pseudonyms to maintain their anonymity. She had been unaware that 'forced name-changing was a common tactic of repression by the Sudanese majority' (Perry, 2011: 911).

As we saw in Chapter 1, in some qualitative research, gaining informed consent from participants needs to be a multi-stage process rather than a straightforward event centred around the signing of a consent form. Some participants, such as people with dementia or other cognitive impairment, or any participant in longitudinal research such as much ethnography, may need to be asked for their consent at several points during the research if consent is to be fully informed (Robinson et al., 2011: 331). Conversely, in research with some communities, consent will be needed from several people. In schools you may need initial consent from the head teacher to do research on the premises, then consent from department heads and/or class teachers to do research with their pupils, then consent from the pupils themselves (Agbebiyi, 2013: 537). In a village in Botswana a researcher may need consent from a research ethics committee, then from a village chief (who in turn will seek consent from the village council) and then from potential participants (Chilisa, 2020: 242).

For some researchers, a 'duty of care' involves paying participants for their input (Kara, 2018: 100–1). For others, payment can cause a range of problems, such as poorer quality data, changed relationship between researcher and participant and difficulties for other researchers who don't have a budget for paying participants (Colvin, 2014: 62; van Wyk, 2014: 208; Weeks, 2014: 144). Different disciplines have different views on this: medical researchers and psychologists are generally in favour of paying participants, while lawyers and anthropologists are not (Back, 2015: 66; Colvin, 2014: 61). What is generally accepted is the need to reimburse participants for any out-of-pocket costs they may incur as a result of their participation, such as travel fares (Hamilton, 2009: 220).

It is generally not regarded as ethical to gather data covertly, though there are exceptions (Gillham, 2008b: 93–4). Gillham points out that there are two dimensions to consider here: whether observation is overt or covert, and whether it is in an open, publicly accessible setting, or a closed, private setting. He suggests that covert observation in a closed setting has the most potential to be unethical (Gillham, 2008b: 93). This implies that overt observation in an open setting has the least potential to be unethical – though that does not mean this approach is free of ethical considerations. Consent is a problem: if you are studying people's responses to sports, and want to observe spectators at a sporting event in a stadium, you can't ask them all.

Using technology to gather data raises new ethical conundrums. No technology is free from bias because it is created by people who are not free from bias. Even the internet search engine, where most of us start looking for most things these days, is demonstrably biased, not only by the biases of the people who create its algorithms, but also because of its commercial interests in which we, the users, are the product that the organisation behind the search engine sells to the companies who buy their advertising opportunities (Noble, 2018: 162). So we need to make ourselves aware of, and allow for, the biases in the technology we use.

These are just a few of the ethical issues that researchers need to consider when gathering data. I will cover a few more in the next chapter, but this will not be comprehensive; indeed, it could not be – even a whole book on the subject could not be comprehensive. This is because new ethical issues arise with each new qualitative research project in its own unique context. The ethics of qualitative research is a massive topic and, in essence, it is crucial that qualitative researchers are able to think and act ethically throughout their research work (Poth, 2021: 117).

Conclusion

The methods covered in this chapter are the predominant methods in qualitative research. This is partly because they can be used effectively in a lot of research projects, and where this is the case, their use is entirely defensible and appropriate. It is also, though, partly because of a kind of blinkered inertia among researchers and research influencers, such as governments and commissioners, managers and supervisors.

In the early days of qualitative research the only options were questionnaires, interviews and focus groups, with field notes used as data in some disciplines such as anthropology and geography, and case study research also used in some disciplines. The move towards using technology to help gather research data is part of a broader movement to expand the tools available to qualitative researchers. The next chapter will cover some of the more recent methods which offer researchers more flexibility and, from some ontological and epistemological perspectives, more ethical ways to gather data.

Reflective questions

1. Do you feel drawn to one or more of the methods outlined in this chapter?
2. What might you gain from trying any of these methods that are less appealing?
3. How could you mitigate your biases when gathering qualitative data?
4. What barriers might you face in using technology to help you gather qualitative data? How could you overcome those barriers?
5. Thinking about a research project you are working on, or one you would like to undertake, using qualitative data, what are the main ethical considerations you need to bear in mind when gathering that qualitative data?

GATHERING QUALITATIVE DATA: ALTERNATIVE METHODS

┌─ Chapter summary ───

- Introduces the breadth and diversity of what may be defined as 'qualitative data'
- Reviews some options for enhancing interviews and focus groups
- Considers some ways of gathering arts-based data
- Demonstrates the utility of self-reporting methods
- Describes autoethnography
- Discusses embodied data gathering
- Explores multi-modal data gathering
- Outlines some debates around gathering qualitative data using video and other digital methods
- Covers some of the ethical issues raised by the use of alternative methods to gather qualitative data

Introduction

In recent decades, the definition of 'data' in qualitative research has widened considerably, and now includes not only words and numbers but also visual data, audio data, video data, marginalia, ephemera, social media posts, other digital data – pretty much anything that can be gathered and analysed. Indigenous researchers take an even broader view, including stories, proverbs, metaphors, dreams, songs, poems and myths, among other things (Chilisa, 2020: 189–98; Kovach, 2009: 99; Lambert, 2014: 29; Walker, 2013: 304). This diversity and scope offers researchers lots of opportunities and also some challenges. With so many options to choose from, it can be difficult to decide which to use, and so it can be very tempting to select a type of data, or a method of gathering that data, for its appeal. Yet it is important to ensure that the data and methods you choose are those most likely to help you answer your research question(s).

This chapter begins with a discussion of enhanced interviews and focus groups. Then we consider ways of gathering arts-based data, embodied data and multi-modal data. We review some ways to gather qualitative data using video and from social media, and outline some ethical issues that may arise when using alternative methods to gather data.

Enhanced interviews and focus groups

'Enhanced interviews' is a catch-all term for interviews with something extra added for interviewer and interviewee to focus on. This may be something brought by the interviewer, brought by the interviewee or created by the interviewee – or the interviewee and the interviewer together – during the interview. I cannot be certain when the first enhanced interview was conducted, or by whom, but it is likely that the enhancement was photographs taken by the interviewee before the interview. This is known as photo-elicitation or, sometimes, photovoice.

Items that have been used to enhance interviews and focus groups include the following:

- Photos (Box 7.1)
- Icons on postcards (Box 7.2)
- Sets of cards created by researchers (Box 7.3)
- Models made by participants (Box 7.4)

Plus a range of other options, some of which are outlined below. This is not just something researchers do for fun. There are several good reasons for considering enhancement if you are thinking about doing interviews. First, having something external to focus on takes the pressure off the interpersonal elements of the interaction between you. It becomes less like a strangely formal, unusual way to converse, and more like an everyday encounter. Second, some of these methods give participants more control of the data and the stories they tell through their photographs, artefacts, drawings and so on. And third, journal article after journal article on these methods recount how and why the researcher is certain that they got more and better data than they would have done from standard interviewing.

Box 7.1

Photo-elicitation in practice

Erin Smith, Bob Gidlow and Gary Steel used photo-elicitation with 14- and 15-year-old participants, to study their experiences of a school-based outdoor education programme (aka 'school camp') in New Zealand. They began with a pre-camp briefing session in which they explained the project and asked participants to take photos showing 'what school camp was like for them' (Smith et al., 2012: 372), suggesting that they might pretend they were going to post them on social media for their friends to see. The researchers also discussed ethical considerations around photographing other people. They gave the students disposable cameras, asked them to choose a pseudonym, write it on a piece of paper and take one photo of that for practice. Then the researchers collected the cameras to prevent participants using them up in advance or forgetting to bring them to camp, and gave them back to the students the day they left for the camp. After camp the cameras were collected again and the photos developed for use in the interviews, after which they were given to the students to keep. The researchers decided not to look at the photos before the interview, to avoid the possibility of pre-judgements. The photos were given first to the student to select which would be used in the interview, and then the selection was spread on a desk so the student could comment on each one. Then the student was asked to choose one photograph to match each of these statements, which they then completed in writing (Smith et al., 2012: 373):

1. This is my favourite photo from camp because.......
2. This photo from camp makes me feel...... because......
3. This photo of ...... shows what camp was like for me best because......
4. What I liked most at camp was...... because......
5. What I liked *least* about camp was...... because...... (original emphasis)

Participants valued their photographs as a memento of their camp, and appreciated receiving the photos as a direct benefit of taking part in the research. Researchers valued the photographs because they 'seemed to reduce the formality of being interviewed by an adult and encouraged them to articulate their experiences at school camp' (Smith et al., 2012: 376). There were limitations: the cameras were not waterproof so could not be taken along to the water-based activities that formed a big part of the camp experience. And there were ethical issues around privacy and confidentiality which meant that none of the photographs taken could be used in publications. But overall this method yielded rich and useful data.

Box 7.2

Collected cards in interviews

Catrien Notermans and Heleen Kommers studied chronically ill Dutch Catholics, mostly women, who were making a pilgrimage to Lourdes, a shrine to the Virgin Mary who is a very important saint in the Catholic religion. The researchers began by interviewing pilgrims about their feelings for Mary, and were often met with silence or tears. The researchers learned that 'Mary evokes thoughts that are tightly connected with troubles that are silently kept as family secrets rather than publicly expressed everyday life. Mary mirrors the excessive pain people experience in everyday life, and the pain is hard to tell' (Notermans and Kommers, 2012: 614). Clearly this was a problem: no researcher wants to cause distress to their participants. So the researchers collected around 30 cards with different visual representations of Mary to use in their follow-up interviews. The cards included local images of Mary as well as other images from further afield. The researchers presented the cards, in sets of five, and asked interviewees which one from each set they liked best, which they disliked most, and why. Then all the preferred images were put together and interviewees asked how, based on those images, they would describe Mary. This helped 'both the pilgrims and the inter-viewer to elicit the stories that otherwise would probably not have been told' (Notermans and Kommers, 2012: 615).

Box 7.3

Created cards in interviews

Barbara Sutton created 'concept cards' to help elicit the embodied experiences of women in Argentina. She devised a list of words that could be related to the body, such as law, pain and youth, and wrote one on each card. She also offered blank cards for participants to write words that were not in her list but were significant for them. Then she asked participants to choose the cards that seemed most relevant to their own physical experiences – as many cards as they liked – and to tell her why they had chosen them. This enabled participants to cluster the cards and establish relationships between themes (Sutton, 2011: 183). Sutton had intended this as an ice-breaker at the start of the interview, but it 'prompted interviewees to "dive" into the thick of their problems, proceeding to explore their concerns, fears, or traumas' (Sutton, 2011: 186) and proved such a useful way to enable women to talk about sensitive, illegal, contentious or taboo topics that it ended up becoming embedded in the interviews. One downside was that it was hard to remain systematic, even with the support of an interview schedule. Even so, this method generated 'rich and complex narratives' about women's embodied experiences (Sutton, 2011: 177).

Box 7.4

Enhanced focus group in practice

Julie Dalton studied the ways mental health issues can affect teaching and learning for pre-service teacher trainees. As this is a sensitive topic, with mental health problems still being stigmatised, she chose to use structured enhanced focus groups as a supportive environment. The enhancement was making individual models, for which the researcher provided a wide selection of craft materials. The groups were structured by membership numbers and time management: six participants spent 30 minutes together making their models, then each person in turn spoke about their creation for five minutes before a five-minute discussion. This meant each focus group lasted 90 minutes. Some participants were uncertain about their ability to make models, and Dalton (2020) reassured them that 'there was no assessment or judgement being made' (41). Every participant did make a model and this led to them all reporting feelings of pride and achievement. The models enabled safe and detailed discussion of the research topic by moving the focus from the personal to the artefact.

You will remember from Chapter 1 that Q methodology uses cards bearing statements for participants to sort into piles. Researchers have also used all sorts of cards in different ways to enhance their interviews. These may be cards collected or created by researchers, as shown in Boxes 7.2 and 7.3.

Cards are of course artefacts. Researchers are also using many other kinds of artefacts in interviews, which may also be collected or created. Canadian ethnographer Jennifer Rowsell asked her 11- to 14-year-old participants to bring one or more valued artefacts from home. She found that these artefacts 'brought family narratives and attachments to life' (Rowsell, 2011: 340). As we saw in Box 1.6, Indigenous Welsh researcher Dawn Mannay asked her participants to take photos or make maps or collages to represent 'their worlds inside and outside of the home' (Mannay, 2010: 97). Mannay held individual interviews with each participant, with their artwork as the focus, which enabled her to gain 'a more nuanced understanding of the mothers and daughters' worlds' (Mannay, 2010: 100) than she would have obtained through standard interviews. For Mannay, this is because participants had control over their own artworks, what they depicted and how, which meant she learned about aspects of the participants and their environments that she might not have thought to ask about if she had defined all the interview questions herself.

More recently, researchers have begun to bring these methods of enhancement to focus groups as well as interviews. Again, it makes the encounter more fun and informal, and gives participants more control of what they disclose and the stories they tell. And, as with enhanced interviews, researchers are sure the data from enhanced focus groups are greater in quantity and richness than they would have been from a standard focus group. Box 7.4 shows an example of an enhanced focus group.

There is really no limit, creatively speaking, to the ways in which researchers can approach enhanced interviews and focus groups. I spoke to an organisational researcher once who had a bag of assorted pebbles from the beach, and asked participants to use them in interviews to represent their colleagues and the relationships and power dynamics between them. The researcher told me it worked really well, participants had no difficulty with the task, and she was able to photograph the result and label the photograph with job roles and/or pseudonyms. I myself was a participant in a focus group where the researcher brought a random selection of items from home – I remember a screwdriver, a lemon, an egg-cup; that kind of thing. The researcher put them all out on the table, and invited participants to choose one that seemed relevant, for them, in response to the research question. Again, participants had no difficulty with the task, and it elicited a rich and useful discussion.

Gathering arts-based data

Arts-based data encompass visual arts, written arts, textile arts, modelling, mapping and sound. We have already seen examples of some of these earlier in the chapter, such as Smith et al. (2012) using photos, Mannay (2010) using photos, maps and collages, and Dalton (2020) using modelling.

Visual arts include drawing, painting, stencilling, print-making, collage, graffiti, among others – as well as photography and video which is where art meets technology. Drawing or sketching are often preliminary stages for painting, stencilling and print-making. Drawing and sketching lead to considerations of 'perspective, interpretation and gaze', which can be key considerations for many researchers (Heath et al., 2018: 714). Photography is differently selective: the camera angle is chosen, and then, within the frame, everything visible is included, whereas an artist may emphasize some details and omit others.

There are many ways of collecting, constructing and using visual data. Boxes 7.5 and 7.6 show two very different approaches, to give you a flavour of the range of available options.

It is rare to find a child who doesn't want to draw, but it is not so rare with adults. In Eggleton's research, two participants felt uncomfortable in drawing (Eggleton et al., 2017: 988). In general, when you plan to ask people to create art for your research, it is important to make your proposal clear from the outset, avoid judgement, and where possible have an alternative option to offer anyone who finds they are uncomfortable with the activity.

The *written arts* include poetry, fictional stories, play and screenplay scripts. Poetry and fiction are most commonly used for data gathering; play and screenplay scripts for

Box 7.5

Gathering arts-based data in practice

Newell Wright and Val Larsen studied the experience of American business students attending a semester-long 'study abroad program' (SAP) in Antwerp, Belgium. On the last day of a semester, each departing student was invited to decorate a brick in the stairwell of their hall of residence, and offered coloured magic markers and paint. Two hundred students did this over seven semesters. Each graffito was photographed and the photos were analysed by the researchers. They also conducted in-depth elicitation interviews with 13 former students, using each student's graffito, to generate further insight. This enabled the researchers to conclude that travel, 'magic moments', and *communitas* (i.e. the development of close and strong personal bonds), meant more to the students than their academic experiences (Wright and Larsen, 2012: 137).

Box 7.6

Participatory arts-based data in practice

Kyle Eggleton studied people's experiences of using general practice waiting rooms as patients in northern New Zealand. Eggleton is a white man, while most of the participants were Māori, many were female and had mental health problems. The researcher was careful to take a culturally sensitive approach. The participants chose the setting for the research encounter, mostly in their own homes or on their *marae* (tribal meeting place). The researcher observed cultural protocols by removing his shoes before the meeting, bringing food to share and offering a gift to each participant. For the research interviews, he used the culturally appropriate *hui* process of sharing information about where he came from and who his family were, including ancestors, plus his life experiences and aspirations, and his participants did likewise (Eggleton et al., 2017: 980). Then he asked participants to draw an idealised representation of making an appointment for general practice, and enquired into its meaning through open-ended questions while avoiding any judgement of the drawings. Participants also asked questions of the researcher, such that the interviews became more like conversations. This process was then repeated for interactions with receptionists and for spending time in the waiting room. Eggleton provided coloured pencils, crayons, paint, marker pens, and paper. He also made his own drawings of these experiences and shared them with participants after the interviews. This culturally and ethically careful approach demonstrated respect for participants and for their drawings and stories. Participants reported finding the drawing process deeply significant, and said it helped them to understand their experiences differently (Eggleton et al., 2017: 981).

analytic work (more on this in Chapter 9). Poetry is more often created by researchers, and fictional stories by participants, though there are exceptions in both directions, and in some cases both researchers and participants write poetry or stories. Rich Furman used his own adolescent poems, written some years earlier, as data for studying adolescent identity and development, alongside other poems created by colleagues from the analysis of the initial dataset (Furman et al., 2007: 301). Box 7.7 offers an example of poetry created by participants, and Box 7.8 shows an example of fictional stories created by participants.

Box 7.7

Poetry created by participants

Emily Bishop and Karen Willis used a range of creative approaches, including poetry, to investigate the hopes of 171 young people aged 11–16 years attending schools in Tasmania. They asked each student to write an acrostic poem, a sense poem, a free verse poem, or a story about hope. The acrostic poem had four lines beginning with the letters H.O.P.E. The sense poem completed the phrases 'Hope tastes like... Hope sounds like... Hope smells like... Hope looks like... Hope makes me feel... each on a separate line (Bishop and Willis, 2014: 8). The structure of the free verse poem could be determined by the student. The researchers took care to tell the students that they were not looking for great works of art. Most students who chose poetry wrote a structured poem, with only ten students writing free verse poems, yet those ten poems provided more nuance and insight than the larger number of structured poems (Bishop and Willis, 2014: 12).

Box 7.8

Fictional stories created by participants

Psychologists Virginia Braun, Victoria Clarke and Naomi Moller studied the way people made sense of COVID-19 lockdown restrictions in the United Kingdom and New Zealand. The researchers were particularly interested in when and why people might obey or break the rules, and what sense they or others might make of those actions. They devised six brief 'story stems' of a few sentences to introduce one or more characters and their situation, each of which involved the character or characters contemplating or witnessing potential rule breaking. Asking for fictional stories was deemed more ethical than asking for direct personal accounts that could compromise participants' welfare. In creating the 'story stems', the researchers drew inspiration from lockdown breaches they had read about in social and mainstream media. Participants were asked to complete two stories, allocated at random, with particular emphasis on the main character's decisions and their consequences. The researchers suggested that participants could spend about 10 minutes writing each story. They received 285 stories, from 144 adult participants, with a surprising amount of detail, richness and length (Braun et al., 2020).

The story completion method used by Braun et al. was initially devised over a century ago by clinical psychologists for use within quantitative research to reveal aspects of the story teller's psychology, with a complex coding system used to convert narrative detail into numerical data for statistical analysis (Braun et al., 2020). Qualitative researchers have been using the method since the mid-1990s to focus on social issues.

Textile arts are a more recent addition to the suite of available creative methods for gathering qualitative data. They are now used by researchers from a range of disciplines, often within a participatory framework – which is not surprising when you consider that 'collective textile making is a well-established practice with a long history' (Shercliff and Holroyd, 2020: 6). Textile arts include knitting, sewing, weaving, quilting, and crochet, among others. Arts outputs themselves may form all or part of the data gathered, alongside conversations that take place while making, associated journals, and other diverse forms of data (Shercliff and Holroyd, 2020: 12). Box 7.9 shows an example of participatory textile making in research.

Box 7.9

Participatory textile making in research

Fiona Hackney and her colleagues in the United Kingdom were concerned about the adverse impact of fast fashion on people, communities and the environment. They formed a five-person team including researchers from fashion, politics, and design. The team decided to investigate whether the process of participatory textile making itself might be able to help consumers learn why and how they could make more sustainable choices when buying clothes (Hackney et al., 2020: 36). They designed one-day workshops to 'replace standard notions of production and consumption with material, sensory and emotional practices generated within communities' (Hackney et al., 2020: 38). These workshops focused on a range of participatory textile activities including knitting, pattern cutting, mending, repurposing and upcycling of clothing and textile artefacts such as purses and aprons. The aim was to highlight the skill, labour, quality and environmental impacts of wearable and usable textile creations – aspects overlooked by standard discourses around fast fashion. The workshops enabled participants to learn new skills, polish up rusty old skills, develop confidence in repairing and making textiles, form new friendships to help them continue doing this and think more about sustainability and 'the environmental and ethical impacts of their clothing choices' (Hackney et al., 2020: 47).

The use of textiles as research data is not restricted to textile-related topics. They have also been used in studying topics as varied as occupational therapy, human–computer interaction and sustainable development (Shercliff and Holroyd, 2020: 10). Also, textile arts can be useful in the representation of quantitative data, and this will be discussed further in Chapter 11. For those interested in using textiles in participatory research, Amy Twigger Holroyd and Emma Shercliff have produced some good practice guidelines as part of their funded research project, Stitching Together (Holroyd and Shercliff, 2020).

Qualitative researchers have used *modelling* as a way of generating data for some decades now, usually within interview or focus group settings. This is actual, physical modelling, using materials as varied as playdough, pipe cleaners and Lego. We saw an example in Julie Dalton's work in Box 7.4.

Maps drawn or annotated by participants, or by participants and researchers together, can generate qualitative data, or quantitative data, or both. Most people probably think of geographic maps, such as Google Maps or road maps, but there are many other kinds of maps. Those that may be useful in research include the following:

- Cognitive maps, which represent people's perceptions of place and distance
- Concept maps, which show links between ideas
- Pictorial maps, which privilege aesthetics over accuracy
- Social maps, which show relationships between people and networks, communities and/or organisations
- Thematic maps, which show variations on a social theme between geographic areas, such as levels of homelessness
- Topographical maps, which show links between places without accurate distances or routes (like the London Underground map)
- Transect maps, which show the location and distribution of resources and land/ space uses

Maps are not used in all cultures, so it is important to understand potential participants' likely levels of comprehension before deciding whether to use maps (Powell, 2010: 543). Where applicable, mapping can be useful for revealing complex relationships between places, objects, concepts, thought and emotion (Newman, 2013: 228). Using mapping for data gathering can help researchers to gain insight into the ways participants see their worlds: 'what is important to them, what their lived social relations are, and where they spend their time' (Powell, 2010: 553). Maps can be incredibly complex, or very simple indeed. Sara Eldén used five concentric circles on a sheet of paper as a basis for children aged 5–12 years to map their personal networks of care and support (Elden, 2012: 71). Maps can also be useful for unearthing information that could otherwise be hard to find. Jacqui Gabb made floor plans of participants' homes and coloured emoticon stickers representing love/affection, anger, sadness and happiness. She used these with families to find out where emotional experiences or interactions had taken place in the home. The maps were appealing and easy for both adults and children to use, and revealed some private acts such as children moving into adults' beds during the night, or moments of shared intimacy, which would not usually be accessible for researchers (Gabb, 2010: 463–4). We see a different example of this in Box 7.10.

Box 7.10

Maps in qualitative research

Lee-Ann Sutherland wanted to study hobby farmers in a rural parish, or municipality, of Scotland; an area approximately 3 km wide and 8 km long. 'Hobby farmers' are non-commercial, lifestyle farmers who work on small holdings. In Scotland, there is no official list or register of hobby farmers, so they can be difficult for researchers to find. Sutherland began with a key informant, a local agricultural consultant, and used snowball sampling to identify participants. She interviewed each participant and began each interview with a detailed map of the local area showing all roads, houses, forest and field boundaries, and bodies of water (Sutherland, 2020: 133). She asked participants to identify the owners or occupiers of neighbouring properties, who she then contacted to ask if they would participate in her research. In this way, she was able to interview 56 land holders including representatives of 31 small holdings of two or more hectares. As an incentive to participate, Sutherland offered participants a copy of the completed map, which would include the names of the land owners and occupiers who she had been able to identify. She used an anonymised and more detailed version of the map in her research.

Another option is body mapping, where arts-based and embodied methods meet (see below for more on embodied methods). In body mapping, a line is traced around someone's body on to paper to create a life-sized outline which can be filled in to represent all kinds of different data: people's experiences of place, their feelings about bodily experiences such as violence or dance, or their relationship to nature (de Jager et al., 2016: 14).

Sound as primary data usually comes in the form of field recordings, also known as 'soundscapes', a word coined in the 1960s by R. M. Schafer and now used by researchers in a wide range of disciplines (Radicchi et al., 2017: 105). Today 'soundscape' has an ISO definition: 'the acoustic environment as perceived, experienced, and/or understood by people, in context' (Radicchi et al., 2018: 106). An example is given in Box 7.11.

Box 7.11

Soundscapes in qualitative research

Antonella Radicchi, Dietrich Henckel and Martin Memmel wanted to involve city-dwellers in identifying, assessing and planning quiet areas in the Reuterkiez district of Berlin, Germany. The lead investigator developed a free app called 'Hush City'. Participants with smartphones used the app to collect 30-second soundscapes and then complete brief questionnaires to evaluate, and provide contextual information for, each soundscape. The researchers offered interviews and group soundwalks for participants who did not have smartphones. In a pilot study, they received 104 datasets from the Hush City app plus data from some interviews and soundwalks. The initial evaluation of all this data yielded a more complex understanding of urban quietness than that based on decibel levels, with places promoting relaxation and social interaction, and characterised by a mix of natural and human sounds, described as 'everyday quiet areas' (Radicchi et al., 2018: 114).

Researchers can also gather secondary data in sound form from the sound archives held by some libraries and other organisations.

Self-reporting methods

Self-reporting methods are tools a researcher can give to participants for completion in their own time. These include email interviews, diaries and cultural probes.

Email interviews are particularly useful for research with participants who routinely use email and where an in-person interview would be difficult to arrange or manage, even by telephone or online. Participants with disabilities or chronic illness may find it easier to answer one question at a time, when it is convenient for them, than to take part in a full interview. People who work at night, or are in different time zones from the researcher, may also find email interviews more accessible than in-person interviews. Also, this method saves time and costs for the researcher as no travel or transcription is needed.

Although email interviews take less time for researchers, they are likely to take more time, overall, for participants than an in-person interview. Also, the researcher cannot draw on visual and aural information such as the participant's body language or the tone and pitch of their voice. And technology can malfunction – not every email that is sent is received, and connectivity problems or hardware breakdown can cause delays or other problems.

An example of email interviews in practice is in Box 7.12.

Box 7.12

Email interviews in practice

Janice Hawkins used email interviews with nurse educators across the United States in research designed to describe their experiences in developing and implementing educational partnership enrolment programs for coursework undertaken by students at two different institutions concurrently. This method was appropriate for her participants, busy professionals who routinely used email and were scattered across a huge country. She conducted semi-structured interviews through iterative email exchanges with 17 participants over a two- to four-week period (Hawkins, 2018a: 497). The resulting data were rich, detailed and highly relevant to her research question, despite containing significantly fewer words than equivalent in-person interviews (ibid). This is probably because her participants 'were able to carefully craft responses and revise and edit before sending' (Hawkins, 2018: 498). She also found that the prolonged engagement with her participants was useful for follow-up questions and clarification. As she conducted interviews concurrently over an extended time period, rather than sequentially, and acquired data that were immediately usable, Hawkins was able to code and analyse data while still conducting her interviews, and explore resulting themes with participants before she finished gathering data (ibid).

Diaries have been used in social research for a long time, such as in the United Kingdom's Mass Observation Archive which has been collecting material about everyday life in Britain, generated by British citizens, since 1937 (see Appendix 1 for the Mass Observation Archive URL). In recent years, researchers have been taking more creative approaches to the use of diaries in research. Box 7.13 shows an example.

Diaries need not only be kept in writing. Nicola Jones and her colleagues conduct longitudinal research into gender and adolescence in the Middle East and North Africa. When the COVID-19 pandemic hit in 2020, they could no longer travel to or in countries such as Jordan, Lebanon or Palestine, so they had to move their research online. They introduced diaries into their methods of gathering data, and offered participants who chose this method the option of written or audio diaries. These were 'structured around open-ended question prompts to help young people to outline their daily experiences and to express their experiences, feelings and reflections on different issues' and could be 'written or recorded according to adolescents' preference and literacy capabilities' (Jones et al., 2020).

Also during the pandemic, Naomi Clarke and Debbie Watson in the United Kingdom studied 'crafting during coronavirus' to capture people's stories of how making helped them to respond to, and cope with, the crisis. Their participants were

Box 7.13

Diaries in practice

Charlotte Kenten used diaries to gain insight into the day-to-day ways in which les-
bians and gay men in a rural part of the United Kingdom become aware of their
sexual orientations. She began with semi-structured in-depth interviews asking about
various aspects of their experience and feelings around their sexual orientations.
Then she asked if they would be willing to keep a daily diary for two weeks, to note
down their day-to-day experiences of their sexual orientation. Kenten had created an
A4 paper diary with one page for each day and prompts such as 'what happened to
make you aware of your sexuality?' and 'how did it make you feel?' (Kenten, 2010: 5).
To begin with, those participants who agreed to keep diaries thought they might not
have much to write, but in the event they found they had more to say than they had
expected. This was followed up with a further set of 'diary interviews', to ask participants about their experiences of keeping their diaries, and to enable participants to
reflect on the experiences they had documented in those diaries. For Kenten, this
method offered 'an insight and a depth that other methods may not produce'
(Kenten, 2010: 15).

told 'it is completely up to you how to complete it (digitally, handwriting, crafting it, a
mixture of them all or another way entirely)' (see Appendix 1 for the URL for this web
page). The researchers received diaries 'in diverse formats including handwritten
accounts, email diaries, PDFs, videos, audio diaries and stitch diaries' (Clarke and
Watson, 2020). (If you are unfamiliar with the concept of a stitch diary, I recommend
looking at Clare Danek's stitch journal online; the URL is in Appendix 1 under the
heading for Chapter 5.) Photo diaries are another option (Mizen, 2005). Carlie Goldsmith, whose research we saw in Box 1.3, used photo diaries to enable her participants
to communicate without the need for a spoken language in common, and to have the
freedom to document their lives as they chose. Her participants were refugees, asylum
seekers and migrants, and the photo diaries proved very effective in providing insights
into the emotional and psychological dimensions of their lives, particularly issues of
mental health and social isolation (Goldsmith, 2015: 16).

Cultural probes were developed by design researchers Bill Gaver, Tony Dunne and
Elena Pacenti. A 'probe' is an artefact for a participant to interact with, such as a
postcard bearing a question to answer, a map with stickers to show where someone has
been or would like to go, a digital camera or a structured diary with prompts for writing
responses at particular times (Gaver et al., 1999: 22–4). The cultural probes are presented to participants as a set or collection, and participants are invited to interact with
whichever probes they wish, in whatever way they prefer. Gaver and his colleagues first

developed the cultural probes for an EU-funded project investigating ways to increase the presence of older people in their local communities in Norway, the Netherlands, and Italy. The researchers were not working towards a commercial product or a solution to a problem, but 'to provide opportunities to discover new pleasures, new forms of sociability, and new cultural forms' (Gaver et al., 1999: 25). The cultural probes helped them to do this in all three communities.

The process of using cultural probes for gathering data 'disregards traditional utilitarian values in favour of playfulness, exploration and enjoyment' (Boehner et al., 2014: 194). The method has spread from design research into the social sciences, and is sometimes just called 'probes'. A recent example of its use is in Box 7.14.

Box 7.14

Cultural probes in practice

Louise Couceiro's doctoral work investigates how UK children aged 7–10 years respond to collective biographies of women such as *Goodnight Stories for Rebel Girls*. She had made arrangements to gather data from children in an educational setting, but then the pandemic hit and she had to find a new way to gather data remotely. Cultural probes formed the basis for a 'reader response toolkit', an 'electronic toolkit of open-ended, arts-based activities... designed with participants' enjoyment and interests at the centre' (Couceiro, 2020). She asked participants for input into the toolkits, which she supplemented with ideas of her own, and emphasised that the toolkit should be used as a springboard; they could actually respond to the texts in any way they liked (Couceiro, 2021: personal communication). The toolkit included a short introductory video, encouraging participants to interact with the activities that appealed to them, and reminding them to email photographs or videos of their curations to Couceiro. She sent the toolkit, with four books, by post to participants, who responded with drawings, re-designed book covers, comic strips, a silent LEGO movie, a hand puppet, a research project, a play script and many other creations. Then Couceiro held interviews online to learn more about participants' responses and give participants 'an opportunity to contribute to analysis of their creations' (Couceiro, 2020). She found that their creations offered a useful basis for discussing the texts in the interviews, and that participants' explanations of the creations and the process of producing them were essential for analysis (Couceiro, 2021: personal communication).

Autoethnography

Autoethnography was devised by Carolyn Ellis in the 1990s and is now widely used, particularly in the arts and social sciences. It is 'an approach to research and writing that seeks to describe and systematically analyze personal experience in order to understand cultural experience' (Ellis et al., 2011: 1). The word 'autoethnography' is made up of the Greek words for 'self', 'folk/people' and 'write'. Using yourself as the basis of enquiry enables you to sidestep the awkward ethical problems raised by representing or speaking for others (Lapadat, 2017: 589). However, if not practised rigorously, autoethnography can be self-indulgent and irrelevant (Denzin, 2014: 69–70). One way to countermand this is through collaborative autoethnography which offers 'a path toward personally engaging, nonexploitative, accessible research that makes a difference' (Lapadat, 2017: 589). Also, ethnography can be used as part of a multi-modal study (Leavy, 2009: 38).

The only prescribed method is descriptive writing. Beyond that, autoethnographers may use any appropriate method or methods of gathering and analysing data. These data need to be linked with wider concerns such as inequalities, history, relationships and culture (Chang, 2008: 132–7; Denzin, 2014: 7–8). The findings should be linked with theory and practice or policy (Kara, 2018: 41). When autoethnography is rigorously practised and appropriate links are made, it becomes an excellent research method which can have a demonstrable impact on practice and policy (Chang, 2008: 52–4; Lenza, 2011).

Embodied data gathering

Embodiment is a comparatively new concept in qualitative research. Some researchers argue, quite reasonably, that we cannot do research without our bodies; that the conventional idea of research as somehow 'disembodied' has serious limitations (Ellingson, 2017: 7; Thanem and Knights, 2019: 10–11). Therefore, it is arguable that all data gathering is embodied because no researcher can gather data without their body. Whether sitting at a desk tracking down data online, or walking to an interview with a participant, or standing to introduce an arts-based activity to a group, we use our bodies to gather our data. Also, we can gather data through our bodies: we gather observational data primarily through our eyes, soundscapes with our ears and so on.

Much qualitative research using this concept focuses on highly embodied topics such as illness, grief, pregnancy and childbirth. Another option is the guided tour method which has been used since the late 1970s (Thomson, 2018: 515), predominantly by information and library science researchers. Box 7.15 shows how this can work in practice.

The argument that we cannot gather data without our bodies is of course a valid one. However, we also have a choice about whether – and, if so, how much – to foreground embodiment in qualitative research. Understanding the concept will give us a firm basis for making good decisions about its use in our work.

Box 7.15

Embodied research in practice

Leslie Thomson, who is based in the United States, reviewed the literature on the guided tour to compile advice for others who might wish to use the method. The guided tour involves a participant leading a researcher around a location, often one that is more relevant to the participant than to the researcher. During the tour the participant will describe the location and its features, answer the researcher's questions, and think aloud about the ideas, thoughts and feelings which arise in connection with the location (Thomson, 2018: 511). Therefore this method 'rests upon the embodied copresence of and the interaction between a researcher and participant' (Thomson, 2018: 515). Locations where guided tour research has taken place include museums and art galleries, libraries and home offices including digital spaces, among many others. Thomson (2018: 523–4) has identified seven steps for designing and conducting a guided tour:

1. Define your aims in a clear statement.
2. Plan data gathering and ensure you have all the equipment you will need.
3. Give a full explanation to potential participants and ensure they have time to prepare for the tour.
4. From the start of the tour, use direct and open-ended requests, which can be vague ('Show me whatever you like') or specific ('Please show me how your information is organised').
5. Prioritise participants' voices.
6. Use open-ended verbal probes, such as 'Can you say more about this?'.
7. Keep a visual record through photographs, videos or sketches.

The guided tour is unlikely to be useful as a sole method of gathering data. However, used alongside other methods, it 'addresses and connects spatial, material, and embodied concerns well' (Thomson, 2018: 530).

Multi-modal data gathering

A multi-modal approach can be particularly useful for research with a high level of complexity (Omona, 2018: 23; Ritchie and Ormston, 2014: 45). We have already seen examples of multi-modal data gathering in Box 7.13, where Charlotte Kenten gathered diaries and interviews from adults, and Box 7.14, where Louise Couceiro gathered children's creations. These research projects were entirely qualitative, though qualitative multi-modal research may also include quantitative data.

Multi-modal data gathering requires more resources for both data gathering and data analysis than gathering data using a single method. Also, it needs careful planning – but it can yield rich rewards.

Video and digital data

Video data can be collected using a variety of equipment such as smartphones, hand-held cameras, cameras worn on the head or body, vehicle dashboard cameras, fixed cameras or aerial cameras also known as drones. Of course video data are used in quantitative research, such as the research of Xin Gu and colleagues which uses video data gathered by a drone with Bayesian modelling to identify predictors of crash risks for car drivers travelling through a multi-lane road interchange (Gu et al., 2019). And video data are also used in qualitative and multi-modal research. Video data are easy to collect but can be challenging to analyse (see Chapter 9 for more on this) so it is wise to plan your analytic strategy before you gather large quantities of video data.

One digital method which is very new, and as yet not much used, is the collection of data through video gaming. Geographers Phil Jones and Tess Osborne assert that building game environments to help answer research questions is unexpectedly easy (Jones and Osborne, 2020: 291). Some games engines, such as Unity, are free for non-commercial uses, and offer a selection of packages allowing even technically inexperienced researchers to build a small and simple digital environment. Advice for beginners is available online through discussion boards and YouTube. Furthermore, many students are keen gamers and enjoy building virtual environments (ibid).

A more established method is ethnography in digital spaces, also known as 'netnography' (Kozinets, 2010). This is used in a variety of fields such as tourism and computer science. Like conventional ethnography, the aim is to learn from spending time with people in a community, but in a digital rather than a geographical place. Barry Ardley and Eleanor McIntosh spent three months in Facebook groups for adult fans of LEGO (AFOLS) to investigate how value was created within these communities. They gathered evidence from posts and comments in the group, and made field notes throughout. This enabled them to show how AFOLS create value in digital spaces, 'not only for members but for the LEGO brand as a whole' (Ardley and McIntosh, 2021: 2).

There is a plethora of opportunities for collecting data from digital spaces, which include hundreds of platforms, thousands of discussion groups, and millions of blogs, not to mention all the other interactive digital options such as online petitions (Briassoulis, 2010), sales listings, dating sites and so on. Also, social media companies and others enable swift digital gathering of large datasets through allowing access to their application programming interfaces, or APIs. These are easy to learn to use through the 'API University' on The Programmable Web online (Kara, 2017: 129) (see Appendix 1 for the Programmable Web URL). Perhaps because APIs enable researchers to gather a large amount of data in a short space of time, data gathered in this way have mostly been used in quantitative research, but they also have a great deal of potential for qualitative research (Lomborg and Bechmann, 2014: 257).

In this section I aimed to give an overview and an idea of the potential of video and other forms of digital data. Because they offer so much scope to qualitative researchers, it would be possible to write a whole book on this topic without covering all the available ground. The references provided should enable you to follow up any methods of interest.

Ethics of gathering qualitative data using alternative methods

Many of these alternative methods of gathering data, such as enhanced interviews and focus groups, arts-based methods and self-reporting methods, and participatory video research, can be used as an ethical choice because they give participants more control over defining and shaping the data and therefore the answers to research questions. This is in contrast to the mainstream methods of gathering qualitative data, covered in Chapter 6, where the research agenda is set mostly or entirely by researchers. Unless you are using mainstream methods with a participatory methodology, it is likely that researchers will write all of the questions for questionnaires and for interview and focus group schedules, and will design any technological aids such as apps to help them gather data. This can be seen as paternalistic, and – as we saw in the section on enhanced interviewing earlier in this chapter – many have argued that being less directive and giving participants more agency within the research process leads to richer data and more interesting and useful findings.

This illustrates that alternative methods can solve some ethical problems, though they also generate others. Some people may be reluctant to participate in arts-based or embodied data gathering because they dislike the proposed activities or fear that their skills are inadequate (Dalton, 2020: 41). And some may not be able to take part; for example, certain types of dyslexia make it impossible to write poetry, and some visual impairments can make drawing difficult. We are not in the research business to make participants uncomfortable, and fortunately there are ways to mitigate these difficulties (Kara, 2020: 103). Explain your method clearly so that potential and actual participants understand what you expect from them. It is good practice to offer a choice of activities, or choice within the activity, as Louise Couceiro did to such good effect in Box 7.14 above, because this enables more people to participate with confidence. And of course participants must be able to withdraw if they wish.

Using digital methods for data gathering also generates new ethical difficulties. The distinction between private and public is different in digital spaces than in geographical spaces. Information that is publicly accessible may still be considered private by someone who has set up a blog to keep their family informed about their travels or chatted with a friend on Twitter. Ardley and McIntosh, when collecting data from Facebook groups, were careful to obtain consent in three ways: from the groups' administrators, from the groups as a whole, and from individuals whose posts they proposed to quote (Ardley and McIntosh, 2021: 10). This is very good practice and contrasts sharply with researchers who have chosen to undertake covert research online. Some argue that covert online research is defensible for some reasons and/or in some circumstances (Schembri and Latimer, 2016: 635; Schrooten, 2012: 1803). However, I would advise extreme caution because there is evidence that people who generate information online are not necessarily content for that information to be used for research purposes (Condie et al., 2017: 147; Harris, 2016: 68; Kramer et al., 2014: 8788). The Association of Internet Researchers advises that 'Special care should be taken when collecting data from social media sites in order to ensure the privacy and dignity of the subjects' (Franzke et al., 2020: 12).

If a participant agrees to connect with a researcher through an online platform, such as by becoming 'friends' on Facebook, they may inadvertently give that researcher access to their content on other sites, through lack of awareness of the links that exist between some social media platforms (Rooke, 2013: 267). In a worst-case scenario this could compromise participants' safety. Also, even though online research has many potential benefits, it can also be detrimental to researchers' well-being (Grant, 2019: 54). Working with participants through social media can improve the quality of the relationships between researchers and participants, but it can also make demands on researchers outside of working hours and beyond the life of the research project (Mainsah and Prøitz, 2019: 274, Nguyen et al., 2021: 196).

These are just a few examples of the considerable ethical complexity in digital research. Perhaps because of this complexity, research ethics committees are not always able to offer effective advice and support to researchers who want to gather data online (Harris, 2016: 63; Samuel et al., 2018: 453). Fortunately there is helpful advice available online, such as the Internet Research Ethical Guidelines 3.0 produced by the Association of Internet Researchers (Franzke et al., 2020).

Conclusion

By the end of this chapter, your head may be spinning with possibilities. You may even have come up with a new method of gathering qualitative data which you would like to try out – or you may do so in future. As we saw in Chapter 1, all methods of gathering data were invented by someone, somewhere, sometime, so there is no reason why you cannot devise one yourself.

All this innovation can be very exciting, but it is important not to get carried away. Always remember that the methods you choose must serve your research purposes, not the other way round. Also, the methods you use to gather your qualitative data will have implications for the methods you can use to analyse that data, and it is essential to think this through at the outset rather than enthusiastically gather a load of data and then wonder what to do next. The following Chapters 8 and 9 cover the analysis of qualitative data and I recommend reading them thoroughly before you gather any data for your research.

Reflective questions

1. When might you use alternative rather than mainstream methods of gathering data?
2. This chapter uses a broad definition of 'data'. What are the implications of this for your research?
3. Could methods other than interviews and focus groups, whether alternative or mainstream, be enhanced? If so, how, and to what ends?
4. How do you feel about gathering data using arts-based methods? Why do you feel that way? What can you learn from this?
5. What is your reaction to the concept of embodied data gathering? Why? What can you learn from this?

QUALITATIVE DATA ANALYSIS: CONSIDERATIONS

┤Chapter summary├

- Introduces the pre-analysis steps of qualitative data management, storage, preparation and coding
- Outlines the basic principles of qualitative data management and storage
- Covers the preparation of audio, video and visual data
- Discusses the two main methods of coding qualitative data: framed and emergent coding
- Sets out the main pros and cons of the most commonly used computer software packages for qualitative data analysis
- Explains the processes of manual qualitative data analysis
- Compares the pros and cons of digital and manual analysis
- Considers the role of collaboration in qualitative data analysis
- Reviews some of the ethical issues around qualitative data analysis

Introduction

In quantitative research, data are usually analysed to answer the question: Can we disprove this hypothesis? In qualitative research, data may be analysed to answer a variety of questions, such as: How does this phenomenon happen? Why does this intervention work? How does this process operate? Which circumstances are optimal for this treatment to have the most effect?

Qualitative data can come in small homogenous datasets, or in large quantities and varying formats. We saw an example of the latter in Box 3.2. Being faced with a big pile of diverse data is daunting for even the most experienced qualitative researcher, and even small homogenous datasets need careful and skilled attention. You can see an example of this in Box 8.1.

Data analysis is arguably the hardest part of qualitative research work, and the most important. Some people love the intellectual challenge, others find it a tedious process. And it is a process: of data management, storage, preparation and coding before you even get to analysis. This means there are several decisions to make and steps to take before you can do any actual analytic work. You need to be able to answer questions such as:

- How will you manage your data? Where will they be stored? Who will have access to them, and when?
- Will you work with your data manually or using software? Why? What are the tools you will employ to help you?
- What preparation does your data need before they can be coded and analysed? How will you do this?
- How will you code your data?
- Will you code and analyse your data alone or in collaboration with others? Why? If in collaboration, how will that collaborative work be done?

This chapter will help you to answer these questions. The next chapter will review methods of analysing your prepared and coded data.

Data management and storage

You probably already know that good data management is an ethical imperative for researchers. Whether data are digital or in hard copy, they should be securely stored. If you have made promises of confidentiality and anonymity to participants, these should be maintained during data storage.

If you belong to an institution, it may have a data storage or data management policy or procedure, setting out the requirements to which you must adhere. If you don't belong to an institution, at a minimum, hard copy data should be stored in a locked cupboard or filing cabinet. Digital data should be stored on a device that is only used by the researcher or research team, and the device should be password protected. Digital data should also be backed up to a similarly secure location. This may be a data repository, as research funders are increasingly requiring data to be made available for re-use, and this includes qualitative data (Hughes and Tarrant,

2020a: 5). There are online data repositories around the world, including some specialist archives for qualitative data (Edwards et al., 2020: 80–1; Kara, 2017: 124–5).

You also need to abide by prevailing legislation, such as (at the time of writing) the General Data Protection Regulation (GDPR) which applies if you or any of your students/clients/customers are in the European Union, the Data Protection Act (1998) in the United Kingdom, the Personal Information Protection and Electronic Documents Act (2000) in Canada and equivalent legislation in some other countries.

Data preparation

Some data arrive ready for analysis, such as data from online chats or documentary data. However, most data need to be prepared before they can be analysed. This may mean converting them into a different format, such as by transcribing audio data or scanning images, completing a metadata form or both. It is essential to have some kind of system to help you trace your converted data back to the source, so that you can check in case you spot any error that may have crept in. This system can often be quite simple, such as by numbering each piece of raw data and giving an equivalent number to each piece of prepared data.

It is essential to be meticulous about data preparation. You know how a single error in a quantitative dataset can completely change your findings. Equally, when you are working with textual data, a single typo can cause a dramatic change of meaning. Consider this interview excerpt:

'I went to the game to see the chaps.'

A typographical error here could yield:

'I went to the game to see the chaos.'

P and O are next to each other on a QWERTY keyboard so this would be an easy mistake to make. Errors of omission can be just as bad or even worse, as in the phrase 'public administration' with the L left out from the first word. Neither of these errors would be picked up by a computer spell-checker. There are also errors of commission (putting something in which shouldn't be there), transposition errors (putting two letters, words or numbers in the wrong order) and misreading and substitution errors, respectively caused by incorrect reading or writing (Kara, 2017: 163). It is helpful to be aware of these possibilities, and to do what you can to guard against them.

Audio data, from interviews or focus groups, usually need to be transcribed. This is a time-consuming process: a standard rule of thumb is to allow four hours for transcribing every recorded hour. It can be tempting to outsource this work, particularly if you have the budget to pay a professional transcriber. Transcription software is a cheaper option. However, both can introduce errors into your data. Doing your own transcription is likely to be more accurate, and is also a great help in familiarising yourself with your audio data.

Transcription sounds straightforward, as if all you have to do is listen to the recording and type what you hear. In fact, it is not so simple and there are a whole load of decisions to make. Will you record non-speech utterances such as laughter, coughs, sighs and so on? If so, how? If not, why not? Will you record pauses? If so, will you record the length of each pause, or just note that a pause occurred? Why? How will you deal with unclear speech? And so on. There is no set or 'best' way to transcribe audio data (Hammersley, 2010: 556); you need to identify the method that is most appropriate for your research. Some analytic techniques have specific transcription conventions and techniques, and this is covered in more detail in the next chapter. Also, some organisations have transcription protocols for their researchers to follow; we see an example of this in Box 8.1 below.

Video data also usually need to be transcribed and this is even more complicated. Do you include information about the environment? People's clothing and hairstyles? Their gestures and other body movements? Facial expressions? Interactions? What else do you need to consider? How do you identify these features and the speakers/actors in your transcript, and how do you lay that out on the page (Hammersley, 2010: 556–7)? There is no standard rule of thumb about how long it takes to transcribe video data, because it depends on the complexity of your transcription system. But, unless you are only transcribing words (in which case you might as well have used audio recording), it is bound to take longer than transcribing audio data; perhaps much longer.

Visual data, such as photos, drawings, painting or collage, can be turned into text for analysis by writing a description of what you see. Alternatively, they can be scanned and loaded into a software program such as NVivo or MAXQDA which enables coding of images. (There is more information about relevant software later in this chapter.) Or the images can be scanned and coded by hand. Scanned copies can be enlarged and/or duplicated, which can be helpful if the data are very detailed. Again, you need to figure out which system is likely to work best for your research.

A metadata record can be helpful, particularly for analysis by hand (Kara, 2017: 161). You would need to devise your own metadata record to meet the needs of your research. There is an example in Figure 8.1.

You can use one metadata form for each image and this will help you to count, compare and contrast the significant features in the data. Leaving some blank rows at the end of the form is good practice because, as you prepare your data, you may think of significant aspects which you didn't consider at the start. For example, you might decide you want to record the mood of the sketch using a simple triad such as upbeat, neutral or gloomy, or you might want to record the type of sketch using categories such as minimalist, doodle, rough, line drawing or detailed. You could use equivalent systems to record the metadata of other forms of data such as documents or interview transcripts.

Sketch number	
Date sketch created	
Sketch created by*	
Place in sketch	
Buildings in sketch	
People in sketch	
Animals in sketch	
Objects in sketch	
Distinctive features	
Any other comments	

Figure 8.1   Metadata record for data in sketch form. (*name or, if anonymity promised, ID code or pseudonym.)

Data preparation is time-consuming and can be quite boring. However, it is essential to work attentively and carefully, to guard against errors. On the plus side, data can be prepared in small chunks of time: even 5 minutes is long enough to complete one metadata form or transcribe a few sentences of audio data. If much preparation is needed, it is best to prepare your data as you collect them, rather than waiting until you have a big pile of data.

When you have prepared all your data, it is sensible to spot-check a selection for any mistakes. Pick a manageable amount of data – say, 5% of the total – at random, and check that they are error free. If they are, you can be fairly sure the whole dataset is free from mistakes. However, if you find errors, you will need to correct them and then make further spot-checks until you are confident there are no more mistakes in the dataset.

Coding qualitative data

Working with quantitative data is generally more straightforward than working with qualitative data. Much quantitative data do not need coding as they are in a numerical form, so you only need a code to identify any missing data. Where coding is needed, you can often continue to use numbers, or something similarly straightforward such as letters of the alphabet.

Coding qualitative data is a more complex process which involves assigning labels, known as codes, to sections of the data. Some people use software to help with this process, which means that if you are working with textual data, you can label anything from a single letter to an entire document with a code, and more than one code can be applied to the same section of data. Most data analysis software also allows you to import data in other formats, such as images or sound clips, and to code them directly without converting them into text.

Other researchers prefer to code data manually, working with printouts and pens, highlighters, Post-It notes and so on. This is particularly favoured by some embodied researchers (Thanem and Knights, 2019: 116) (see Chapter 7 for more on embodied data, and Chapter 9 for more on embodied analysis). If you want to code manually – or you need to because you don't have access to software – it helps to print out textual data in double spacing with wide margins, to make space for annotations. Images should be printed at a good size and ideally in colour. If the data are complex, you might need two or three copies to code effectively.

Coding can be divided into two kinds: framed coding and emergent coding. For the former, you use a coding 'frame', which is in fact a list of words and phrases. Then you look for sections of data which relate to the words and phrases in your list. There are various ways to devise a coding frame. For example, you could:

- use academic, policy or other relevant literature to identify key words and phrases
- create key words and phrases from your research questions
- work through a small section of your data using emergent coding (see below for more on this) to create a coding frame for use with the rest of the data

Suppose I was studying the school and non-school elements of science education of children aged 13–14. My coding frame might look like this:

Classroom
Biology
Chemistry
Physics
Geology
Environment
Hypothesis
Experiments
Data
Results

Learning

Home

Internet

TV

Citizen science

Then here is a piece of transcribed data from an interview with a young person.

'Science in school last week was so-o-o boring. The teacher talked about solids, liquids and gases, and we had to do an experiment to see how long an ice cube took to melt. Bo-ring! But then with my Mum at the weekend we helped with a big experiment that people were doing all over the country. We had to sit in the park for an hour and write down all the birds we saw, then send it to a website. That was really fun'.

Figure 8.2 shows how that piece of data might look when coded using the frame above.

Data	Code(s)
Science in school last week was so-o-o boring.	Classroom
The teacher talked about solids, liquids and gases,	Classroom Physics
and we had to do an experiment to see how long an ice cube took to melt. Bo-ring!	Classroom Physics Experiment
But then with my Mum at the weekend	Home
we helped with a big experiment that people were doing all over the country.	Citizen science
We had to sit in the park for an hour and write down all the birds we saw	Biology Environment
then send it to a website. That was really fun.	Internet

Figure 8.2 Data coded using a frame

By contrast, in emergent coding, you don't use a coding frame; the codes 'emerge' from the data. In other words, you code the data with whatever you perceive therein. So, using emergent coding, the data might look as shown in Figure 8.3 below.

The first example begins to show that framed coding can be systematic and yield useful results. The second example demonstrates that emergent coding offers more nuance than framed coding. With emergent coding, we can pick up different teaching methods (presentation), a research method that is not in the coding frame (observation) and some of the emotional dimensions of science (boring/fun). The trade-off here is that using a coding frame is generally quicker, but emergent coding is usually deeper. One way to balance this trade-off is to use some emergent coding to help develop a coding frame. Box 8.1 shows an example of this in practice.

Data	Code(s)
Science in school last week was so-o-o boring.	Classroom Boring
The teacher talked about solids, liquids and gases,	Classroom Physics Presentation
and we had to do an experiment to see how long an ice cube took to melt. Bo-ring!	Classroom Physics Experiment Boring
But then with my Mum at the weekend	Home Family
we helped with a big experiment that people were doing all over the country.	Citizen science National
We had to sit in the park for an hour and write down all the birds we saw	Biology Environment Observation
then send it to a website.	Internet
That was really fun.	Fun

Figure 8.3 Data coded using emergent coding

Box 8.1

Data preparation and coding in practice

Ningshi Xie and colleagues in Canada studied mental health nurses' perceptions of barcode medication administration technology in in-patient settings. This technology had been adopted in other health settings and has the potential to improve patient safety by reducing scope for errors when administering drugs. Ten interviews were conducted, audio recorded and transcribed verbatim by Xie 'following an organizational standardized Qualitative Data Preparation and Transcription Protocol' (Xie et al., 2019: 327) from the Centre for Addiction and Mental Health in Toronto, Ontario. One of Xie's colleagues reviewed three of the transcripts against the recordings to ensure that they were accurate. Then three interview transcripts were used to create a coding frame, and Xie and a colleague each used this frame independently to code all of the transcripts. If a section of data was found where no codes from the frame could be applied, new emergent codes were created (Xie et al., 2019: 327).

You may be wondering isn't all of this terribly subjective? Yes it is, like all research to a greater or lesser extent, as we saw in Chapter 1. Nevertheless, there are steps we can take to mitigate our subjectivity. Working consistently and systematically, like Xie et al. in Box 8.1, is one such step. Being aware of and acknowledging our own biases and preferences is a second step. This requires us to work reflexively (see Chapter 2 for more on reflexivity). Victoria Clarke and Virginia Braun, highly experienced data analysts and teachers of data analysis, suggest that before doing any analytic work, it is helpful to reflect and make notes on three things: first, the assumptions (if any) that you hold about the research topic; second, your values and relevant life experiences; and third, how all of those might influence the ways in which you perceive and interpret your data (Clarke and Braun, 2013: 122). The point of this is not only to guard against bias but also to help you gain more insight into your data (ibid). A third step is to write a full and honest account of your methods as well as your results, and to make your own positionality clear (see Chapter 10 for more on reporting research).

Using software for qualitative analysis

Computer-aided qualitative data analysis software (CAQDAS) comes in many forms. An important point to understand is that no form of CAQDAS does the work for you or takes any element of control, such as through the use of algorithms (Silver and Lewins, 2014: 17). You still have to code and analyse the data yourself; the software offers tools to make this quicker and easier. That said, coding data digitally is not much quicker than coding data manually. However, the great advantage of CAQDAS is: once the data are coded, it becomes very quick and easy to interrogate that data. Therefore, with CAQDAS, you should be able to do more analytic work with your data than if you are coding and analysing manually.

Writing about software in books is a doomed endeavour as by the time you read this no doubt there will have been changes. That said, CAQDAS software is more stable and slower-moving than many types of software. I will run through some packages here as an overview, though please note this is of course all 'at the time of writing' and I recommend making your own checks online. URLs for each package are in Appendix 1.

Full disclosure: I have been using NVivo since 2003, and I stick with it because it works well for me, plus most software is expensive and learning new software is time-consuming. However, several colleagues have told me that they find MAXQDA more intuitive and user-friendly than NVivo. Quirkos is much more affordable than most CAQDAS options, though at present it only supports the coding and analysis of text. Ultimately the selection of software is a personal choice – unless your institution, funder, colleagues or others require you to use a particular package, in which case you can skip this step.

NVivo is arguably the market leader, and is trying hard to do all things for all qualitative and mixed-methods researchers. It handles data in a wide variety of formats including text, audio, video, images, spreadsheets, online surveys, web pages and social media. Users can classify, sort, arrange, search and visualise their data, and identify and examine relationships within the data. There are functions for writing memos, making links and creating models and diagrams. NVivo for Windows is available in seven languages, and NVivo for Mac is available in five, but NVivo is not available for Linux. NVivo also has add-ons for collaboration, so teams with people in different locations can work together on the same dataset, and for transcription.

MAXQDA is also targeting qualitative and mixed-methods researchers. Its functionality is similar to NVivo's in terms of the types of data it handles, though its website claims it is 'the mixed methods leader' with more quantitative research functionality and better linkage of quantitative and qualitative data. MAXQDA also claims to be the only form of CAQDAS which is 100% identical on Windows and Mac computers, and its interface is available in 15 languages which is helpful for international teams. It is not available for Linux. Add-ons include a module for quantitative analysis of text, and a statistics module for descriptive and inferential statistics.

ATLAS.ti is also designed for qualitative and mixed-methods researchers although, judging from the information available online, it seems stronger on the qualitative aspects. Its website claims it is 'the most intuitive and easy-to-learn software' for scientific, market and user experience research, and that it can handle larger projects than any of its competitors. ATLAS.ti offers software for Windows and Mac computers, and also has a web-based cloud version, but is not available for Linux. The interface is available in five languages.

Dedoose, again, is designed for qualitative and mixed-methods data analysis, and seems to offer much the same functionality as those listed above. One difference is they offer a single monthly fee for all their services. Their website claims they have the most responsive support in a variety of media including emails, forums, Facebook and Twitter. Also, they operate on Linux as well as Mac and Windows. Dedoose is entirely cloud based, which they claim as an advantage but in fact it has both pros and cons. On the plus side, being cloud based means any updates take immediate effect. On the minus side, working in the cloud requires a stable good quality internet connection and power supply which is not available to all researchers. Also, there is a risk of temporary or permanent data loss if the Dedoose system fails, and of data theft if hackers find their way around the security. The security seems solid, and there are arrangements for data to be backed up nightly and retained for two years. However, the section about data breaches on the security web page says (at the time of writing) that Dedoose will deal with the breach and 'to the extent reasonably practicable, restore the integrity of all Dedoose project data that had been affected'. So they acknowledge that they can't give a 100% guarantee. This is not specific to Dedoose; it applies to all cloud-based services. If you habitually work with cloud-based services and find the benefits are worth the low level of risk, Dedoose may suit you well.

QDA Miner is for qualitative research using data in the form of documents or images. It claims 'more computer assistance for coding than any other qualitative research software' and has add-ons for content analysis and text mining, and for statistical analysis. There are data visualisation options, and you can add time and location information to your data too, plus it works with right-to-left languages. There is a module for 'geocoding' which enables you to create different kinds of maps to present your data. It is available for Windows and Mac, but not for Linux. They offer a free version, QDA Miner Lite, with basic features plus an interface and help file in three languages.

Quirkos works only with text data, but on the plus side it is simple, intuitive and works on Linux as well as Windows and Mac. It is much more affordably priced than most CAQDAS packages, with a one-off price for an unlimited licence. Another feature unique to Quirkos is that it gives you the option of working in the cloud or on your local computer with the same platform and interface. Working in the cloud is useful for collaboration as team members can see updates in real time. And Quirkos has built-in support for working with any kind of script, including right-to-left and pictographic languages.

In qualitative research, non-text data include images (photographs, drawings, paintings, collage, etc.), videos, artefacts, maps, audio recordings and so on. Essentially, anything that could help a researcher to answer a question may be classified as data. As we have seen, some CAQDAS support work with a wide range of non-text data, such as NVivo; some support work with a narrow range, such as QDA Miner; and some only work with text data, such as Quirkos. So if you are using non-text data and you want to use CAQDAS to help you code and analyse those data, you will need to select your CAQDAS package accordingly.

Several CAQDAS packages offer the option to import data from some or all of the others, which suggests that people may switch between packages or use more than one. Also, this is not an exhaustive list; there are others, some of which are free and/or open source. And this is emphatically not a review section. I have tried to present an overview of the features and, as I see them, the pros and cons of each package. Most paid-for packages offer reasonably generous free trials and I suggest you make good use of these to help you figure out which software is best for you.

Analysing qualitative data manually

Some researchers argue that you can reach a better understanding of your data if you code and analyse them by hand. Torkild Thanem and David Knights (2019: 116) give an eloquent explanation of one way to do this:

Get your field notes out. Type up your interview recordings and print them out along with any photographs that you have taken and any documents that you have collected. Read through your hard copies, take notes in the margins, and highlight key words and expressive quotes. Use different colours if you like. Mark important pages with stickies and write key words on catalogue cards. Type up or photocopy notes pages containing key quotes and observations. Take a pair of scissors and cut out separate quotes and observations. Lay it all out on the floor. Add artefacts that you have collected during the research process. Step into your empirical material, get on all fours and work with it, play with it. Arrange it according to themes and sub-themes without getting stuck in one structure. Draw maps and diagrams, and take photographs so that you can arrange and rearrange your material whilst keeping track of the different linear and non-linear connections that start emerging.

I can see the appeal of this hands-on approach, though Thanem and Knights make three assumptions that may not be true for you. First, they assume you have enough available floor space to lay out all your data. Second, they assume that you are able-bodied and so can crawl around among your data. Third, they assume that you have a dataset that is small enough to manage manually. If you have a dataset of a suitable size, enough floor space and an able body, then this is an option worth considering.

Laura Ellingson points out that if you are unable or unwilling to use an approach like Thanem and Knights', and you are also unable or unwilling to use CAQDAS, another option is to use a hybrid of digital and manual analysis. This involves converting any hard copy data into digital form, and working on screen, perhaps in a word processing program. Then you can cut, paste, copy, annotate and highlight digital copies of data; change the colours of backgrounds, text and highlights; use different fonts for different participants; hyperlink between texts, images and web pages to create connections; and so on (Ellingson, 2017: 160). One advantage of this approach is that you can work with larger volumes of data than for purely manual analysis (Ellingson, 2017: 161). Other advantages are that you don't need a big floor space or a body that can stand, kneel and crawl.

I would advise every qualitative researcher to experiment with both manual or hybrid and CAQDAS-supported coding and analysis before you settle on one or the other, or on the combination you prefer.

Collaborating on data analysis

Collaboration can be very useful in data preparation, coding and analysis (Lemon and Salmons, 2020: 128). One obvious reason for this is the old saying that 'two heads are better than one'. Another, perhaps less obvious, reason is that collaboration tends to help researchers work more ethically (Kara, 2018: 118).

People often work alone when they are preparing, coding and analysing data. Even if they are working in a team, they often work individually rather than collaboratively, and – as with quantitative raters – use standard techniques to assess the level of reliability between individual coders in an effort to achieve consistency. This lone working may be why data analysis is a phase of the research process where researchers seem particularly susceptible to ethical breaches such as data manipulation or falsification. The Retraction Watch website and database contain thousands of examples – see Appendix 1 for the URL.

When collaborating, people act as a moderating influence on each other (Kara, 2018: 118). Our collaborators can support us in resisting the pressure we feel from the agendas of participants, managers, funders and so on. Collaborators can also enable us to withstand our own inevitable temptations to help the findings along a little here and there. Also, collaborating with others can help us to identify and countermand each other's biases (Croskerry et al., 2013: ii67). In these ways, collaborating on data preparation, coding and analysis can help us avoid ethical breaches. Indigenous researchers say it is better to collaborate on data analysis than to work alone (Smith, 2012: 130; Walker, 2013: 303–4).

That said, collaboration brings its own ethical challenges, which are not often considered in literature or practice (Kara, 2018: 78). For ethical collaboration, we need mutual respect, effective communication and clear shared expectations. It is also essential to spend time articulating, sharing and understanding each other's ontological and epistemological positions (Chilisa, 2020: 91) (see Chapter 2 for more on these concepts). When this shared understanding is not achieved, problems can result (Box 8.2).

Box 8.2

Problematic research collaboration

Åshild Lunde and her colleagues in Norway studied a research project in which a team of experienced health researchers from different disciplines conducted empirical studies of athletes with knee injuries. This was known as 'the knee project'. The knee project team included physiologists and clinician researchers. The physiologists used observation and measurement to understand physical changes. The clinician researchers used interviews to understand patients' experiences.

The physiologists classified the research participants as 'copers' and 'noncopers' (Lunde et al., 2013: 207). However, the clinician researchers' findings from the interviews suggested that participants classified as 'copers' by the physiologists could in fact be characterised as 'noncopers'. These contradictions were not seen as a potential resource by the knee project team; instead, the project foundered on the researchers' inability to agree on an analytic narrative.

(Continued)

Lunde and her colleagues conducted a piece of meta-research – researching the knee project – to find out what went wrong. They interviewed members of the knee project team to find out about their role in, contribution to, involvement in and perception of the project. All team members expressed a sense of failure and disappointment (Lunde et al., 2013: 201). The meta-researchers found several reasons for the knee project's collapse, including lack of strong leadership and professional cultural differences between academic and practitioner-researchers in the team. They also acknowledged that individual personalities were likely to have played a part beyond that which they could identify through their research. However, the main problem was the lack of understanding of each others' ontological and epistemological positions. As one of the participants said (Lunde et al., 2013: 209):

> It is first in retrospect that we became aware of all the differences that we have not been explicit about. It is not just about what kind of questions you ask – it is about a completely different understanding.

Other barriers to collaboration are budgets and timescales, which may preclude thorough collaborative work. However, even an element of collaboration can be surprisingly helpful for qualitative analysis: perhaps a short time spent discussing some aspects or examples of your data, or each team member coding an excerpt of data followed by a discussion of the codes used to establish a collectively agreed coding frame that one researcher can apply to all the data. There is more information about collaboration in analytic work in Chapter 9.

Ethics in qualitative data analysis – part 1

You already know that analysing data is a difficult task, and analysing qualitative data can be even more difficult. Most of the ethical problems you could encounter can be sidestepped by following the principles of good research practice: store your data safely, prepare them meticulously and code them carefully. Make considered decisions about whether to use software or analyse by hand or combine the two, and collaborate when you can.

Also, be aware that you are likely at one point or another to feel tempted to manipulate or even fabricate data. If you feel such temptation, as I believe many researchers do – I know I have – then acknowledge, but do not act on, the feeling. Such temptation may be a particular risk for activist researchers, but all researchers are at some level of risk here, not least because we often do analytic work alone.

Having said that, it is important to clarify that these feelings of temptation do not arise because we are riddled with vices. Daniele Fanelli and his colleagues in the United

States, Canada and Europe conducted a large international study into unethical duplication of images in journal articles. They found that the factors affecting scientific integrity were 'academic culture, peer control, cash-based publication incentives and national misconduct policies' (or the lack of them) (Fanelli et al., 2019: 771). They also found a lower risk of unethical duplication of images in countries where incentives to publish are linked to career progression and institutional prestige (Fanelli et al., 2019: 775). This suggests that structural factors, rather than individual vices, are the main causes of misconduct in research.

Even so, it is not OK for us to discard our own responsibilities. Knowing about these structural factors can help us, as individual researchers, to resist any temptation to manipulate or fabricate data, because that knowledge can enable us to understand the source of such temptation and find ways to resist.

Conclusion

Now you know how to manage, store and prepare your data; how to code your data; and why and when you might collaborate during that process. Perhaps more importantly, you know there are a number of tasks to complete with qualitative data before you can start your analytic work. This knowledge is essential for planning and costing research projects.

In the next chapter, we will review the main methods of analysing qualitative data.

Reflective questions

Think about a research project you are working on, or one you would like to undertake, that uses qualitative data.

1. What are the main ethical considerations you need to bear in mind when preparing and coding your qualitative data?
2. What steps could you take to ensure that your data are prepared accurately?
3. Could you usefully introduce one or more collaborative elements to your data preparation? If so, what, and why?
4. Do you feel more drawn towards digital, manual or hybrid data coding? Why? What might you gain from trying the other ways of coding data?
5. Could you usefully introduce one or more collaborative elements to your data coding? If so, what, and why?
6. Other than by working collaboratively, how can you guard against bias in coding your data?

TYPES OF QUALITATIVE ANALYSIS

┌─ Chapter summary ─────────────────────────────────────

- Reviews debiasing strategies
- Introduces the many methods of analysing qualitative data
- Looks at the role of theory in qualitative data analysis
- Covers content analysis, conversation analysis, discourse analysis, narrative analysis, thematic analysis, grounded theory analysis, textual analysis and collaborative analysis
- Considers innovation in qualitative data analysis, including arts-based analysis, multi-modal analysis, embodied analysis, digital approaches to analysis and participant involvement in analytic work
- Explores some of the ethical issues in qualitative data analysis

Introduction

This chapter will give you an overview of qualitative data analysis and its interpretative component which is the core of our work as qualitative researchers. Analysing qualitative data is a complex process of intellectual dance, tracing links between codes, theory or theories, emotions, categories, memories, themes and knowledge. That knowledge may come from academic literature, professional experience, personal experience – any relevant knowledge may be brought in to help the enquiry.

In this dance, we need to guard against bias, as far as possible. There are some strategies which can help (Croskerry et al., 2013: ii67–8) offer the following:

- Make sure you have all the information you need, because biases have more room to operate where information is insufficient.
- Use predetermined and tested structures, such as checklists, to ensure rigorous thinking.
- Be aware of how your emotions are affecting your analytic work, and do what you can to minimise their influence on decisions.
- Value scepticism. Remember that if something looks too good to be true, it probably is.
- Ask for others' opinions, particularly on complex topics or where you are unsure – or very sure.
- Think about who you are accountable to and how they might view the decisions you are taking.
- Use deliberate slow thinking, sometimes called 'mindfulness', to help overcome the biases caused by automatic fast thinking.

Reflexivity is another strategy that can help with debiasing which is increasingly used by researchers of all kinds, as we saw in Chapter 2. While reflexivity is useful at all stages of the research process, it is perhaps most useful at the analytic stage. You will find specific suggestions in Chapter 8. Writing plays a key role here, keeping field notes (sometimes called 'memos' for analysis) of your thoughts and decisions. See Chapter 5 and Box 5.1 for more detailed information about field notes.

There are many ways to analyse qualitative data, and how you choose is related to your ontological and epistemological positions (see Chapter 2 for more on this) and perhaps your theoretical perspective (covered in Chapter 3). This chapter will describe the most common types of qualitative data analysis: content analysis, conversation analysis, discourse analysis, narrative analysis, thematic analysis, document analysis, grounded theory analysis and textual analysis. (There are many other types of qualitative data analysis, such as interpretive phenomenological analysis, semiotic analysis and framework analysis, but they are beyond the scope of this chapter.) We will consider some examples of innovation around which aspects of data to analyse, and the role of collaboration in analysing qualitative data. Then we will discuss arts-based and multi-modal data analysis. Embodiment in qualitative data analysis will be considered, and the role of technology. The ethical aspects of analysing data will also be discussed.

Theory in analysis

We saw in Chapter 3 that theory and analysis are intimately linked, in several possible ways, either using existing theory or building theory from research data or findings.

- Existing theory can be used as a lens for viewing your data, codes and findings.
- Existing theory can be used as an organising framework to help arrange and connect data (Collins and Stockton, 2018: 4).
- Theory can be built from data or findings, as in grounded theory which is based on inductive reasoning (Belgrave and Seide, 2019).
- Theory can be built from data or findings by considering as many options as possible before reaching a conclusion, using abductive reasoning (Saldaña, 2015: 25).

Overall, theory helps you to steer a course from research questions to findings (Evans et al., 2011: 289) and analysis is a key part of that journey. Long before you embark on analytic work, you should be clear about the way or ways in which you are working with theory. Then, when you do your analytic work, use your theory to guide you, or to help build your theory, in accordance with your plans.

Content analysis

Content analysis may be familiar to you as it is a quantitative technique which is also used in qualitative research, generally with text or visual data (Silverman, 2020: 387). It is quite simple: all you have to do is take your codes and/or categories, and count the number of instances in each (Silverman, 2020: 120). If you use software, this is very quick to do; it will take longer if you are analysing data by hand, but it is not difficult. It can be useful if you have a lot of data to explore, so is often used with secondary data such as media or archival data (Kara, 2017: 178). If your data are available in digital form, content analysis can be very straightforward, and may even be done without preliminary coding if you have text data, as most software will enable you to search for specific words and phrases and then tell you how many there are.

The utility of content analysis is limited, as it only gives you a superficial descriptive sense of *what* is in your data, and does nothing to explain *why* those phenomena occur (Kara, 2017: 178). Therefore, in qualitative research, content analysis is usually used in a multi-modal analytic approach, rather than on its own. (Multi-modal analysis is covered later in this chapter.)

Conversation analysis

Conversation analysis, or CA, draws on techniques from cognitive anthropology, which investigates how language is used, and from linguistics. CA is founded on the premise that talk structures our world, rather than the other way around, and that talk itself has an organisational structure. Conversation analysts are interested in how this structure operates.

Conversation analysts have identified some specific features of talk. These include the following (Bryman, 2016: 529–30):

- Turn-taking – a way in which talk is structured, based on codes understood by both or all people conversing
- Adjacency pairs, such as reciprocal greetings or question and answer
- Preference organisation – generally speakers prefer acceptance and agreement over rejection and disagreement, and conversation will be structured accordingly, with acceptance or agreement being quicker and requiring fewer words than rejection or disagreement
- Accounts – descriptions of actions, interactions, thoughts and/or events and
- Repairs – ways to manage interruptions, hesitations, mis-speaking and other disruptive phenomena while maintaining the rules of turn-taking

Data for CA are usually recorded real-life talk rather than talk specifically designed for research such as research interviews. CA uses a detailed system of transcription including notations to mark all the different aspects of a conversational soundscape. These include audible in- or out-breaths, the length of pauses, long-drawn-out sounds which may be within or separate from words, overlapping talk, incomprehensible talk and changes of pitch. There is no set convention for these notations. Because the analytic work of CA is so detailed, it is usually used with small datasets.

You can see from the example in Box 9.1 that CA is a very detailed type of analysis. This means it can only be used with small datasets. However, because it is so detailed, it is a good way to get a lot of information from a little data.

Box 9.1

Conversation analysis in practice

Seuren and his colleagues used CA to conduct a microanalysis of seven video consultations via FaceTime with patients who had heart failure. They wanted to find out how well the video consultations worked, where there were challenges and how those challenges could be addressed. They drew their transcription conventions from Jefferson (2004) and these were as follows:

For vocalised interaction:

(1.0)	Silence in tenths of seconds
(.)	Micropause
[ ]	Brackets mark start and end of overlapping talk.

.	Falling intonation
,	Slightly rising intonation
?	Strongly rising intonation
;	Slightly falling intonation
↑↓	Brief rise or fall in intonation
:	Vowel or consonant is held longer
___	Underlining indicates emphasis
LOUD	Capitals signify relatively loud speech
°°	Degree signs signify relatively soft speech
>talk<	Contracted or relatively fast speech
tal-	A hyphen signifies a cut-off in mid-production, typically audible as a glottal stop
.hh	Audible in-breath. Each *h* denotes about 200 ms.
( )	Parenthesis indicate hard-to-hear talk

For embodied interaction:

⋆ ⋆	
+ +	
$ $	Gestures and descriptions of embodied actions are delimited between two identical symbols (one symbol per participant) and are synchronised with correspondent stretches of talk
*--->	
--->*	The action described continues across subsequent lines, until the same symbol is reached
>>	The action described begins before the excerpt's beginning.
--->>	The action described continues after the excerpt's end
.....	Action's preparation
----	Action's apex is reached and maintained
,,,,,	Action's retraction
nur	Participant doing the embodied action is identified when they are not the speaker

Here is an example of a patient reporting their oxygen saturation readings to a nurse, over video, using this transcription system:

60	(0.2)
61	Patient:.mlk ninety three:.

(Continued)

62	(0.7)
63	Nurse: £yea:£. uh[:u hu
64	Patient: [ninety fi:ve.
65	Partner: uh::hu hu
66	(0.5)
67	Patient: ↑ninety fi:ve;
68	(0.5)
69	Nurse: that's great.=
70	Partner: =↑ninety six;=
71	Patient: =it's ninety six; yeah.
72	Nurse: ↑wee::h; the dizzy heights;

This method enabled the researchers to 'identify the challenges of remote physical examination over video, and the verbal and non-verbal communication strategies used to address them' (Seuren et al., 2020).

Discourse analysis

Like conversation analysis, discourse analysis focuses on language, but unlike conversation analysis, it includes more kinds than spoken dialogue alone. In discourse analysis, a 'discourse' refers to all of the communication on a particular topic and/or from a particular viewpoint. This may include spoken or signed dialogue, as well as documents, broadcasts, advertisements, performances, social media posts and so on. So the 'haute couture' or high-end fashion discourse would include glossy magazines, fashion shows, television programmes featuring haute couture and all discussions of high-end fashion, among other things. Discourse analysts claim that the language used in such discourses is so central to our social lives that studying it in detail is essential for us to understand how we function socially (Robson and McCartan, 2016: 371).

Discourse analysts do not only analyse what is said or conveyed, but also how it is said or conveyed, and what the communicator is trying to achieve through their communication. Across a variety of disciplines, a wide range of sub-types of discourse analysis are in use, drawing on different theoretical approaches and using different methods and sources of data (Leipold et al., 2019: 447–9). Box 9.2 shows an example of discourse analysis in practice.

The analytical work of Simon Joss and his colleagues was much richer and more detailed than the summary overview in Box 9.2 might suggest. Space precludes a fuller discussion, but it is worth saying that they were able to build up a rich picture of what

---

Box 9.2

Discourse analysis in practice

Simon Joss, Matthew Cook and Youri Dayot used discourse analysis with the Smart City Standard issued by the British Standards Institution (BSI) in the mid-2010s, to investigate the way citizenship was represented in the Standard. The Standard was commissioned by the UK Government, and comprised six inter-relating documents which were collectively devised through public consultation and expert consensus. It was the first such Standard in the world, and therefore important to analyse because it was likely to be used as a template for work in other countries. The questions formulated by the researchers were, 'What kind of citizenship regime is constructed discursively by the standard and what might the effects of such constructions be' (Joss et al., 2017: 32). Drawing on the work of Jenson (2009), the researchers set out three intersecting dimensions in terms of which to examine and interpret the citizenship regime set out in the Standard: the 'responsibility mix' (distribution of responsibility between individual, community, market and state), rights and obligations (forming the boundary of a political community) and governing practices, including ways of engaging citizens and providing access to the state (Joss et al., 2017: 32). The researchers used quantitative and qualitative methods in a close textual analysis of the Standard. The quantitative analysis involved calculating the frequency of the term 'citizen(s)' in the six individual documents and in the text as a whole; comparing this with the frequency of other actors, such as 'business' or 'customer', to show the relative weight given to citizenship and looking at the frequency of word associations (Joss et al., 2017: 34). The qualitative analysis involved initial manual analysis and theoretical work to identify codes, then coding to identify smart city discourse frames and citizens' subject positions. The researchers found five smart city discourse frames: 'governance reform' occurred most frequently, then 'digital innovation', 'economic growth/competitiveness', 'city as complex system' and lastly 'resource efficiency/sustainability' (Joss et al., 2017: 36). They found 10 citizens' subject positions: 'consuming public services' occurred most frequently, and others included 'being empowered by data', 'collaborating with city', and lastly 'pursuing "common good"' (Joss et al., 2017: 39).

---

the Standard says about citizenship, how it says those things and what it is aiming to achieve in the world.

Narrative analysis

Narrative analysts search for, collect and analyse stories. These may be any kind of story from a brief narrative extracted from a single paragraph of written data to a full life history. This is a more complex process than it might at first appear. For a start, story is not one thing but many: a powerful educational medium (Archibald, 2008: ix); a translation of experience into selected words, such that both the experience and the words must be attended to (Simpson, 2016: 95); a way of making and remaking meaning (Phillips and Bunda, 2018: 7); a social practice (Phillips and Kara, 2021: 43) and more. Stories are truth and not truth. Stories may be gathered from participants or from documentary sources, analysed in a number of different ways and their components used as ingredients for new stories we tell in our writing and our talk. We all tell and listen to stories, all the time, and stories beget stories.

There are a bunch of different ways to approach narrative analysis, and debates about everything from definitions to methodology. Some people argue that narrative and story are not the same, because 'narrative' implies chronology while 'story' does not. Others argue for a typology to categorise the different ways to approach narrative analysis, though there is at present no agreed or even dominant typology. It is beyond the scope of this book to review all of these debates. Box 9.3 shows an example of narrative analysis in practice.

Box 9.3

Narrative analysis in practice

Cecilia Pasquinelli and Marapina Trunfio, from the University of Naples in Italy, studied the role of the media in representing, and shaping public and policymakers' understandings of, overtourism. The term itself was introduced by the international media, and by focussing on certain aspects of the phenomenon, the media 'influence how, and to what extent, local communities and policy-makers perceive, conceive, and respond to' overtourism and its challenges (Pasquinelli and Trunfio, 2020: 1806). The researchers used narrative analysis within a multi-modal analytic design to investigate ways in which online news media portray the causes and effects of overtourism and attempts to manage the problem. They collected 56 articles from 35 online sources over a 15-week period in May–August 2018. Relevant narrative fragments were extracted and grouped into three pre-determined categories: causes of overtourism, effects of overtourism and actions to solve the problem. Then the narrative fragments within each category were reconnected into stories that framed the 'overarching representation of overtourism' (Pasquinelli and Trunfio, 2020: 1811). This was complemented by a quantitative analysis of the text including the most frequent words and their co-occurrence with 'overtourism', which enabled the researchers to identify key topics and stakeholders in their dataset (Pasquinelli and Trunfio, 2020: 1811–2). Integrating the findings from the quantitative and narrative analyses enabled the researchers to identify a range of causes and stakeholders held to be responsible for overtourism, some of the effects of overtourism and actions being taken to try to solve this problem. The narrative analysis was particularly helpful in revealing some of the complexity of the situation.

Thematic analysis

Thematic analysis offers a way to find, analyse and interpret patterns in qualitative data. As with narrative analysis, there are different ways of doing this, and little agreement about which is best, even within disciplines, let alone between them.

However, at its most basic, thematic analysis is quite straightforward. Virginia Braun and Victoria Clarke wrote an article on thematic analysis in psychology (Braun and Clarke, 2006) which has become foundational in the discipline and beyond, with over 100,000 citations at the time of writing. They offered a process with six steps:

1. Become familiar with the data through transcribing (if necessary), reading and re-reading, and making notes of initial ideas.
2. Systematically code interesting features of the data.
3. Search for themes by collecting codes into potential themes.
4. Review themes by moving between coded extracts and the data as a whole to check if the themes work – revise them as necessary.
5. Define and name the themes, again revising as you go if necessary until you are confident that you have themes which can help you tell the story of your data.
6. Write a report outlining the analysis and explaining how it relates to your research question and context (Braun and Clarke, 2006: 87).

These steps are not necessarily taken consecutively in a linear process. In particular, a researcher may move forward and back between steps two and five, perhaps many times, particularly if they are working with a large and complex dataset (Maguire and Delahunt, 2017: 3354). Box 9.4 shows an example of thematic analysis in practice.

Box 9.4

Thematic analysis in practice

Veterinary scientists Agnese Balzani and Alison Hanlon used thematic analysis with a transdisciplinary literature review in a study of the factors influencing farmers' views on farm animal welfare. They searched PubMed and Web of Science, from September to November 2019, and found 96 relevant articles published worldwide from 1989 to 2019. Analysis of these articles yielded 29 codes and three themes: farmers' views of farm animal welfare, internal factors (farmers' characteristics) influencing their views and external factors influencing their views. These enabled the researchers to answer their research questions: 'What do farmers think about farm animal welfare?' and 'What are the factors that influence their thinking?' (Balzani and Hanlon, 2020: 6). They were also able to make three recommendations which would help farmers and others in the industry to put extra safeguards in place for the welfare of farmed animals (Balzani and Hanlon 2020: 18–9).

In 2020, Braun and Clarke published a follow-up article identifying ten problems that appear in published research which either cites, or claims to follow, their approach. These include conceptual issues, misunderstandings, problematic assumptions and problems with the process or practice of thematic analysis. Some examples: assuming thematic analysis is atheoretical, assuming thematic analysis is allied with a particular theoretical stance, confusing codes and themes or themes and topics and even claiming to follow the procedure set out in the 2006 article while in fact doing something completely different. Braun and Clarke (2020) have constructed a set of 20 questions to help article reviewers and journal editors evaluate submissions incorporating thematic analysis (18–9). This is also a useful resource for researchers intending to use thematic analysis.

Document analysis

We saw in Chapters 3 and 7 that documents can be used as data for research. Analysing documents can be a complex undertaking. There is no single way to analyse documents, and indeed some of the analytic techniques already discussed can be used with documentary data, such as content analysis, discourse analysis and narrative analysis (Grant, 2019: 29). But there are some aspects of analytic work which are particular to document analysis.

First, it is useful to record each document's metadata: who wrote it, when and why? What was the document's intended audience or audiences, and what was it created to achieve? There may be other questions too that you can devise for your particular dataset. Carol Cardno suggests 18 questions for the analysis of educational policy documents, under the headings of document production and location, authorship and audience, policy context, policy text and policy consequences (Cardno, 2018: 631).

If you have enough documents, you can use descriptive statistical calculations with this metadata – in which case it is worth keeping your records in a digital spreadsheet, as that makes counting, sorting and calculations quick and easy. Either way, the metadata enables you to describe your dataset and help your readers understand.

Then, if you are using framed coding and you have digital documents, it is also quick and easy to search each document electronically for each code and then select and extract the relevant text. With hard copy documents this takes longer, because you have to search by eye, but it is still a straightforward task.

With emergent coding, the process takes longer still, regardless of whether you are using digital documents, or hard copy, or a combination. You need to examine each document thoroughly, reading and re-reading it carefully, to identify and extract relevant sections (Bowen, 2009: 32).

Either way, once you have extracted all the relevant parts, you need to read over the extracts to look for patterns, categories and themes to use in interpretative work, in accordance with your chosen analytic technique.

Box 9.5 gives an example of document analysis in practice.

Box 9.5

Document analysis in practice

Penny Mackieson and her colleagues in Australia, whose Codebook is featured in Box 5.1, used a form of thematic analysis with the official records of parliamentary debates in the Australian state of Victoria relating to the introduction of Permanent Care Orders. These offer an alternative to adoption for children living away from, and unable to return safely to live with, their parents. Official records are generally trust-worthy and good quality (Mackieson et al., 2018: 968). The records were in PDF format, but the researchers chose to convert them to Word for analysis, which they did in three stages. The first stage involved reading the whole dataset, identifying preliminary themes, translating the preliminary themes into defined codes and mapping those codes and the relationships between them. In the second stage, the researchers took an iterative approach to re-reading the dataset, refining themes and adjusting, applying and confirming codes, and systematically sampling to check for consistency or discrepancies. This yielded 27 thematic codes. In the third stage, they counted and analysed the frequency of use of their codes, re-read and electronically searched their dataset to find quotes to illustrate each theme, and interpreted their findings with guidance from a pre-existing typology of ideological perspectives (Mackieson et al., 2018: 977). Throughout this process, they recorded every decision made, and the rationale for it, in the Codebook they had devised (see Box 5.1 for details). This method, while quite laborious, was also rigorous, transparent and replicable (Mackieson et al., 2018: 979).

Grounded theory analysis

We saw in Chapter 3 that grounded theory is a systematic way of building theory as data are being gathered and analysed. The conventional view of qualitative research is that data analysis happens after all the data have been gathered together. However, in grounded theory research, analysis begins as soon as any data have been gathered, and the results of that analysis are used to inform ongoing data gathering, and so on, in an iterative process (Belgrave and Seide, 2019: 302). The foundation of grounded theory analytic work is 'constant comparison', where data and codes are constantly compared with each other, and short memos written to capture the researcher's analytic thoughts as data are coded and recoded (Belgrave and Seide, 2019: 305). Codes may be combined into categories which are then integrated into a theoretical framework, and during this process, the constant comparison continues, between the more abstract categorisation and theorising and the more concrete data and coding (Belgrave and Seide, 2019: 314).

Grounded theory was devised by Barney Glaser and Anselm Strauss while they were studying terminally ill patients in a California hospital. The patients had different levels of knowledge about the fact that they were dying. Glaser and Strauss wanted to understand how patients dealt with the knowledge that they were dying, and the reactions of their healthcare staff (Tie et al., 2019: 2). Although both researchers had been trained in the scientific method, they questioned its appropriateness for this kind of research. This ethical concern led them to develop the method of constant comparison, and that in turn led them to understand and write about the way theory can be inductively generated from data.

Later, Glaser's and Strauss's views of grounded theory diverged, with Glaser continuing to teach and advocate for the original approach, and Strauss developing from the initial post-positivist stance towards a more constructivist method (Ralph et al., 2015: 4). The method has continued to evolve, though constant comparison and memo writing are consistent elements (Ralph et al., 2015: 2). However, there are no specific requirements for grounded theory analysis in terms of epistemological or ontological position, theoretical lenses to use, types of coding and so on. Also, grounded theory research may be qualitative or multi-modal, and can include some quantitative data if appropriate. And some researchers use analytic techniques from grounded theory within other types of research. We saw an example of this in Box 1.4 outlining a multi-modal project involving surveys, an RCT, focus group discussions and in-depth interviews. Within this project, one researcher used grounded theory analysis with part of the data, a set of 60 interview transcripts.

Perhaps because grounded theory has roots in post-positivist medical research, it has proved more attractive to STEM researchers than some other qualitative methods. Box 9.6 below shows an example of this in practice. In this example, the use of open, axial and selective coding marks out Grace Mbuthia and her colleagues as adherents of Strauss's approach to grounded theory (Ralph et al., 2015: 2).

Textual analysis

Textual analysis deals not only with words but also with other features of texts such as images, symbols and language. Also, textual analysis doesn't only deal with written data, but also with visual, audio-recorded or video-recorded data (Hawkins, 2018b: 1754). Textual analysis is used by researchers from a wide range of disciplines, and incorporates a variety of methods, both manual and digital, sometimes including

---

Box 9.6

Grounded theory analysis in practice

Grace Mbuthia, Charles Olungah and Tom Ondicho wanted to investigate health-seeking behaviours and other factors contributing to delayed diagnosis of tuberculosis (TB) for people in West Pokot County in western Kenya on the border of Uganda. Participants, who were patients newly diagnosed with pulmonary TB, were recruited with the help of nurses from various TB clinics in the county. Data were gathered through in-depth interviews and complementary focus group discussions, all of which were conducted in Kiswahili, later translated into English and transcribed in both languages (Mbuthia et al., 2018: 4). Analysis was conducted concurrently and the interview questions were amended for later interviews to gather more information about emerging themes. The analytic procedure involved reading and re-reading transcripts while identifying and coding the data. Three types of coding were used: open coding to identify codes, axial coding to group-related codes into sub-categories and selective coding to integrate sub-categories into theoretical constructs. Then 'The axial and the selective coding were used to explore the relationships between the subcategories and tie the concepts together to generate a conceptual framework through comparative analysis' (Mbuthia et al., 2018: 5). This enabled the researchers to create a 'conceptual framework of a pathway of delay', showing that individual, socio-cultural and structural factors can all contribute to delayed diagnosis, leading to more transmission of the disease and greater individual suffering (Mbuthia et al., 2018: 8).

---

quantitative techniques. The aim is to understand how people create meanings with, and communicate through, texts of all kinds. Textual analysis is often used with secondary data, though it can also be used with primary data such as interview or focus group data; we saw an example of this in Box 1.4. Box 9.7 below shows an example of textual analysis with secondary data. This offers an interesting example of multi-modal research, with qualitative data, a multi-faceted quantitative analytic process and qualitative findings.

Collaborative analysis

The journal article reporting Balzani and Hanlon's work (Box 9.4 above) makes clear that the coding was done by Agnese Balzani (Balzani and Hanlon, 2020: 7). Data analysis is often conducted by one person because that is the most cost-effective and time-saving method. Yet there are often good reasons for working with others to analyse qualitative data where different perspectives can usefully enrich analytic work, reduce bias and help the research to stay ethical (Odena, 2013: 365; Smith, 2012; 130;

Box 9.7

Textual analysis with secondary data

Pongsak Luangaram and Warapong Wongwachara, from Thailand, used textual analysis to explore the nature of communication from central banks about monetary policy. The researchers were particularly interested in how readable and under-standable this communication was; the key themes discussed and how positive was the economic outlook portrayed. They used digital methods with multiple established measures from computational linguistics, including formulae and algorithms, to analyse the post-meeting monetary policy statements of 22 central banks from 2000 to 2015 (English language versions only, for standardisation) (Luangaram and Wongwachara, 2017: 4). Their sample included central banks from countries with both advanced and emerging market economies in North and South America, Europe, Asia and Australasia. They collected over 3,000 statements, and digital analysis made this large dataset manageable. The sophisticated approach they took to analysing their data enabled them to uncover hidden complexities in monetary policymaking and communication (Luangaram and Wongwachara, 2017: 37).

Walker, 2013: 303–4, citing Begay and Maryboy, 1998: 50–5). However, collaborative work can raise new ethical problems, particularly if there is an unequal power balance between collaborators (Kara, 2018: 115).

Collaboration in analytic work is usually with colleagues and sometimes with participants. Box 9.8 shows an example of researchers and a participant collaborating on analysis.

There are other ways to collaborate with participants and/or their representatives in analytic work. We saw in Box 7.14 that Louise Couceiro, with her reader response toolkits, gave her young participants the chance to contribute to the analysis of their creations during discussions of those creations in online interviews. Carlie Goldsmith, whose work with refugees, asylum seekers and migrants in London is in Box 1.3, consulted with over 80 delegates at a Refugee and Migrant Conference as part of her analytic work. She presented themes emerging from her research and examples of her data, to support in-depth discussions which were a great help in informing her analysis (Goldsmith, 2015: 16). (Seeking feedback from participants or their representatives is sometimes known as 'member checking'.) These are just a few examples. In partici-patory research, collaborating with participants is essential throughout. Of course, involving participants or their representatives in qualitative data analysis is not always possible – but it is often worth considering.

Box 9.8

Collaborative analysis in practice

Sports researcher Mary Ann Kluge worked with two other researchers and their participant, Linda Glick. At the age of 65, and with no experience of athletics or even exercising to keep fit, Linda decided to train as an athlete and compete in the Rocky Mountain Senior Games. She asked her friend Mary Ann to be her personal trainer and coach. Mary Ann and her colleagues were intrigued by this unusual decision and decided, with Linda's agreement, to record and investigate her experience of becoming an athlete. They chose to use video to capture real-time physical activity, and gathered many hours of video data. Also, Linda kept a journal of her thoughts and feelings. The researchers read Linda's journal several times, coded the text and identified themes. Then the researchers and Linda together reviewed the video data several times 'to recognise what visible material is visually significant and how to use it to best reflect the associated narrative' (Kluge et al., 2010: 286). Linda was a full participant in this process, which resulted in a 23-minute film that she also narrated.

There are some other examples of involving participants in analytic work in this chapter and in Chapter 7. In Box 9.8, participant Linda Glick worked with researcher Mary Ann Kluge and her colleagues throughout the analytic process. In Jennifer Lapum's research in Box 9.10, people who had recovered from open-heart surgery helped to analyse data from others' experiences of undergoing such surgery. And in Box 7.14, Louise Couceiro's young participants contributed to the analysis of their creations during their online interviews. These examples show us that participants, or their representatives, can be involved in analytic work in a range of different ways. Participants may be involved directly, in part of the work (as with Couceiro) or in all of the work (as with Kluge et al.). Or their representatives may be involved, either because it would be inappropriate to ask participants to be involved (asking people who have recently undergone open-heart surgery for data is burden enough) or because it is difficult to keep track of participants from transient populations (migrants, asylum seekers, refugees, homeless people, nomads and so on). And there are other ways, too: a group of participants may be convened to give input during analytic work, or partic-ipants' representatives may be involved in all the analytic work to bring both fresh eyes and good contextual knowledge. That said, it is not always necessary or appropriate to try to involve participants or their representatives in analysing qualitative data. But it is often worth considering because this kind of involvement can enrich analysis and improve the quality of findings.

Innovation in analysing qualitative data

The research methods literature contains many examples of innovation in qualitative data analysis. These include innovations around which aspects of data to analyse, and innovations around re-using data. Focus group data were initially analysed from transcripts as if they were interview data, but in the early 21st century, some researchers began also to analyse the interactions between people in focus groups to find out what that might add to the analysis of the text itself (Belzile and Öberg, 2012; Farnsworth and Boon, 2010; Halkier, 2010). Others began to do analytic work with silences, pauses or omissions to try to uncover what might have been left unsaid and why (Frost and Elichaoff, 2010).

Re-analysing existing qualitative research data is a burgeoning approach in many areas, recently encouraged by the COVID-19 pandemic with associated movement restrictions necessitating new methods for desk research. Other drivers of this increase include requirements from funders, publishers and Governments for maximum use to be made of data to reduce the burdens that data gathering places on participants and researchers (Bishop and Kuula-Luumi, 2017: 1). Online repositories of qualitative research data are based in Australia, several European countries, the United Kingdom, the United States and perhaps other countries too (Edwards et al., 2020: 80–1; Kara, 2017: 125). It is evident from research reusing qualitative data that 'data from the past can still yield rich, relevant research outcomes' (Bishop and Kuula-Luumi, 2017: 13).

Researchers also began to draw on creative methods in research, which had two implications for qualitative data analysis. First, the analysis of creatively gathered materials, such as the journal plus video footage gathered by Kluge et al. shown in Box 9.8 above. Second, the application of creative methods to analytic work. Here we will focus on the second category which includes arts-based, multi-modal, embodied and digital approaches.

Arts-based analysis often focuses on the written arts, such as stories, poetry, play and screenplay writing, and may also include visual arts techniques such as photography and diagramming. Arts-based analytic techniques range from the comparatively simple to the extremely complex. Box 9.9 shows a reasonably simple approach known as 'I-poems'. It is also possible to construct we-poems, if you are doing pair or couple interviews or working with focus group data, or they-poems if relevant. A more recent innovation has been pronoun poems, using I, we, they, she, you and it (Chadwick, 2017: 65).

Converting prose to poetry, whatever the method, can help researchers to develop new knowledge about their data (Furman et al., 2007: 304; Patrick, 2016: 385). Another technique is the creation of 'found poems' from existing words and/or phrases in the data (Prendergast, 2015: 683). These may be sequential, where the order in which the words and/or phrases appear in the original data is maintained in the poem, or not sequential, in which case the researcher can decide on the order in which the words

---

Box 9.9

Poetic analysis in practice

The I-poem offers a way to assess how participants represent themselves in inter-views, by attending to the first-person statements in the interview transcripts. This method was developed by Carol Gilligan and her colleagues in the United States in the 1990s, and used more recently by Rosalind Edwards and Susie Weller in the United Kingdom in their longitudinal research investigating change and continuity in young people's sense of self over time. To create an I-poem, the researcher needs to read a transcript carefully to find out how the participant spoke about their self, paying particular attention to any statements including the personal pronoun 'I'. The researcher can highlight every 'I' plus any relevant accompanying text that might help them to understand the participant's sense of self. These highlighted segments are then copied from the transcript and pasted or written into a new document, in the same sequence, each one on a new line to create a kind of poem. I-poems help to identify a participant's sense of self by foregrounding the voice, or voices, that they use to speak about their self. This technique is adaptable for use with participants of different genders, ages, abilities, backgrounds and so on (Edwards and Weller, 2012: 206). However, it can be quite time-consuming, so is best used with a small sample or sub-sample (Edwards and Weller, 2012: 215).

---

and/or phrases appear in the poem. Another option is 'poetic transcription' (Ellingson, 2009: 63–5), in which a researcher will use participants' own words, in poetic form, to represent the participants' views and experiences. This can be done with interview or focus group transcripts, and can yield different insights for researchers from other types of analytic work (Faulkner, 2019: 215). Or researchers can simply write poems, using a poetic form or free verse, inspired by all or part(s) of their data.

Multi-modal arts-based analysis can be much more complex. Box 9.10 shows a very complex approach. This analytic approach is very unusual in its team-based working and its complexity and thoroughness. I present it to you here, not as something to try to emulate (though if you want to, be my guest!), but as an outlier which is useful to understand.

Multi-modal analysis can take many forms, as we have already seen in Boxes 9.2, 9.3, 9.7 and 9.10 above. It usually leads to richer findings than one type of analysis so, for some researchers, multi-modal analysis is a good way to reflect the complexity of human experience (Kara, 2020: 141). However, it is of course more resource-intensive than using a single method, so should only be used when appropriate and when resources permit.

Box 9.11 shows an interesting example of multi-modal analysis of video data using qualitative and quantitative techniques within qualitative research.

Box 9.10

Multi-modal arts-based analysis in practice

Jennifer Lapum worked with a transdisciplinary team in Canada to investigate patients' experiences of open-heart surgery. Data were gathered through two post-surgery interviews, one while the patient was in hospital and another 4–6 weeks later when they were recovering at home, and in between the interviews, the participants kept a journal of their experiences (Lapum et al., 2012: 102). The transdisciplinary team included a heart surgeon, a poet, researchers, healthcare staff and former open-heart surgery patients, among others. The team analysed the data, using a complex iterative method, over an entire year. They began by using reflective discussions to imagine how patients could have felt, physically and emotionally, during their experiences. The data presented participants' stories in chronological order, so the team used this as an organising framework. The framework had five phases: pre-operative, post-operative, discharge from hospital and early and later recovery at home. Within this framework, the team documented and categorised keywords, phrases and ideas, which were then used to form poems in free verse. Then they developed concepts for photographic images to highlight the main narrative idea of each poem. Corresponding photographs were taken which, with the poems, formed a new set of data. The team then held more reflective discussions, based around this new dataset, to imagine the patients' experiences more fully. Then the images were further developed and the poems revised to 'further illuminate the complexities, ambiguities, defining features, tensions, and sensory details' of participants' stories (Lapum et al., 2012: 104). The team did this through 'a process of iterative dialogue, systematic inquiry, visualization, concept mapping, and metaphorical interpretation' (Lapum et al., 2012: 104). The researchers discussed, wrote and drew their findings as visual and diagrammatic metaphors.

Integrating findings is often a key aim for multi-modal researchers, but it is not the only option. Sabela Petros interviewed older South African people caring for children and grandchildren affected by HIV/AIDS about their experiences. He also interviewed senior managers from the government and NGOs about policy and legislation around HIV/AIDS. He analysed both datasets separately before comparing them to assess the level of corroborated and divergent findings. This helped to contextualise carers' experiences, describe differences between carers' and officials' views of the situation, identify gaps in public policy and suggest ways these could be remedied (Petros, 2012: 290–1).

Petros shows us one alternative to the integration of findings. Another is to use the concept of diffraction instead of aiming for integration. As we saw in Chapter 3, the concept of diffraction was brought into social research by the American physicist and

Box 9.11

Multi-modal analysis of video data

Jessica DeCuir-Gunby and her colleagues in the United States were making a lon-gitudinal study of mathematics teachers' professional development. They filmed mathematics lessons given by three cohorts of teachers, then coded the data using a three-step process:

1. Lesson mapping: describing each lesson's organisation and structure, with categories based on teachers' interactions in the classroom, for context and to identify changes over time. Categories included 'whole-class sharing' and 'small-group instruction'.
2. Lesson rubric coding: quantitative examination of teacher-initiated verbal communication in specific categories, based on a rubric created by the researchers, to capture the frequency of use of each category by each teacher. Categories included 'extensions of tasks' and 'relevance making'.
3. Transcription of verbal communication from the lesson rubric-coded data, to capture what was said within each category.

ANOVAs and Bonferroni tests were used to analyse the quantitative data from this coding system and identify any significant differences between the three cohorts of teachers.

As well as the videotaped lessons, the researchers also kept field notes of what happened in the classrooms before, during and after each lesson, and videotaped group interviews with teachers. All of these qualitative data were analysed using a five-step method for each individual lesson:

1. Use lesson mapping categories to provide structure and framework for the lesson.
2. Pair lesson rubric codings within events highlighted by lesson mapping.
3. Place comments from field notes within lesson mapping categories.
4. Match events of lesson with the teacher's statements from group interview.
5. Integrate findings from first four data sources to create individual cases.

The quantitative analysis enabled DeCuir-Gunby and her colleagues to offer an overall view of what happened in the cohorts' classrooms, while the qualitative analysis enabled them to scrutinise each individual teacher and lesson (DeCuir-Gunby et al., 2012: 212). This mixing of methods also enabled the researchers to identify and describe several aspects of complexity within the data, such as instances of some teachers' data corroborating, complementing or contradicting other data (DeCuir-Gunby et al., 2012: 207).

social theorist Karen Barad, and is useful in helping to conceptualise complex situations. Multi-modal research is also useful for complex projects, and this complexity itself can make integration difficult (Uprichard and Dawney, 2019: 20). Emma Uprichard and Leila Dawney propose that diffraction can provide a useful alternative when integration is difficult or impossible. Jessica Gullion suggests that in analytic work, diffraction requires researchers to 'think with and through' their data, consider 'patterns and difference' and explore 'dynamic unfoldings' to gain 'insight into processes of change' (Gullion, 2018: 125–6).

Archaeologists Rachel Crellin and Oliver Harris argue for the use of diffraction in helping to analyse ancient DNA (aDNA). They value conventional analytic approaches to large-scale aDNA projects, such as isotope analysis, sequencing and radiocarbon dating. However, they 'identify three critical issues' which may be, or become, barriers to aDNA fulfilling its empirical and conceptual potential in archaeology (Crellin and Harris, 2020: 39). The first is nature and culture being viewed as a binary. The second is an essentialist understanding of identity as singular and fixed. The third is the desire of researchers to create tidy narratives through which to present their work. Crellin and Harris suggest that diffraction could be useful in helping archaeologists embrace the contradictions, overlaps, tensions and complexity of identity and history (ibid: 47), and so create fuller, more insightful analytic work.

As with data gathering (Chapter 7), there is an argument that all data analysis is embodied (Ellingson, 2017: 150) because we can't do anything without our bodies. Others argue that an embodied approach is an option in data analysis (Jewitt et al., 2017: 38). These concepts are quite new and there is as yet no established way of conducting *embodied data analysis*. Much of the focus is on the processes involved in qualitative analytic work, such as transcription (Chadwick, 2017: 60; O'Dell and Willim, 2013) and coding and categorising (Ellingson, 2017: 150; Thanem and Knights, 2019: 116). There is some encouragement for researchers to listen and look for, reimagine and rethink the bodies that appear in our data (Chadwick, 2017: 58; Jewitt et al., 2017: 51; see also Box 9.10 above). And the researcher's own body may figure as an analytic element (Jewitt et al., 2017: 51; Thanem and Knights, 2019: 113). These approaches to analysis are comparatively new and there is not yet much literature describing how they are used in practice (Chadwick, 2017:54). Box 9.12 offers an example.

We have already seen some examples of the use of *technology in data analysis* in this chapter, such as in Box 9.5 where Mackieson et al. used electronic searching to identify quotes, and in Box 9.7 where Luangaram and Wongwachara used digital analysis to manage a large dataset. This demonstrates that there are micro and macro uses of technology in analysing qualitative data. No doubt other researchers whose work is featured in this chapter used qualitative data analysis software, as described in Chapter 8, and/or other technological aids such as spreadsheets, not to mention the ubiquitous email and online meetings.

Box 9.12

Embodied data analysis in practice

Rachelle Chadwick interviewed middle-class and low-income women in South Africa about their experiences of childbirth. In analysing her interview data, Chadwick found the theoretical work of Julia Kristeva very useful as a framework for thinking and writing about the embodied voices of her participants. Kristeva is a transdisciplinary theorist, combining psychoanalytic and linguistic concepts in 'an attempt to think [about] subjectivity, bodies, language and ideology' simultaneously (Chadwick, 2017: 59). Kristeva argues that it is not possible to separate language from its speaker whose living energy gives meaning to the language they use. Further, she insists that bodily energies and rhythms are an inseparable part of making meaning, and so Kristeva fuses the speaking body and language firmly together. This provided a strong theoretical framework to help Chadwick take an embodied approach to her interview data, but she still needed an analytic method (Chadwick, 2017: 60). She devised a method of transcription that aimed to reproduce the 'embodied, performative and breathy qualities of speech' and its 'messy and lively qualities', to focus not only on the content of the data, but also on the ways in which participants told their stories (Chadwick, 2017: 61). This meant her transcripts were 'open and sensory texts rather than closed, realist and empirical reflections' of the participants' experiences (Chadwick, 2017: 64). Then she drew on the listening guide developed by Carol Gilligan and her colleagues to help her take an embodied approach to analysis. The listening guide involves three consecutive 'listenings' (listening for the plot, listening for the 'I' through I-poems and listening for different voices) and this 'tunes our ear to the multiplicity of voices that speak within and around us' (Gilligan and Eddy, 2017: 76). Chadwick found that this enabled her to attend to the contradictions and 'moments of narrative excess' (Chadwick, 2017: 65) in her data, which are often glossed over in qualitative analysis. Her development of the I-poems into pronoun poems provided 'a different way of listening for the fleshy voices present in narratives' (Chadwick, 2017: 70).

Technology offers very useful tools to researchers, though the amount of choice can feel daunting, and the frequent necessity for learning new skills and techniques can feel wearing, and the technology failing to work as it should can feel frustrating. But overall, the opportunities technology offers to researchers definitely outweigh the challenges.

Ethics in qualitative data analysis – part 2

Analysing data can be one of the most complex parts of qualitative research. You need to work systematically, carefully and thoroughly, while balancing competing priorities such as the voices of your participants, the agendas of other stakeholders, the demands of your superiors and your own feelings and needs. There are many ethical and other decisions to be made, and the whole process can be quite exhausting.

This is a point in research at which reflexivity can be particularly useful. Reflexivity is 'the examination of both the structural and personal conditions which help us understand the knowledge we create' (Dean, 2017: 10–11). This requires us to pay attention to the influences on our work, such as our personalities, identities, experiences and institutions, as we analyse our data (Doucet and Mauthner, 2012: 130; Hammersley and Traianou, 2012: 33–4). Chapter 8 offered some guidance on how to practice reflexivity. At the analytic stage, involving other people can also help; either through collaborative analysis as set out above or, if that is not possible, through a 'debrief', i.e. a meeting with someone who can help you to think reflexively about your analytic work (Kara, 2018: 118).

Research ethics committees and institutional review boards are often more concerned about the safe storage of data than about ethical analytic practices. Yet interpreting data is at the core of our work as qualitative researchers, and it is an area where we have a great deal of power (Kara, 2018: 114). As a quantitative researcher, I expect you are keenly aware of how statistics can be, have been and are misused, and how this misrepresents data. The variety of qualitative research makes it difficult to identify equivalent examples. However, when you are carrying out qualitative analytic work, it is ethically essential to stay true to your data and participants, and to other stakeholders such as collaborators and funders. This is easy to say, but in practice, it can be a tricky balancing act.

Conclusion

We saw in Chapter 7 that you can devise your own method of gathering qualitative data. Similarly, you can devise your own method of analysing qualitative data. Curie Scott did this in her doctoral research when she used participatory drawing to study perceptions of ageing among older adults. She had multi-modal data including drawings, audio and video recordings, field notes and photographs, and devised a seven-stage method of analysis. The first three stages involved different types of transcription, in the fourth she analysed aspects of drawing, in the fifth she developed categories of description and the sixth and seventh involved provisional and final ordering of those categories (Scott, 2018: 169).

This may all seem rather overwhelming if you're used to a much smaller set of options, such as between parametric or non-parametric statistics, with many choices being made for you, perhaps because of sampling technique or size. The essence of good practice in qualitative analysis is to use theory and reflexivity as guides and analyse your data carefully, thoroughly and systematically.

Reflective questions

1. Which methods of analysing qualitative data appeal to you, and why?
2. How do you think you could most usefully use theory in your own research?
3. How can you ensure that your analytic work is high quality and ethical?
4. Is arts-based analysis *real* analysis? Why?
5. Could you involve participants in your research? Why? If you could, how would you do this, and what might you gain?

10

REPORTING ON QUALITATIVE RESEARCH

Chapter summary

- Introduces the concept of reporting research and the importance of stories
- Outlines the similarities and differences between reporting on quantitative, qualitative and multi-modal research
- Discusses good practice in research reporting
- Explores the role of fictionalisation
- Covers the potential for research reporting of poetry, play scripts and screenplays, video, animation, zines, comics, podcasts and blogs
- Distinguishes multi-modal reporting from multi-modal research
- Reviews some key ethical issues in reporting on qualitative research

Introduction

Reporting on research used to be referred to as 'writing up'. Writing certainly plays a crucial part in all Euro-Western research reporting, but it is no longer the whole story. Now qualitative – and quantitative – research is also reported through video, performance, animation, comics, podcasts and so on. And written reporting is no longer confined to the standard outputs of reports, journal articles, chapters and books, but may also encompass blog posts, poetry, social media updates, zines, self-published e-books, play scripts and other written media.

This is not to say that every researcher must be fluent in all of these methods of reporting. But it is important for us, as researchers, to be aware of the options, and to understand when and how we might use them, alongside the methods we are all familiar with, such as dissertation, thesis, research report or journal article.

Some good examples of this kind of reporting are produced by the Wellcome Centre for Integrative Parasitology at the University of Glasgow. This Centre was established in 1987 and was the first UK-based collective funded by Wellcome, a grant funder that focuses on science and health. The Centre reports its research through a blog, podcasts, videos and comics, all of which are freely available online. (The URLs for the Centre and for its research reporting webpages are in Appendix 1.) In doing this, they are making use of the evidence showing that stories are a good way to communicate ideas and experience economically, directly and vividly; to share knowledge and to make sense of complex situations (Gabriel and Connell, 2010: 507–8).

In fact, stories are hardwired into our individual and collective existence. Neuroscientists have shown that our brains are compulsive story-making machines (Storr, 2020: 115, drawing on the work of David Eagleman, 2011). Evolutionary psychologists have demonstrated that stories were and are essential to the survival of humanity (Storr, 2020: 138, drawing on the work of Robin Dunbar and his colleagues from the 1990s and 2000s). We all tell and learn from stories every day so, whether you are writing a conventional report or a comic, a video script or a blog post, it makes sense to use stories as the basis for reporting research.

Reporting on qualitative and multi-modal research

The main similarity between reporting quantitative research findings, and reporting qualitative or multi-modal research findings, is that writing and stories are key to good research reporting. As you will know, quantitative researchers cannot simply present their audiences with pages of equations and figures; they need to present their findings in tabular or graphical form, and write an accompanying narrative explaining what this trend means and why that outlier is important. Writing this narrative, like all writing, is a creative process. I also argue that writing is a research method, so ubiquitous that we don't notice or name it as such – but I cannot imagine a Euro-Western research project that would make no use of writing. Indigenous research, by and for communities with an oral tradition, may not need to use writing. But in the Euro-Western paradigm, we write our research designs, funding and ethics applications, literature reviews or other context-setting documents, analyses, reports and endless emails.

The main difference between reporting quantitative research and reporting qualitative or multi-modal research is that with the latter there is often more to report. This is particularly so with multi-modal research because more methods, more to report on. It also holds true with qualitative research because qualitative data and its analysis are generally more complex than in quantitative research, so more words are needed to communicate it adequately. Some people argue that it is difficult to communicate qualitative and multi-modal research effectively because it is so 'messy' (Bloomberg and Volpe, 2012: xix). Yet there are many examples of good communication of qualitative and multi-modal research.

It is really at the reporting stage of research that the distinctions between quantitative, qualitative and multi-modal research break down, because all forms of reporting can be used for every type of research. It is perhaps arguable that quantitative researchers are more likely to use conventional reporting methods, and that qualitative researchers are more likely to be open to using, say, arts-based methods of reporting. But really there is no type of reporting that is more or less applicable to quantitative than to qualitative research. The key consideration here is which methods of reporting will work best for the readers or viewers.

Good practice in research reporting

Good practice in reporting research is no different for qualitative or multi-modal than for quantitative research. Even so, it is worth briefly reviewing the main principles of good practice (Phillips and Kara, 2021: 106–7).

- Consider your audience. Who are they? What do they need to help them understand the story you have to tell? You may need to use some imagination if you don't have full information, but this imaginative work is worth doing, because it will help you decide on the best method or methods of reporting.
- Craft your story for that audience in the plainest, simplest language possible. Use short words and sentences. Only use specialist terminology if essential (or if you know your audience are all specialists), and then give plain language definitions. This helps everyone, and it particularly helps any members of your audience whose first language is not the language in which you are writing.
- Structure your story carefully; make sure it has a good narrative arc with a clear beginning, middle and end.
- Describe your own positionality or standpoint so that others can judge your work more accurately.
- When you have a draft, ask for feedback from others. This should tell you what you are doing well, what needs improving and how those improvements could be made.
- Use the feedback to improve your work.
- Edit carefully to ensure your report is free from mistakes.

- Avoid cliches, and repetition: reiterate points only when your audience will need reminding to help them understand.
- Do not plagiarise other people's work.
- Represent your data, analysis, participants and findings as faithfully as possible.

O'Brien et al. (2014) have produced a useful set of standards for reporting qualitative research which are based on an iterative and rigorous research process. The standards consist of 21 points, each with definitions, explanations and examples. These are too long to reproduce here, but are clearly written and useful in supporting high-quality and transparent research reporting. They are available online and the URL is in Appendix 1.

Fictionalisation

Fiction and non-fiction are often thought of as entirely separate types of writing. Yet non-fiction writers use many of the same skills as fiction writers (Stein, 1998: 7). Sensory language, metaphor, repetition for effect, conflict, delay, tension – these are just some of the techniques used regularly by fiction writers which can also make non-fiction prose more engaging for its readers. Of course, they will be used differently in reporting research: you are unlikely to be reporting conflict between characters (though, of course, that can happen), but there is often scope for setting up conflict between two intellectual positions, or between two apparently opposing findings, and then not resolving that conflict immediately, using delay to cause tension which makes your writing more compelling for the reader. Another way to do this is to pose a question and then not answer it immediately; either say you will come back to it later, or simply leave it hanging for the time being.

There can also be ethical reasons for fictionalising, such as to protect the anonymity of participants (Piper and Sikes, 2010: 572). This can be particularly useful if you have gathered data online, perhaps from social media. With this type of data, anonymising your participants does not protect them if you use direct quotes, because if one of those is put into a search engine, it can lead straight back to its originator. So instead you could create a fictionalised, composite quote by 'selecting representative elements from the dataset and composing a new original that is not traceable back to the originals' (Markham, 2012: 5).

Fictionalisation raises questions about truth. In English, we sometimes say, 'What's the real story?' This neatly encapsulates the distinction between 'literal' truth – the real – and 'authentic' truth – the story (Pickering and Kara, 2017: 299). There is truth in stories. Think about a film or a television drama you have enjoyed; that enjoyment would be based partly on how true the story felt to you. And here I am talking about authentic rather than literal truth: it could have been a science fiction film, or a historical drama, but if you can relate to the characters and understand their actions, then that story 'rings true'.

Fictionalisation is often used in reporting qualitative or multi-modal research through the creation of a composite narrative, such as a fictionalised case study where elements are drawn from data provided by several individuals (Saldaña and Omasta, 2018: 194). This helps to protect participants' anonymity and preserve their confidentiality. However, using this approach can make it difficult for researchers to show that their accounts are faithful to their data (Willis, 2019: 474). Box 10.1 offers a route to overcoming this problem.

Box 10.1

Composite narratives

Rebecca Willis interviewed 14 current and former Members of the UK Parliament in 2016, to find out how they understood their political roles and how they approached the issue of climate change. She promised them anonymity and decided to create composite narratives to help her keep that promise. Peer reviewers supported this approach but asked for more clarity about how the narratives were derived from the data. In response, she developed a four-stage process for composing narratives:

1. For each composite narrative, she grouped 3–5 interview transcripts together based on some similarities, such as all interviewees being new in role or all being experienced senior politicians.
2. She took all quotations directly from the interview transcripts.
3. She took other details, such as interview location and conversation structure, directly from one of the source interviews in the group.
4. She took any judgements, motivations or feelings directly from the interview transcripts (Willis, 2019: 474–5).

This method enabled Willis to maintain her participants' anonymity while producing complex, situated accounts that conveyed the richness and nuances of politicians' experiences. These accounts were also readable and understandable, and so could be used within and beyond academia. Both scientists and practitioners found Willis' work to be insightful, and helpful in practice (Willis, 2019: 477).

Where anonymity is not required, it can be helpful to include case studies within research reports. Case studies can be useful for illustrative purposes or to highlight alternative perspectives. They can be produced in writing or as an audio or video recording. These kinds of case studies are different from the case study research covered in Chapter 6. They have been called 'popular case studies' (Yin, 2018: 19) because they are often used by journalists, bloggers and other media producers.

Poetry

Poetry can be very accessible, though as an art form, poetry can also be complex, even intimidating to some people. Even so, poetry can be really useful in reporting research. Poems, or text presented poetically, can have a different impact on audiences than the same information presented as prose (Kara, 2017: 174; Patrick, 2016: 385). And poetry has the potential to reach beyond academic and professional audiences (Eshun and Madge, 2016). There is an example of this in Box 10.2.

Box 10.2

Research poetry

Penelope Carroll and her colleagues in Aotearoa/New Zealand studied the experiences of people living in marginal housing, such as sheds, garages, tents and caravans, in urban and rural areas. They conducted 40 in-depth interviews and a policy-focused thematic analysis. Then they reviewed the interview recordings and transcripts to reveal stories and contexts which had been obscured by the policy focus. They wrote down phrases and sentences which illustrated unique life events or participants' perspectives, and also noted descriptions from field notes. Then they created 34 'prose poems' (one per 'household') by forming these into stanzas while keeping faith with the central themes in, and the flow and meaning of, the participants' narratives (Carroll et al., 2011: 628). The researchers aimed for clear and understandable poems rather than poems of literary merit. The poems, and the process of creating them, helped the researchers to reach a greater understanding of the complexities of living in marginal housing in Aotearoa/New Zealand. The researchers shared the poems with participants who described them as accurate and meaningful. The poems were used in reporting the research findings to academic, practitioner, policy and general audiences.

Play scripts and screenplays

Plays are conventionally written for theatrical productions, or for radio, television or other media. Theatre imposes the most constraints: all the action has to happen in one place, or two or three consecutively. Usually there are only a small number of actors, and it is difficult to perform crowd scenes, or actions such as travelling, with any credibility. Radio and other audio formats present different constraints, as not only the action but also the context must be conveyed through sound alone, and a character who is silent for too long may be forgotten by the audience. Television is more like film and there are fewer constraints apart from the budget.

Screenplays, which produce the scripts for films, have the fewest constraints, partly thanks to computer-generated imagery. In a film, you can move from one planet to another, live under the sea or include an army of bus drivers mounted on unicorns. Research reported in play or screenplay formats may or may not be intended for performance; the scripts may simply be intended for reading.

Verbatim plays use the words of research participants or others. These were first used as a kind of documentary theatre (Paget, 1987: 18) and more recently for reporting research, such as Michael Richardson's research into the intergenerational issues of Irish men (Richardson, 2015). Another method used for reporting research is called 'recorded delivery'. In its simplest form, this involves transmitting the speech of research participants into headphones worn by actors who mimic the original speakers to reproduce their speech as accurately as possible. Material from recorded interviews is selected, edited and arranged to produce a dramatic composition (Shah and Greer, 2018: 61).

Verbatim plays and recorded delivery are intended for performance. Box 10.3 gives an example of reporting research using a play script which was not intended for performance.

Box 10.3

Research play script

Katrina Rodriguez and Maria Lahman studied the ways in which messages from family and peers influence Latina US college students' understanding of the intersections of their ethnicity, class and gender, and of the value of education. They conducted 15 individual interviews, three with each of five female student participants, and held a two-hour culturally responsive focus group in the form of a traditional Mexican dinner in the home of one of the researchers. They reported their findings in the form of a full-length three-act play script entitled *Las Comadres: Cuentame su Historia* (which means 'Girlfriends: Tell Me Your Story'). The researchers originally planned to construct the play script entirely from quotes from the interview and focus group transcripts, but these sounded 'flat and sanitised' (Rodriguez and Lahman, 2011: 611). So the researchers combined the quotes with fictional dialogue they created themselves. Although the play was not intended for performance, the researchers worked hard to ensure that the script would work if it was ever performed, while maintaining the integrity of participants' experiences and messages. They enlisted the help of colleagues in reading the script aloud during the writing process, which helped to increase the authenticity of the characters' dialogue and interaction.

Video

Video is accessible for audiences, and much easier for researchers to produce than it used to be, though editing does require a little technical know-how. But that is easy to acquire; there is plenty of information and advice online. And publishing video is very straightforward on sites such as YouTube and Vimeo.

Video reports of research findings can be created in a range of ways. The simplest option is probably a one-take 'talking head' video shot on a smartphone. The outputs of some types of qualitative research, such as digital storytelling (covered in Chapter 6), can serve as video reports of research findings. And there is also scope for much more sophisticated video reporting, which is particularly useful for qualitative research into complex real-world phenomena. An example is shown in Box 10.4.

Box 10.4

Video report of research

Ethnomusicology is a sub-genre of ethnography which focuses on the study of music in its social and cultural contexts. Ethnomusicologists David Irving and Jenny McCallum studied the Cocos Malay people of the Cocos (Keeling) Islands, one of the most isolated archipelagos in the world, to examine 'the role of music and dance in maintaining cultural identity in the face of changing political context' (Irving and McCallum, 2020: 3). These islands were colonised in 1826 by a Scottish trader who brought with him dozens of enslaved Malay-speaking people from Malaysia and southern Africa, though he lost control to a Scottish rival by 1834. The islands were annexed by the British Empire in 1857, and transferred to Australia in 1955, though all that time they were still controlled by one family of Scottish origin. The Australian government bought the islands from the family in 1978, and in 1984 the islanders voted to become part of Australia. There is very little tourism. Because of their history and isolation, the music of the islands is unique, merging Scottish and Islamic music and dancing. Irving and McCallum video-recorded public performances of music and dance in the mid-2010s, and also researched archival footage and conducted ethnographic interviews in Malay and English. Then they produced 'a documentary film that records a range of living traditions and practices' of Cocos Malay culture, to 'investigate the ways in which music and dance reflect the processes of cultural and political traditions in a small postcolonial community' (Irving and McCallum, 2020: 3). The documentary is called *The World of Cocos Malay Music and Dance* and can be viewed online; the URL is in Appendix 1.

Animation

Animation is very accessible and can reach a wide audience. There are many different kinds of animation such as stop motion, hand-drawn and digital animation. It is not difficult to create, but it is time-consuming, so if you want to use animation for reporting, you need to be able to invest either a lot of time or a lot of money. For this reason, animated research reports are usually short, which means they can only make a few points and may not include much detail or nuance (Phillips and Kara, 2021: 139). Yet animations are often engaging and memorable and for some, this is a worthwhile trade-off. Box 10.5 shows an example of an animated research report.

Box 10.5

Animated report of research

Stacy Bias is a fat and queer activist, artist and animator. She studied fat people's experiences of travelling by plane for her undergraduate dissertation, with 795 survey respondents and 28 interviews which she recorded on video. She wanted to report her research in a way that included 'the wise and creative voices' of her participants (Bias, 2021: 146) but the recordings she had weren't great quality, and some of her participants were nervous about sharing their experiences in public. She chose, instead, to create an animation, incorporating the voices of consenting participants. When she published her animated research report *Flying While Fat* online, it was picked up by the mainstream press and went viral, reaching over two million viewers worldwide in under three weeks (Bias, 2021: 150). (The URL for *Flying While Fat* is in Appendix 1.)

Of course, not all animations will have such a wide reach, and not all animated reports of research are made publicly available. *Animated Thinking: I Feel Different* is an animation reporting on research into the identities and experiences of autistic girls. This was published on the BBC iPlayer for a year from November 2020, and so at the time of writing, it was only accessible to people with a UK TV licence, or to those who were able to attend webinars arranged by the researchers.

Zines

'Zine' is short for 'magazine' and refers to a self-published pamphlet or booklet, usually with text and illustrations. There are genres of zine such as the 'fanzine', produced by fans of public figures or groups, such as musicians or sports teams and given by hand to other fans at concerts or matches, and the 'perzine' which is personal and autobiographical (Bold, 2017: 224). Zines were originally handmade in small quantities, though zine publishing has expanded enormously in the last couple of decades (Barton and Olson, 2019: 205).

Zines are available on almost every subject and are studied in a range of academic fields across the social sciences, arts and humanities (Stockburger, 2015: 223). They can be sole authored, co-authored or produced as an edited collection. Zines are sold in bookshops, archived in bricks-and-mortar or digital libraries or distributed online to be read on screen or downloaded and printed.

There are no rules for zine production: a zine can be long or short, any size or colour, rough and scrappy or polished to perfection. Perhaps because zines were historically an outlet for topics not covered by the mainstream media, and for writers who were unable to write for the mainstream media (Bold, 2017: 215), they are often used in research done by or with marginalised groups. They also seem to have considerable appeal for activist researchers. However, these are far from the only contexts in which zines are used, as we can see in Box 10.6.

Box 10.6

Research zines

Project Orange is a research-led architecture and interior design studio in London, England. Project Orange identified a problem with the split between academia, which sees the reality of building as quite mundane, and architectural practices, which see academia as indulgent and providing graduates with inadequate preparation for real-world work. Also, mandatory continuing professional development for chartered architects in the United Kingdom focuses on technical know-how and ignores the importance and value of design and the wider societal impact of architecture (Soane, 2019: 50). Project Orange asked each studio member to identify an area in which they were personally interested, and then to research and report on this with reference to projects they had worked on. A senior lecturer in architecture at a local university was brought in to offer guidance, encouragement and an academic perspective. The lecturer edited the reports into a zine called PO Box 1. This was shortlisted for the Royal Institute of British Architects' President's Award for Research in 2011 (Soane, 2019: 51). Over the intervening years, this process was repeated three times, with a different focus and a different academic editor each time. This generation of research from practice has been disseminated through several conferences and has influenced academic teaching (Soane, 2019: 53). All four zines are available for download from the Project Orange website; the URL is in Appendix 1.

Comics

Like zines, comics are useful for communicating complexity, including contextual information, in very accessible ways (Rainford, 2019: 255). There is evidence that the use of pictures to support text aids retention of information (Aleixo and Sumner, 2017: 79; Caldwell, 2012: 6; Duncan et al., 2016: 44). There is also evidence that reading comics uses both brain hemispheres at once which enables both visual and verbal learning (Aleixo and Sumner, 2017: 80; Blanch and Mulvihill, 2013: 39). Evidence from a professional setting shows that providing information to adults in comic form assists comprehension (Botes, 2017: 1). All of this means that comics, like zines, are an excellent way to report research, not least because they make findings accessible to participants and the wider public (Sou and Hall, 2021: 99). An example of this is shown in Box 10.7.

Box 10.7

A research comic

Gemma Sou and her colleague Felix Aponte-Gonzalez spent a year doing ethnographic research in Puerto Rico after Hurricane Maria, following 16 low-income families to find out how they recovered from the disaster. Gemma Sou fictionalised the research findings, creating a composite family and telling their story in a 20-page comic which was drawn by John Cei Douglas. This enabled Sou to portray her participants ethically by offering nuanced representations of their personalities, experiences and context, thus providing a useful counterpoint to the homogenised and dehumanising portrayal of suffering in the mainstream media. The narrative, dialogue and experiences of the composite family were entirely based on the research data (Sou and Hall, 2021: 101). The comic, *After Maria*, was made freely available online in English and Spanish; the URL is in Appendix 1. Also, over 1,500 hard copies were sent to educators and academics worldwide, and it has been used as a teaching resource in over 20 countries (Sou and Hall, 2021: 102).

Podcasts

Podcasts are gaining in popularity, perhaps partly because of the increase in mobile devices that offer more opportunities for people to listen to podcasts in different situations. They are particularly useful if you want to reach audiences who have difficulty with reading, or cannot easily read in the language you are using or are visually impaired. Podcasts are not difficult to produce and share online. As with zines, the format is very flexible: a podcast can be as long or as short as you like, and can involve one person speaking, or two or more in conversation or an interview format (Salmons and Kara, 2020: 205).

As we saw earlier in the chapter, the Wellcome Centre for Integrative Parasitology in Glasgow, United Kingdom, uses podcasts, among other media, to report its research findings. The URL for the webpage where these podcasts are hosted is in Appendix 1.

Blogs

Blog posts offer an increasingly popular way for researchers of all kinds to report their findings (Kara, 2020: 178). They can be useful for reaching many types of audience, including research participants (Salmons, 2016: 171). Setting up your own blog is only advisable if you are sure you can produce regular good-quality content and reach a wide audience. There are many high-profile research blogs which already have a big following and are happy to publish well-written guest posts.

Radiology researchers Jenny Hoang and her colleagues compared the numbers of people who viewed online versions of research articles in academic journals and a blog. The journals were two peer-reviewed radiology journals, *the American Journal of Neuroradiology* and *the American Journal of Roentgenology*, and the blog was *Radiopaedia.org*, a radiology blog promoted via social media. They found that the blog had six times as many page views as both journals put together (Hoang et al., 2015: 760).

Multi-modal reporting

Reporting itself can be multi-modal, using different methods of communication within a single output. This applies to quantitative research as well as qualitative and multi-modal research. Piper Harron is a mathematician whose doctoral thesis contains jokes, puns, analogies, metaphors and comic strips. Some sections are written three ways: for lay people, for her peers and for her professors (Harron, 2016). Box 10.8 shows an example of multi-modal reporting of qualitative research.

Box 10.8

Multi-modal reporting

Helen Owton investigated the relationship between sport and asthma, which are both embodied phenomena. In one of her research reports, an academic journal article, she used narrative 'found poetry', created from interview transcripts, and a hand-drawn illustration, alongside conventional academic prose. Her aim was to align and unite these three methods on the page, to offer new ways of knowing and seeing (Owton, 2013: 600). This served to represent her participants' experiences more fully than she could have done using conventional prose alone, and to engage her readers' emotions as well as their intellects and so enrich their experiences of the story she was telling.

Multi-modal research may be reported multi-modally – or using a single method, if that is more appropriate. Equally, qualitative research can be reported using a single method or multiple methods.

The ethical aspects of research reporting

Reporting research is an ethical act in itself, particularly if the research has been funded through public money or charitable donations. There is a publication bias in research because research that is 'successful' is more likely to be published. (There are debates about what constitutes 'failure' in research that are beyond the scope of this book.) This publication bias is driven by a combination of imperatives from funders, publishers and academia, and is fundamentally unethical. Of course, there may at times be good reasons for withholding research findings from publication, or placing an embargo on their publication until a future time. Indeed, premature publishing has led to unethical outcomes, as with the Belfast Project. This was an oral history archive set up in the United States to capture and store personal accounts of the late 20th-century Northern Ireland conflict. Contributors were given guarantees that their contributions, and the archive itself, would be kept secret until after their deaths. However, nine years after the archive was set up, its director reported findings from two accounts in a book which was accompanied by a TV documentary. The two contributors concerned had died, but other contributors were still alive, and this publication brought the archive to the attention of the media and the criminal justice system. Legal activity ensued which eventually forced the archive to release some accounts to the UK police (Inckle, 2015), and as a result several people were arrested and questioned, and some were charged. This unusual case raises a whole bunch of ethical questions but the key point here is that reporting qualitative research findings is not a trivial affair; it can change people's lives.

Research ethics committees still, often, take the paternalistic approach of insisting that participants are anonymised, rather than recognising that participants may be better able to weigh the risks and benefits of anonymity or disclosure for themselves (Gerver, 2013: 135). There is movement on this in some guidance, such as Canada's national *Tri-Council Policy Statement: Ethical Conduct for Research Involving Humans*. This statement allows that there may be times when 'individual attribution, with consent, is appropriate' and acknowledges that 'Privacy protections in research are evolving' (TCPS2, 2018: 127). For many Indigenous researchers, it is an ethical imperative to name any participant who wishes to be named (Wilson, 2008: 10).

Writing may be largely a solitary pursuit, yet it is always a relational activity (Tierney and Hallett, 2010: 683). When you are writing, you are creating your relationship with your audiences. It is not only good practice but also ethical, to understand who your audiences are and aim for your reporting to meet their needs. Similarly, when you are reading or viewing material, you are creating a relationship with the writer. To cite others' work ethically, you need to understand it fully and represent it accurately (Löfström, 2011: 263).

Quantitative research is commonly reported using a single authorial voice. Qualitative and, in particular, multi-modal researchers often prefer to include multiple voices. Some Euro-Western scholars of ethics (Kuntz, 2015: 79; Rhodes, 2009: 667; Warren, 2014: 65) argue that for qualitative research reporting to be truly ethical, it 'should focus on multiple voices offering contextualised questions, thoughts, possibilities, ambiguities and openness, rather than a single voice giving answers, generalisations, prescriptions and closure' (Kara, 2018: 131). And some Indigenous researchers, such as Wilson (2008), Kovach (2009) and Lambert (2014), work in precisely this way.

Reporting on any kind of research requires a lot of decisions. What is the story you want to tell? What is the best way to tell that story? What elements are you excluding by choosing to tell that story rather than another possible story? What are the implications of those exclusions? How can you represent your data and your participants accurately and fairly? Embedded in these decisions is power. As we report on research, we have the power to choose the elements to include and the order to put them in. And with this power comes responsibility (Kara, 2018: 123): to our participants, their communities, our communities, colleagues, managers, supervisors, commissioners, funders, families, friends and other stakeholders. Reporting ethically requires us to maintain awareness of our authorial power and of how we choose to use that power (Kara, 2018: 131).

Reflective questions

1. Which methods of reporting research appeal to you, and why?
2. What skills do you have, and/or what skills would you like to acquire, that could help you report on qualitative research?
3. How could you mitigate your biases when reporting on qualitative research?
4. How do you think you could help your audience(s) to understand your research findings and their context?
5. Should qualitative research reporting be done collaboratively, with colleagues and/or participants? Why?

11

PRESENTING AND DISSEMINATING RESEARCH

Chapter summary

- Distinguishes between presentation and dissemination
- Introduces creative approaches to presentation
- Covers good practice in presenting and disseminating research findings
- Focuses on performative, complex, multi-modal, collaborative and arts-based presentation methods
- Considers how dissemination can be linked with other aspects of research
- Outlines arts-based and multi-modal dissemination
- Looks at how dissemination may be carried out by people other than researchers
- Discusses some of the ethical aspects of presenting and disseminating qualitative research findings

Introduction

I distinguish between presenting research in person to a live audience, whether in a room together or online, and disseminating research, when you send research outputs to people or publish findings in any format. In reality, there are not always clear distinctions between disseminating, presenting and reporting findings. However, these categories are useful in helping us to think and talk about how we report on and share our findings.

As with reporting, all forms of presenting and disseminating research findings can be used for quantitative, qualitative or multi-modal research. More creative methods of presentation and dissemination are perhaps more readily associated with qualitative than with quantitative research. Yet researchers using quantitative and laboratory science methods can, and do, use qualitative ways of presenting and disseminating their findings. There is an example of this in Box 11.1.

Box 11.1

Qualitative presentation and dissemination of scientific research

Colleen Campbell is a field biologist who spent 20 years studying coyotes and grizzly bears in the Canadian Rocky Mountains. Her work involved the humane capture, recording, tagging and tracing of wild animals, and analysing their DNA. As is often the case with scientists studying animal species, she cared very much about the animals she studied, and wanted to share information about them with the general public 'to foster respect for other creatures' (Campbell, 2019: 21). Campbell is also a talented artist and she created a range of artworks to report and disseminate some of her findings. These included 'wanted' posters, modelled on the posters historically used to publicise alleged criminals with pictures of the person from different viewpoints. Campbell chose this format because coyotes and grizzly bears are feared and hated by many humans. Each poster contained detailed drawings of the animal from different angles, plus text giving information about the animal, including its 'transgressions' (why people don't like it) and 'redemption' (positive features of the animal's existence in the world). She also drew on historical, geographic and linguistic data to create an 'ursagraphic'. 'Ursa' is Latin for 'bear', and Campbell's ursagraphic is a map of Canada showing each place, region or geographic feature which is named after 'bear' in every language she has been able to discover. The ursagraphic shows very clearly how the lives of bears and humans have been intertwined throughout the history of the country we now call Canada. These artworks and others by Campbell were disseminated through a public exhibition in Jasper, Canada, in 2019.

Creative approaches to presentation, such as those used by Colleen Campbell (Box 11.1), have been shown to increase audiences' engagement with, and retention of, research findings (Evergreen, 2014: 18).

Good practice in presenting and disseminating research findings

As with reporting, the key point when presenting and disseminating research is to use the method or methods which will be most effective for your audiences. Whatever the method, though, again as with reporting, the common element is storytelling (Kara et al., 2021: 126). This is because a story is an accessible way to present information (Kovach, 2009: 131). Stories are effective in making sense of complexity, and so can be a good way to convey your arguments. (See the section on fictionalisation in Chapter 10 for a discussion of stories and truth in research.)

There is always more than one story you can tell from any research project, so you will need to decide which story is relevant for which audience. Then tell your story as simply and clearly as you can. Most forms of presentation and dissemination include other elements beyond the actual storytelling: PowerPoint slides for a conference presentation, citations for a journal article and hyperlinks for a blog post. These other elements should be used sparingly and only to support your story. They should never take over and become the main event.

PowerPoint slides seem to be loved and hated in equal measure. They are used in most conference presentations, yet you have no doubt heard the phrase 'death by PowerPoint'. There are a few good practice points worth keeping in mind:

- Keep text to an absolute minimum.
- Keep graphs, charts, etc. to a minimum too, and make sure they are legible.
- Use images rather than text where possible; there are millions of free images on the internet these days from websites such as Pixabay or Unsplash.
- Do *not* read the text from your slides aloud to your audience.

Disseminating research findings is good practice in itself. Research institutions and funders are taking this much more seriously these days, as are researchers ourselves. Publishing of all kinds is useful, though open access publications are of most use. You may have career or other defensible reasons to publish in a paywalled journal or newspaper, which is fine, but then consider writing a blog post or recording a podcast about your article and your research to inform people who don't have access to that journal or newspaper. And it is also important to think about your audiences who may not be online much or at all. For some researchers, this includes participants, in which case it may be necessary to go in person to present findings to participants (Lambert, 2014: 215–6; Wilson, 2008: 48 – see also Box 11.6 below). This is not always possible, for example, where participants are geographically scattered or come from transient populations. Here, again, creative approaches can be helpful. One researcher, whose participants were geographically scattered, created posters which could be printed and circulated by local organisations (Kara, 2018: 136). A group of researchers, whose participants were homeless, created a graphic novel from their data (Dahl et al., 2012). They self-published the book using Lulu online, and handed out copies to homeless people they could find in the hope that those copies would reach as many of their participants as possible.

It is worth reiterating here that dissemination requires planning at an early stage. Dissemination is time-consuming, and can also be expensive, so allocations should be made in timeframes and budgets. Dissemination is crucial to achieve the purposes of research and, as the old saying goes, failing to plan is planning to fail.

Presenting research findings

Research findings are most commonly presented at conferences, in webinars, seminars or meetings. Presenting research is always embodied (Ellingson, 2017: 1). Also, presenting is always performative (Kara et al., 2021: 215). Even a standard talk with PowerPoint slides is, in one sense, a performance to an audience. However, some researchers take the performative element further, as shown in Box 11.2.

Box 11.2

Performative presentation of research findings

Education researcher Cate Watson studied interprofessional working with school-children and their families. Watson was asked to present some of her work at a research seminar on professional development for inclusion in education. She decided to focus on the home–school partnership, and to illustrate this through the narrative of a mother whose child was diagnosed with Attention Deficit Hyperactivity Disorder (also discussed in Chapter 3). This narrative explained the diagnosis as resulting from a sequence of trivial events, while the professionals' narrative of the diagnosis explained it as resulting from the family's deviance. Watson (2011) decided to draw on Hogarthian satire to script a series of scenes documenting the family's progress (402). Her aim was to highlight the absurdity of claiming to be rational in an irrational world. When it was time for her presentation, Watson invited members of the audience to take the various roles and present the scenes to the rest of the audience. This worked well, and audience feedback showed it had been a powerful and effective presentation.

Another interesting facet of Watson's presentation is that it was collaborative. Collaborative presentation can be as simple as two people taking turns to speak, or very much more complex. An example of the latter is in Box 11.3.

Box 11.3

Complex presentation of research findings

Victoria Foster conducted participatory research with parents and carers at a Sure Start programme. Sure Start was an early 21st century UK Government initiative for multi-agency teams to work with families of children under five in areas of deprivation. Foster's participants decided that they wanted to present their findings in the form of a pantomime. This is a form of theatrical production involving musical and slapstick comedy, jokes (often topical), cross-gender acting and audience interaction. Panto-mime was designed to entertain whole families so it was appropriate for the research context. The pantomime was called *The Wizard of Us* and was written, rehearsed and performed by Foster's participants with the support of a local amateur dramatist. *The Wizard Of Us* was also recorded on video. Programme staff and local community members gave the pantomime a warm reception, finding it authentic and powerful, and the video was well received by academic communities (Foster, 2013: 49).

One difficulty with presenting research in brief conference or seminar/webinar slots is that there is only time to tell one short story from your research. This means you are likely to conceal more than you reveal, particularly about the multi-faceted messiness of research. Researchers have been experimenting with ways to convey more of the complexity of the research process to their audiences. This often involves multi-modal presentation methods (Buckley and Waring, 2013: 168–9; Mandlis, 2009: 1358). An in-person presentation can be accompanied by images on slides; an online presentation can include links to other online content; either can include a short video. A word of caution, though: it is important to use visual elements to clarify and enhance rather than to obscure and confuse (Kara et al., 2021: 127). Overcrowded slides, or a video playing while you talk, are unlikely to help convey the messages you want your audiences to receive.

Multi-modal presentations can be collaborative or may be given by one person alone, using different tools and techniques to help their audience absorb and remember their messages. There is an example of this in Box 11.4.

Box 11.4

Multi-modal presentation of research findings

Janice Fournillier studied the experiences of immigrant women in US higher edu-cation. She moved from Trinidad to the United States at the age of 50 to conduct her studies, and found it painful to experience the 'divide and rule' culture of US higher

(Continued)

education, in which white people hold most of the power and it can feel very risky for people of colour to speak authentically. During her time in the United States, she received an invitation to participate in a conference with a theme of 'the plantation'. As Fournillier's own heritage is one of slavery, the 'plantation system', with its masters and slaves, seemed like a direct parallel with the academy and so offered a conceptual framework for her own research. She chose to draw on her heritage and perform her presentation as a stream-of-consciousness monologue in a Trinidadian dialogue. She also incorporated the Caribbean musical form of calypso, singing a highly regarded traditional song about the horrors of slavery and the search for freedom through rebellion. To make her presentation interactive, Fournillier asked her audience to participate in a call-and-response style. There were real risks in taking such a creative and authentic approach, yet her courage paid off as 'the audience responded lustily and shook their heads and shed a tear' (Fournillier, 2010: 59).

Fournillier's work demonstrates that presentation aids do not have to be visual or technological. Also, presentation aids may be visual but not technological. Everyday household items can be used to help people visualise research findings, as demonstrated by designers such as Jose Duarte from Colombia and Nadeem Haidary from the United States. You could use tall glasses filled with coloured liquid to different levels, in the same way as bars on a bar chart, to show different proportions. This can be particularly powerful if you can use a colour, or a liquid, relevant to your findings. So if you were reporting on research into pollution in rivers, you could use murky brown water; if you were reporting on ways to increase the yield of orange trees, you could use orange juice. Precision is difficult with this kind of approach, but Duarte says that as long as the proportions are approximately correct, you can convey your message clearly which is the most important thing.[1]

Textile arts have also been used to present research information (as distinct from the use of textiles as data, discussed in Chapter 7). Throughout 2018, a German office clerk working in a travel agency, Claudia Weber, knitted a 'train delay scarf' to represent her commute from her home town of Moosburg into the city of Munich. Each evening she added two rows, one for each journey. She used grey wool for a delay of under five minutes, pink for 5–30 minutes and red for a delay of more than 30 minutes. By the end of the year, her scarf was four feet long and offered a clear graphical representation of her year's commuting experience. This approach has been taken up with enthusiasm by researchers using textiles. At the British Educational Research Association conference in 2019, Dr Abigail Parrish presented a poster with a knitted graph showing the motivation levels of school students in different years. This is shown in Figure 11.1.

---

[1] www.handmadevisuals.com/about/ (accessed 8 October 2014).

Figure 11.1 Knitted graph of motivation levels. (*Thanks to Dr Abigail Parrish of Bishop Grosseteste University for permission to reproduce this image.*)

Textiles are also used to good effect by some quantitative researchers. Hyperbolic geometry is the geometry of two- or three-dimensional planes or spaces involving curves. This is not a minority interest: it is 'used by statisticians when they work with multidimensional data, by Pixar animators when they want to simulate realistic cloth, by auto-industry engineers to design aerodynamic cars, by acoustic engineers to design concert halls' (Perez, 2019: 311). Mathematicians learned to model hyperbolic space using paper and tape, but these models were fragile and therefore difficult to handle. Latvian mathematician Dr Daina Taimina realised that textiles could be used to model hyperbolic space. She began with knitting, but found she needed too many stitches for her needles, so she turned to crochet (Henderson and Taimina, 2001: 17). This enabled her to create durable models that were easy to manipulate. She now crochets entire coral reefs and has produced an interesting TEDX talk about her work (the URL is in Appendix 1). Further, her 'crochet thinking' is now influencing work in other disciplines, such as architectural design (Baurmann and Taimina, 2013).

Disseminating research findings

Dissemination methods are not covered as thoroughly in the methods literature as some other aspects of research (Vaughn et al., 2012). Most research is disseminated in writing (Kara et al., 2021: 143), but there are numerous other ways to disseminate research such as animations, podcasts and comics.

Disseminating qualitative findings may be an end in itself, or dissemination can be looped in with other aspects of research or with other activities such as arts projects. Box 11.5 shows an example of arts-based dissemination combined with data gathering.

Box 11.5

Arts-based dissemination combined with data gathering

Abigail Schoneboom studied skiving, the employee's art of finding ways to have fun in the workplace. To begin with, she had six participants, and she created 'humorous audiovisual accounts' of their skiving practices, which included devising elaborate games and setting up fake meetings with colleagues so they could catch up on gossip (Schoneboom, 2010: 3). Schoneboom disseminated these accounts through an interactive website which she created for an exhibition on work–life balance at the Peacock Visual Arts Centre in Aberdeen, Scotland. Gallery visitors were invited to contribute their own skiving practices by typing directly into a live online database. The interactive website was also accessible by anyone in the world who had an internet connection, and they, too, could add their skiving practices. During the exhibition, 19 skiving practices were contributed: three by people involved in or reporting on the exhibition, five by gallery visitors, and 11 by people from other parts of the world (Schoneboom, 2010: 9). A further 24 skiving practices were contributed online after the exhibition had ended. Schoneboom used these 43 contributions, alongside the original six, as data for an extended study of skiving.

Schoneboom disseminated her extended study through her open access journal article, and probably by other means, too. Multi-modal dissemination is often necessary to reach all the audiences for a set of research findings – or, perhaps more realistically, to reach as many as possible. An example of multi-modal dissemination is in Box 11.6.

Box 11.6

Multi-modal dissemination

Sarah Franzen conducted ethnographic research into community-based rural development in the United States, with particular emphasis on 'how knowledge and information are exchanged between development organisers and local populations in order to implement development projects' (Franzen, 2013: 420). She identified her audiences as participating communities and their neighbouring communities, development organisations, non-profits, extension agents and local government officials (Franzen, 2013: 414). Franzen made ethnographic films for these audiences, based on her findings. Many of her participants did not have reliable internet access, so she presented the films at public screenings. She disseminated them through DVDs given to participants and organisers, and digital and online copies for those with internet access. The films were also used 'for educational, promotional, and community-building purposes' by participants and a key non-profit organisation (Franzen, 2013: 420).

The use of Franzen's films for education, promotion and community-building is another form of dissemination. Also, dissemination may be carried out by people other than researchers. Either way, these kinds of dissemination can have surprising outcomes. Although we are focusing on qualitative research, it is also worth remembering that these points can apply to quantitative and laboratory research, as shown in Box 11.7.

Box 11.7

Dissemination by non-researchers

Marie-Claire Shanahan tells the story of science writer and blogger Ed Yong, who wrote a blog post disseminating the research of Debiao Zhao and colleagues from the University of Edinburgh. Zhao et al. found that chickens could be gynandromorphic, i.e. have an equal balance of male and female cells and behaviours. They published their findings in the journal *Nature*; Yong read the article and decided it merited a post. Various people commented on the post, including one of the scientists who had co-authored the journal article, and a farmer with a gynandromorphic chicken. Yong put them in touch with each other and this led to a full-scale collaboration. The farmer arranged for blood samples to be taken, recorded observations, took photographs and shared all of this with the scientist for use as research data. They also kept Yong informed about their collaboration and its outcomes, which meant that he in turn could update his readers (Shanahan, 2011: 911–3).

From research to practice

Simply telling people about research findings is often not enough for qualitative researchers, particularly those who have been working to find ways to improve a situation. The study of methods for putting research into practice is known as 'implementation science' in the United Kingdom and Europe (and by other terms elsewhere) and is a form of research in itself (Bauer et al., 2015: 1). This is quite a new field, prompted by findings that in some forms of practice such as healthcare, interventions that researchers found to be effective were not then being used to improve the lives of patients. Implementation science research is usually multi-modal with both qualitative and quantitative data (Bauer et al., 2015: 5).

Putting research into practice is a complex business; so much so, in fact, that there is not – and cannot be – any list of rules to follow. Every situation is different, so a creative approach is required, whether you are working to implement qualitative, quantitative or multi-modal research. That said, there are some guiding principles, developed by Laura Damschroder and her colleagues in the United States in the early 21st century as the *Consolidated Framework for Implementation Research* (CFIR). These researchers gathered and analysed theories from the literature on how to put research into practice, and used their findings to produce the CFIR (Damschroder et al., 2009). The principles they put forward are the following:

- Start making plans for how to implement your findings as early as you can.
- Draw on the CFIR for ideas that can be used in the context in which you are working.
- As you do your research, try to identify features of your topic and its context that will enable (or hinder) implementation to create improvements.
- Be aware that there may also be unexpected enablers or barriers to implementation, and aim to respond appropriately and swiftly to any that arise.
- Keep a record of the positive and negative influences on the implementation of your findings, including how and why they occurred and operated.

Even where research findings are implemented, structural factors in society, often related to inequalities, may be a barrier to improvements resulting from implementation. As we saw in Box 5.2, Janice Du Mont and Deborah White conducted global research into the implementation of rape kits. These are standardised tools for gathering evidence of sexual assault that are used by criminal justice personnel, though often not successfully. Du Mont and White found three main reasons for this: professionals' incompetence, corruption in professional settings and contempt for women reporting rape (Du Mont and White, 2013: 1234). In another example, European researchers conducted participatory research with Romani people, nomads who are highly marginalised, to focus on what and how they could contribute to European society. The research was presented jointly by Roma and academic researchers to policy-makers at the European Parliament, and this led (among other things) to the development of a European strategy to ensure that Romani people could 'participate effectively in making the decisions that affect the lives and well-being of Roma communities' in Europe (Munté et al., 2011: 263). Yet ten years later, despite more changes to legislation and strategy at Europe-wide and European national levels, Romani people were still highly marginalised in European society (Kende et al., 2020: 1). In both of these examples, human prejudice is the main barrier to the implementation of research findings leading to improvements in people's lives: prejudice against women in the first example, and prejudice against Romani people in the second.

This can be quite depressing and discouraging for researchers who are working to make a positive difference to individuals, groups, communities and society. We have to remember that social change takes time. Also, there are ways to support implementation, such as knowledge exchange. Like implementation science, there are several terms in use for this (Read et al., 2013: 23). Whichever term you use, this is a more egalitarian approach than dissemination or implementation, which are both activities done by researchers and/or practitioners to or for other people. Knowledge exchange implies a reciprocal process of sharing knowledge between researchers, practitioners, policy-makers, service users and others (Kara, 2020: 231). This is not as easy as it sounds because – as we have seen in Chapter 2 – different people know different things and/or understand the same things differently from each other, and achieving a common level of knowledge and understanding takes time (Martin et al., 2011: 214–6). But knowledge exchange can be worth the effort because it increases the likelihood of implementation (Gagnon, 2011: 28). If knowledge exchange is not possible, another option to support implementation is to involve research participants or their representatives, and potential research users, in planning that implementation (Gagnon, 2011: 25).

The ethical aspects of presenting and disseminating research findings

The ethical aspects of presenting and disseminating findings are written about even less than the methods of presentation and dissemination (Pickering and Kara, 2017: 299). Yet it is essential to present our findings accurately and clearly, and to represent our participants and other stakeholders honestly and fairly, while meeting the needs of our audiences as well as we can, and staying true to our qualitative research. This is a difficult ethical balancing act.

One aspect that is very rarely covered is how presenting and disseminating findings can be very demanding for researchers. Lucie Cluver writes eloquently about this with reference to her large-scale and longitudinal quantitative research with AIDS-affected children in South Africa:

> We present at government policy forums; in small, closed meetings of
> politicians; to UNICEF and WHO and UNAIDS and Save the Children and
> USAID-PEPFAR, which fund many of the programmes with AIDS-affected
> children in our region. We go back to community meetings, to chieftains, to

local hospitals and schools, and explain what these numbers mean for their province. I give the same talk so often that it becomes a blur. I see my students give the same talk, but better than me. Sometimes it feels like being a very minor band on an economy-class world tour: Addis, Dar, Washington, New York, Lagos, Basel, Kampala. We give newspaper interviews and radio interviews and podcasts; we spend three months on a statistical analysis and then simplify it all to a single slide.

(Cluver et al., 2014: 52)

As we saw in Box 10.5, Stacy Bias created a short animation to disseminate her undergraduate research into the experiences of fat people while flying, and made it freely available online. She says the following:

I anticipated it would be well received among the fat activists and individuals for whom the themes resonated but I was amazed to find the press also picked it up with great enthusiasm. Mainstream outlets like *Buzzfeed*, *Cosmopolitan* and *People* magazine delivered surprisingly detailed and sympathetic coverage alongside more traditionally empathic mainstays. Our direct YouTube views jumped to 300,000 in less than 2 weeks, then hundreds of thousands more across embedded media platforms – ultimately reaching a viewership of over 2 million in less than 3 weeks.

(Bias, 2021: 150)

Dissemination does not always go so well. We saw in Box 6.5 that Roland Bannister conducted ethnomusicological research with a unique Australian military band. He took care to ensure that his participants were happy with his dissemination plans, even sending them draft articles to discuss and approve before submitting the articles for publication. Academic publications proved trouble-free, but one article was published in the *Australian Defence Force Journal*, which was regularly read by people connected with the band. When participants were sent drafts and told where the article would be submitted, three expressed enthusiasm, one said 'no problem' and the others did not reply (Bannister, 1996: 54). But when the article was published, one participant – who had checked and approved the draft – rang Bannister to 'express his consternation about the way he was represented' (Bannister, 1996: 54). Later, another participant wrote to Bannister, worried that part of the article would 'bring discredit to the band' (Bannister, 1996: 55).

Cluver, Bias and Bannister do not write explicitly about the personal impact of their presentation and dissemination experiences. Even so, it does not take much imagination to understand that repeated and reductive presentations could be very wearing, or that the roller-coaster ride of high-profile media interest and a video going viral could be both exhilarating and exhausting, or how upsetting and worrying it must be when, even having taken good ethical precautions, some participants are unhappy about a publication. Cases of presentation and dissemination placing a burden on researchers are rare in the literature but much more common in practice. If researchers' findings are controversial, they may receive abuse online, particularly if they are women or people of colour. Self-care is an ethical imperative for all researchers, not only at these late stages of the process but throughout our research work.

Conclusion

Our responsibility for participants' welfare, and that of their communities, is made clear throughout our research training and engagement with formal ethical approval systems. This emphasis is important, but it creates a context in which we can easily forget we are also responsible for the welfare of our data, our findings and ourselves (Kara, 2018: 157–9). Even when we have planned our presentation and dissemination strategies well, subsequent time pressures and other demands may encourage us to sideline some or all of our plans. But there is no point in doing research unless we share and publicise the knowledge we generate. So sharing our findings with others should not be an afterthought, but a carefully planned and executed process designed to maximise the use of those findings, while enabling us to take care of ourselves in our work.

Reflective questions

1. Which of the methods of presentation set out in this chapter could work for your qualitative research? How, and why?
2. Should qualitative findings be presented collaboratively? Why?
3. Which of the methods of dissemination set out in this chapter could work for your qualitative research? How, and why?
4. How could you mitigate your bias when presenting your qualitative findings?
5. What barriers might there be to disseminating your qualitative research, and how could you overcome them?

12

CONCLUSION

The bounded nature of a book like this may give the false impression that qualitative research, too, has clear start and finish points. There is rarely a clear beginning to qualitative research – is it the first idea, the first word written, the first conversation, the design, the funding? *The Lost Ethnographies: Methodological Insights from Projects that Never Were* (Smith and Delamont, 2019) is an edited collection, each chapter telling the story of the work that went into a research project which did not then come into existence, often because of an unsuccessful funding application. There is an inherent paradox in the suggestion that a non-existent research project can provide methodological insights; evidently a great deal of work was done on each of these 'projects that never were'. In her concluding chapter, Katie Fitzpatrick asserts that 'A project is always partial and unfulfilled, begging for further inquiry and, at the end, always denied completion, fullness, the whole story' (Fitzpatrick, 2019: 167). This applies not only to ethnography but to all qualitative research – and, indeed, to books. We can never tell the whole story; the work is never truly finished.

One implication of this is that researchers not only have a duty of care in their work but also a duty of aftercare. This of course applies equally to quantitative researchers, but it is rarely discussed in the Euro-Western research methods literature, though some individual Euro-Western researchers do take it into consideration (Kara, 2018: 151). For Indigenous researchers, however, aftercare appears to be standard practice, some going so far as to suggest that researchers should consider their ethical responsibility to the next seven generations by working out the likely long-term legacy of their research (Kouritzin and Nakagawa, 2018: 684; Smith, 2012: 16). People with oral traditions have longer memories, and so perhaps can more easily envisage a longer future, than those of us who are dependent on the written word. Also, aftercare may come more naturally to researchers with a tradition of working inside their own communities within a relational ontology. Yet I would argue that Euro-Western researchers need to consider aftercare much more than we do, and that while we cannot emulate

Indigenous researchers because of our cultural differences, we do have the opportunity to learn from their approach.

Qualitative research, as it is taught by and to Euro-Western researchers, has an interesting approach to relationality. We are taught to create rapport with participants, to put them at ease and help them feel comfortable with us. Yet looked at another way, this is a very instrumental approach to human relationships: using our friendship skills to get what we want from someone in a form we can then call 'data'. Some commentators have called this the 'commodification of rapport' (Duncombe and Jessop, 2012: 110), and it can seem quite cold-hearted, particularly if your participants are isolated people with few or no actual friends. How ethical is it to create this rapport with a participant, listen carefully to what they have to say – in itself an unusual and welcome experience for many people – and then, just as they are feeling they have a new best friend, drop them like a stone?

In general, qualitative research requires more of our everyday human skills than quantitative research. This makes it more appealing to some people – and less appealing to others. Fieldwork can be particularly messy because people are unpredictable, have and display emotions, tell lies or half-truths and hold opinions and agendas that are different from our own. While there are some techniques that can help you with qualitative fieldwork, such as those outlined in Chapters 6 and 7, throughout the process you will need to draw on all your interpersonal skills – to 'be a human', as Karen Ross and Meagan Call-Cummings say (2020: 507). This would arguably also be beneficial for quantitative research.

We saw in Chapter 1 that qualitative and quantitative research have a lot of similarities and are complementary rather than oppositional. Chapter 2 showed us that the classical version of positivism, on which much quantitative research was based, has been largely discredited, and that quantitative researchers from a range of disciplines have argued for the usefulness of reflexivity to quantitative research as well as to qualitative and multi-modal research. We saw in Chapter 3 that theory operates differently in qualitative than in quantitative research. In Chapter 4, we began to understand the importance of context, flexibility, ethics and creativity for qualitative research. Chapter 5 explained the complexity and utility of context, Chapter 6 highlighted the importance of flexibility and ethics and Chapter 7 expanded our view of creativity in qualitative research. In Chapter 8, we were reminded of the need to work systematically and carefully, and then in Chapter 9, we began to understand the complex intellectual dance that is qualitative data analysis. The relationship between fiction and truth in research reporting lies at the heart of Chapter 10. And in Chapters 10 and 11, we met again the similarities between quantitative and qualitative research because their methods of reporting, presenting and disseminating research need not be so very different.

Having considerable experience of quantitative, qualitative and multi-modal research, I truly think they are not as far apart as we are led to believe. I have shown in this book that, as well as their very real – and very useful – differences, they also have a number of similarities and complementarities. Throughout the book, we have seen examples of qualitative research in conventionally quantitative disciplines, and of qualitative and quantitative methods being used together to good effect.

I am sure many researchers and their work would benefit from a fuller understanding of methods, methodologies, theories and approaches. It is sometimes too easy to stick with those we already know. Perhaps we all need to challenge ourselves, at times, to rethink the way we conduct research in the light of a new research question. Then, even if we do go on to work in the ways we know best, we will have done so as the result of a carefully considered decision, not as a result of laziness or thoughtlessness or external pressures.

Qualitative research is, of course, a serious business; not to be taken lightly. However, people are often surprised to discover that qualitative research can also be a whole lot of fun. Designing an interesting project with like-minded colleagues, using an exciting method to gather data from people with fascinating tales to tell, making unexpected discoveries during analysis, presenting your findings to an interested and engaged audience – experiences such as these can make the process truly joyful.

I wish you great joy of your own qualitative research.

APPENDIX 1

URLs

Chapter 1

Glossary of research terms on the companion website for my 2017 book *Research and Evaluation for Busy Students and Practitioners* (2nd edn; Policy Press): https://policy.bristoluniversitypress.co.uk/research-and-evaluation-for-busy-students-and-practitioners/companion-website/students/glossary

Chapter 5

Giorgia Lupi and Stefanie Posavec devised and tested a method of making field notes based on drawing: http://giorgialupi.com/dear-data

Clare Danek created a stitch journal using textile art: https://claredanek.me/stitch-journal/

Chapter 6

Helpful resources for learning and using participatory action research: https://www.participatorymethods.org/resource/participatory-action-research-health-systems-methods-reader

Digital stories from the people of Rigolet, a remote coastal community in northern Labrador, Canada, about their experiences of climate change: https://www.youtube.com/results?search_query=rigolet+storytelling+%26+digital+media+lab

Chapter 7

Mass Observation Archive: http://www.massobs.org.uk/

Naomi Clarke and Debbie Watson's participant information: https://naomialice.co.uk/my-crafting-during-coronavirus-diary/

The Programmable Web: https://www.programmableweb.com/

Chapter 8

NVivo: https://www.qsrinternational.com/nvivo-qualitative-data-analysis-software/home

MAXQDA: https://www.maxqda.com/

ATLAS.ti: https://atlasti.com/

Dedoose: https://www.dedoose.com/

QDA Miner: https://provalisresearch.com/products/qualitative-data-analysis-software/

QDA Miner Lite: https://provalisresearch.com/products/qualitative-data-analysis-soft-ware/freeware/

Quirkos: https://www.quirkos.com/

Retraction Watch: https://retractionwatch.com/

Chapter 10

The Wellcome Centre for Integrative Parasitology at the University of Glasgow: https://wellcomeopenresearch.org/gateways/wcip

Wellcome Centre for Integrative Parasitology research reporting (blog, podcasts, videos, and comics): https://www.gla.ac.uk/researchinstitutes/iii/wcip/publicengagement/

O'Brien et al. (2014) standards for reporting qualitative research: https://journals.lww.com/academicmedicine/fulltext/2014/09000/Standards_for_Reporting_Qualitative_Research__A.21.aspx

The World of Cocos Malay Music and Dance: https://www.youtube.com/watch?v=OIjAF7Bh6as

Flying While Fat: http://flyingwhilefat.com/

Project Orange research-led architecture and interior design studio in London, England: http://www.projectorange.com/

Project Orange zines available for download: http://www.projectorange.com/publications

After Maria: https://www.hcri.manchester.ac.uk/research/projects/after-maria/

Chapter 11

Daina Taimina's TEDX talk about crocheting hyperbolic geometry: https://www.youtube.com/watch?v=w1TBZhd-sN0

REFERENCES

Agbebiyi A (2013) Tiers of gatekeepers and ethical practice: Researching adolescent students and sexually explicit online material. *International Journal of Social Research Methodology*, 16(6): 535–40. doi:10.1080/13645579.2013.823290

Ahearn A (2006) Engineering writing: Replacing 'writing classes' with a 'writing imperative'. In: Ganobcsik-Williams L (ed.) *Teaching Academic Writing in UK Higher Education: Theories, Practices and Models*. Basingstoke: Palgrave Macmillan, pp. 110–23.

Aleixo P and Sumner K (2017) Memory for biopsychology material presented in comic book format. *Journal of Graphic Novels and Comics*, 8(1): 79–88. doi:10.1080/21504857.2016.1219957

Archibald J (Q'um Q'um Xiiem) (2008) *Indigenous Storywork: Educating the Heart, Mind, Body and Spirit*. Vancouver, BC: UBC Press.

Ardley B and McIntosh E (2021) Netnography, Facebook, and the adult fans of LEGO: Researching value creation processes in an online community. SAGE Research Methods Cases https://methods.sagepub.com/case/netnography-facebook-adult-fans-lego-value-creation-processes-community (accessed 3 March 2021).

Ashley F (2021) Accounting for research fatigue in research ethics. *Bioethics*, 35: 270–6. doi:10.1111/bioe/12829

Back L (2015) *Academic Diary*. London: Goldsmiths Press.

Ball J and Janyst P (2008) Enacting research ethics in partnerships with Indigenous communities in Canada: "Do it in a good way". *Journal of Empirical Research on Human Research Ethics*, 33–51. doi:10.1525/jer.2008.3.2.33

Balzani A and Hanlon A (2020) Factors that influence farmers' views on farm animal welfare: A semi-systematic review and thematic analysis. *Animals*, 10(9): 1524. doi:10.3390/ani10091524

Banks S (2016) Action research for social justice. In Hardwick L, Smith R and Worsley A (eds) *Innovations in Social Work Research: Using Methods Creatively*. London: Jessica Kingsley Publishing, pp. 18–39.

Banks S and Brydon-Miller M (2018) Ethics in participatory research. In: Banks S and Brydon-Miller M (eds) *Ethics in Participatory Research for Health and Social Well-Being: Cases and Commentaries*. Abingdon: Routledge, pp. 1–30.

Bannister R (1995) *An Ethnomusicological Study of Music Makers in an Australian Military Band*. Doctoral thesis. Deakin University.

Barad K (2007) *Meeting the Universe Halfway: Quantum Physics and the Entanglement of Matter and Meaning*. Durham and London: Duke University Press.

Barger M, Wormington S, Huettel L and Linnenbrink-Garcia L (2016) Developmental changes in college engineering students' personal epistemology profiles. *Learning and Individual Differences*, 48: 1–8. doi:10.1016/j.lindif.2016.04.002

Barker M-J and Scheele J (2016) *Queer: A Graphic History*. London: Icon Books Ltd.

Barker M-J and Iantaffi A (2019) *Life Isn't Binary: On Being Both, Beyond, and In-Between*. London: Jessica Kingsley Publishers.

Bassot B (2020) *The Research Journal: A Reflective Tool for Your First Independent Research Project*. Bristol: Policy Press.

Barton J and Olson P (2019) Cite first, ask questions later? *Papers of the Bibliographical Society of America*, 113(2): 205–16.

Bauer MS, Damschroder L, Hagedorn H, Smith J and Kilbourne AM (2015) An introduction to implementation science for the non-specialist. *BMC Psychology*, 3(1): 1–12. doi 10.1186/s40359/015/0089-9

Baurmann G and Taimina D (2013) Crocheting algorithms. *Cornell Journal of Architecture*, 9: 98–106.

Becker H (2007) *Writing for Social Scientists: How to Start and Finish Your Thesis, Book, or Article* (2nd edition). Chicago, IL: The University of Chicago Press.

Belgrave L and Seide K (2019) Grounded theory methodology: Principles and practices. In: P.Liamputtong (Ed.), *Handbook of Research Methods in Health Social Sciences*. Singapore: Springer, pp. 299–316.

Belzile J and Oberg G (2012) Where to begin? Grappling with how to use participant interaction in focus group design. *Qualitative Research*, 12(4): 459–72.

Bias S (2021) Your stories are moving: Animation and affect in creative research dissemination. In: Phillips R and Kara H (eds) *Creative Writing for Social Research*. Bristol: Policy Press.

Bishop E and Willis K (2014) "Hope is that fiery feeling": Using poetry as data to explore the meanings of hope for young people. *Forum: Qualitative Social Research*, 15(1) Art. 9.

Bishop L and Kuula-Luumi A (2017) Revisiting qualitative data reuse: A decade on. *SAGE Open*, 7(1): 1–15. doi:10.1177/2158244016685136

Blanch C and Mulvihill T (2013) The attitudes of some students on the use of comics in higher education. In: Syma C and Weiner R (eds) *Graphic Novels and Comics in the Classroom: Essays on the Educational Power of Sequential Art*. Jefferson, NC: McFarland & Company, Inc, pp. 35–47.

Bloomberg L and Volpe M (2012) *Completing Your Qualitative Dissertation: A Road Map From Beginning to End* (2nd edition). Thousand Oaks, CA: SAGE.

Boehner K, Gaver W and Boucher A (2014) Probes. In: Lury C and Wakeford N (eds) *Inventive Methods: The Happening of the Social*. Abingdon: Routledge, pp. 185–201.

Bogomolova S (2017) Mechanical observation research in social marketing and beyond. In: Kubacki K and Rundle-Thiele S (eds) *Formative Research in Social Marketing*. Singapore: Springer, pp. 125–44. doi:10.1007/978-981-10-1829-9_8

Bold MR (2017) Why diverse zines matter: A case study of the people of color zines project. *Publishing Research Quarterly*, 33(3): 215–28.

Bolton E, Vorajee Z and Jones K (2005) The verismo of the quotidian: A biographic narrative interpretive approach to two diverse research topics. In: Kelly N, Horrocks C, Milnes K, Roberts B and Robinson D (eds) *Narrative, Memory and Everyday Life*. Huddersfield: University of Huddersfield Press, pp. 9–17.

Botes M (2017) Using comics to communicate legal contract cancellation. *The Comics Grid: Journal of Comics Scholarship*, 7(1): 14. doi:10.16995/cg.100

Bowen G (2009) Document analysis as a qualitative research method. *Qualitative Research Journal*, 9(2): 27–40.

Boyles J (2017) Building an audience, bonding a city: Digital news production as a field of care. *Media, Culture & Society*, 39(7): 945–59. doi:10.1177/0163443716682073

Brannelly P (2018) An ethics of care research manifesto. *International Journal of Care and Caring*, 2(3): 367–78. doi:10.1332/239788218X15351944886756

Braun V and Clarke V (2006) Using thematic analysis in psychology. *Qualitative research in psychology*, 3(2): 77–101.

Braun V and Clarke V (2020) One size fits all? What counts as quality practice in (reflexive) thematic analysis? *Qualitative Research in Psychology*, 14: 1–25. doi: 10.1080/14780887.2020.1769238

Braun V, Clarke V and Moller N (2020) Pandemic tales: Using story completion to explore sense-making around COVID-19 lockdown restrictions. In: Kara H and Khoo S (eds) *Researching in the Age of COVID-19*. Vol 3. *Creativity and Ethics*. Bristol: Policy Press.

Briassoulis H (2010) Online petitions: New tools of secondary analysis? *Qualitative Research*, 10(6): 715–27.

Bryman A (2016) *Social Research Methods*. Oxford: Oxford University Press.

Buckley C and Waring M (2013) Using diagrams to support the research process: Examples from grounded theory. *Qualitative Research*, 13(2): 148–72.

Caldwell J (October, 2012). Information comics: An overview. In: *2012 IEEE International Professional Communication Conference*. IEEE, pp. 1–7.

Cameron W (1963) *Informal Sociology: A Casual Introduction to Sociological Thinking*. New York, NY: Random House.

Campbell C (2019) *Once … We Were Allies*. Jasper, AB: Catalogue for Exhibition at Jasper Museum.

Cardno C (2018) Policy document analysis: A practical educational leadership tool and a qualitative research method. *Educational Administration: Theory and Practice*, 24(4): 623–40. doi:10.14527/kuey.2018.016

Carroll P, Dew K and Howden-Chapman P (2011) The heart of the matter: Using poetry as a method of ethnographic inquiry to represent and present experiences of the informally housed in Aotearoa/New Zealand. *Qualitative Inquiry*, 17(7): 623–30.

Chadwick R (2017) Embodied methodologies: Challenges, reflections and strategies. *Qualitative Research*, 17(1): 54–74. doi:10.1177/1468794116656035

Chang H (2008) *Autoethnography as Method*. Walnut Creek, CA: Left Coast Press, Inc.

Charmaz K (2014) *Constructing Grounded Theory* (2nd edition). London: SAGE.

Childers S (2012) Against simplicity, against ethics: Analytics of disruption as quasi-methodology. *Qualitative Inquiry*, 18(9): 752–61

Chilisa B (2020) *Indigenous Research Methodologies* (2nd edition). Thousand Oaks, CA: SAGE.

Clarke V and Braun V (2013) Teaching thematic analysis: Overcoming challenges and developing strategies for effective learning. *The Psychologist*, 26(2).

Clarke N and Watson D (2020) Crafting during coronavirus: Creative diary approaches for participant-centred research. In: Kara H and Khoo S (eds) *Researching in the Age of COVID-19*. Vol 3. *Creativity and Ethics*. Bristol: Policy Press.

Cluver L, Boyes M, Bustamam A, Casale M, Henderson K, Kuo C and Lane T (2014) The cost of action: Large-scale, longitudinal quantitative research with AIDS-affected children in South Africa. In: Posel D and Ross F (eds) *Ethical Quandaries in Social Research*. Cape Town: HSRC Press, pp. 41–56.

Cohen J (2015) *Eating Soup Without A Spoon: Anthropological Theory and Method in the Real World*. Austin, TX: Texas University Press.

Cohen L, Manion L and Morrison K (2018) *Research Methods in Education* (8th edition). Abingdon: Routledge.

Collins C and Stockton C (2018) The central role of theory in qualitative research. *International Journal of Qualitative Methods*, 17: 1–10. doi:10.1177/1609406918797475

Colnerud G (2014) Ethical dilemmas in research in relation to ethical review: An empirical study. *Research Ethics*, 10(4): 238–53. doi:10.1177/1747016114552339

Coltart C, Henwood K and Shirani F (2013) Qualitative secondary analysis in austere times: Ethical, professional and methodological considerations. *Forum: Qualitative Social Research*, 14(1) Art. 18. http://nbn-resolving.de/urn:nbn:de:0114-fqs1301181

Colvin C (2014) Who benefits from research? Ethical dilemmas in compensation in anthropology and public health. In: Posel D and Ross F (eds) *Ethical Quandaries in Social Research*. Cape Town: HSRC Press, pp. 57–74.

Condie J, Lean G and Wilcockson B (2017) The trouble with Tinder: The ethical complexities of researching location-aware social discovery apps. In: Woodfield K (ed.) *The Ethics of Online Research*. Bingley: Emerald Publishing, pp. 135–58.

Condotta JF, Le Ber F, Ligozat G and Travé-Massuyès L (2020) Qualitative reasoning. In: Marquis P, Papini O and Prade H (eds) *A Guided Tour of Artificial Intelligence Research*. Cham: Springer, pp. 151–83.

Connell R (2007) *Southern Theory*. Cambridge: Polity Press.

Cooksey R and McDonald G (2019) *Surviving and Thriving in Postgraduate Research* (2nd edition). Singapore: Springer Nature Singapore Pte Ltd.

Coombes B (2013) Indigenism, public intellectuals, and the forever opposed – or, the makings of a '*Hori* Academic'. In: Mertens D, Cram F and Chilisa B (eds) *Indigenous Pathways into Social Research: Voices of a New Generation*. Walnut Creek, CA: Left Coast Press, pp. 71–88.

Corbin J and Strauss A (2015) *Basics of Qualitative Research: Techniques and Procedures for Developing Grounded Theory*. Thousand Oaks, CA: SAGE.

Couceiro L (2020) Disorientation and new directions: Developing the reader response toolkit. In: Kara H and Khoo S (eds) *Researching in the Age of COVID-19*. Vol 1. *Response and Reassessment* (e-book). Bristol: Policy Press.

Cox S and McDonald M (2013) Ethics is for human subjects too: Participant perspectives on responsibility in health research. *Social Science & Medicine*, 98: 224–31. doi: 10.1016/j.socscimed.2013.09.015

Cram F, Chilisa B and Mertens D (2013) The journey begins. In: Mertens D, Cram F, Chilisa B (eds) *Indigenous Pathways into Social Research: Voices of a New Generation*. Walnut Creek, CA: Left Coast Press, pp. 11–40.

Crellin R and Harris O (2020) Beyond binaries. Interrogating ancient DNA. *Archaeological Dialogues*, 27: 37–56. doi:10.1017/S1380203820000082

Creswell J and Poth C (2018) *Qualitative Inquiry and Research Design: Choosing Among Five Approaches* (4th edition). Thousand Oaks, CA: SAGE.

Croskerry P, Singhal G and Mamede S (2013) Cognitive debiasing 2: Impediments to and strategies for change. *BMJ Quality and Safety*, 2013(22): ii65–ii72. doi:10.1136/bmjqs.2013.002387

Dahl S, Morris G, Brown P, Scullion L and Somerville P (2012) *Somewhere Nowhere: Lives Without Homes*. Salford: Salford Housing and Urban Studies Unit.

Dahlberg H and Dahlberg K (2020) Phenomenology of science and the art of radical questioning. *Qualitative Inquiry*, 26(7): 889–96. doi:10.1177/1077800419897702

Dalton J (2020) Model making as a research method. *Studies in the Education of Adults*, 52(1): 35–48. doi:10.1080/02660830.2019.1598605

Damschroder L, Aron D, Keith R, Kirsh S, Alexander J and Lowery J (2009) Fostering implementation of health services research findings into practice: A consolidated framework for advancing implementation science. *Implementation Science*. http://www.implementationscience.com/content/4/1/50 (accessed 16 February 2020).

Darder A (2019) Decolonizing interpretive research. In: Darder A (ed.) *Decolonizing Interpretive Research: A Subaltern Methodology for Social Change*. Abingdon: Routledge, pp. 3–36.

Davis C, Senechal M and Zwicky J (2008) *The Shape of Content: Creative Writing in Mathematics and Science*. Wellesley, MA: A K Peters, Ltd.

Dean J (2017) *Doing Reflexivity: An Introduction*. Bristol: Policy Press.

DeCuir-Gunby J, Marshall P and McCulloch A (2012) Using mixed methods to analyze video data: A mathematics teacher professional development example. *Journal of Mixed Methods Research*, 6(3): 199–216.

de Jager A, Tewson A, Ludlow B and Boydell K (2016) Embodied ways of storying the self: A systematic review of body-mapping. *Forum: Qualitative Social Research*, 17(2): Art. 22. http://nbn-resolving.de/urn:nbn:de:0114-fqs1602225

de Kleer J (1993) A view on qualitative physics. *Artificial Intelligence*, 59(1–2): 105–14.

de Kleer J and Brown JS (1984) A qualitative physics based on confluences. *Artificial Intelligence*, 24(1–3): 7–83.

Denzin N (2010) *The Qualitative Manifesto: A Call to Arms*. Walnut Creek, CA: Left Coast Press.

Denzin N (2014) *Interpretive Autoethnography* (2nd edition). London: SAGE.

Denzin N and Lincoln Y (eds) (2018) *The SAGE Handbook of Qualitative Research* (5th edition). Thousand Oaks, CA: SAGE.

De Vecchi N, Kenny A, Dickson-Swift V and Kidd S (2016) How digital storytelling is used in mental health: A scoping review. *International Journal of Mental Health Nursing*, 25: 183–93. doi:10.1111/mm.12206

Dingwall R (2016) The social costs of ethics regulation. In: van den Hoonaard W and Hamilton A (eds) *The Ethics Rupture: Exploring Alternatives to Formal Research Ethics Review*. Toronto, ON: University of Toronto Press, pp. 25–42.

Doherty T, Tabana H, Jackson D, Naik R, Zembe W, Lombard C, Swanevelder S, Fox M, Thorson A, Ekström A and Chopra M (2013) Effect of home based HIV counselling and testing intervention in rural South Africa: Cluster randomised trial. *British Medical Journal*, 346: f3481. doi:10.1136/bmj.f3481

Doucet A and Mauthner N (2012) Knowing responsibly: Ethics, feminist epistemologies and methodologies. In: Miller T, Birch M, Mauthner M and Jessop J (eds) *Ethics in Qualitative Research* (2nd edition). London: SAGE, pp. 122–39.

Dreger A (2015) *Galileo's Middle Finger: Heretics, Activists, and the Search for Justice in Science*. New York, NY: Penguin Press.

Du Mont J and White D (2013) Barriers to the effective use of medico-legal findings in sexual assault cases worldwide. *Qualitative Health Research*, 23(9): 1228–39.

Dunbar-Ortiz R (2014) *An Indigenous Peoples' History of the United States*. Boston, MA: Beacon Press.

Duncan R, Taylor M and Stoddard D (2016). *Creating Comics as Journalism, Memoir & Nonfiction*. New York, NY: Routledge.

Duncombe J and Jessop J (2012) 'Doing rapport' and the ethics of 'faking friendship'. In: Miller T, Birch M, Mauthner M and Jessop J (eds) *Ethics in Qualitative Research* (2nd edition). London: SAGE, pp. 108–21.

Edwards R and Weller S (2012) Shifting analytic ontology: Using I-poems in qualitative longitudinal research. *Qualitative Research*, 12(2): 202–17.

Edwards R, Weller S, Jamieson L and Davidson E (2020) Search strategies: Analytic searching across multiple datasets and within combined sources. In: Hughes K and Tarrant A (eds) *Qualitative Secondary Analysis*. London: SAGE, pp. 79–99.

Eggleton K, Kearns R and Neuwelt P (2017) Being patient, being vulnerable: Exploring experiences of general practice waiting rooms through elicited drawings. *Social & Cultural Geography*, 18(7): 971–93. doi:10.1080/14649365.2016.1228114

Eilers S and Johansen R (2017) *Introduction to Experimental Mathematics*. Cambridge: Cambridge University Press.

Elden S (2012) Inviting the messy: Drawing methods and 'children's voices'. *Childhood*, 20(1): 66–81.

Ellingson L (2009) *Engaging Crystallization in Qualitative Research: An Introduction*, Thousand Oaks, CA: SAGE.

Ellingson L (2017) *Embodiment in Qualitative Research*. Thousand Oaks, CA: SAGE.

Ellis C, Adams T and Bochner A (2011) Autoethnography: An overview. *Forum: Qualitative Social Research*, 12(1): Art. 10. http://nbn-resolving.de/urn:nbn:de:0114-fqs1101108

Eshun G and Madge C (2016) Poetic world-writing in a pluriversal world: A provocation to the creative (re)turn in geography. *Social and Cultural Geography*, 17(6): 778–85.

Evans B, Coon D and Ume E (2011) Use of theoretical frameworks as a pragmatic guide for mixed methods studies: A methodological necessity? *Journal of Mixed Methods Research*, 5(4): 276–92.

Evergreen S (2014) *Presenting Data Effectively: Communicating Your Findings For Maximum Impact*. Thousand Oaks, CA: SAGE.

Fàbregues S and Molina-Azorín J (2017) Addressing quality in mixed methods research: A review and recommendations for a future agenda. *Quality & Quantity*, 51: 2847–63. doi:10.1007/s11135-016-0449-4

Fanelli D, Costas R, Fang F, Casadevall A and Bik E (2019) Why do scientists fabricate and falsify data? A matched-control analysis of papers containing problematic image duplications. *Science and Engineering Ethics*, 25: 771–89. doi:10.1007/s11948-018-0023-7

Farnsworth J and Boon B (2010) Analysing group dynamics within the focus group. *Qualitative Research*, 10(5): 605–24.

Faulkner S (2019) Poetic inquiry: Poetry as/in/for social research. In: Leavy P (ed.) *Handbook of Arts-Based Research*, New York, NY: Guilford, pp. 208–30.

Ferrari R (2015) Writing narrative style literature reviews. *Medical Writing*, 24(4): 230–5. doi:10.1179/2047480615Z.000000000329

Finlay L (2011) *Phenomenology for Therapists: Researching the Lived World*. Chichester: Wiley-Blackwell.

Fitzpatrick K (2019) The edges and the end: On stopping an ethnographic project, on losing the way. In: Smith R and Delamont S (eds) *The Lost Ethnographies: Methodological Insights from Projects that Never Were*. Abingdon: Routledge, pp. 165–75.

Fleischmann P (2009) Literature reviews: An example of making traditional research methods user focused. In: Sweeney A, Beresford P, Faulkner A, Nettle M and Rose D (eds) *Survivor Research*. Ross-on-Wye: PCCS Books, pp. 82–97.

Flick U (2018) *Designing Qualitative Research* (2nd edition). London: SAGE.

Foster V (2013) Pantomime and politics: The story of a performance ethnography. *Qualitative Research*, 13(1): 36–52.

Fournillier J (2010) Plus ca change, plus c'est la meme chose: An Afro Caribbean scholar on the higher education plantation. *Creative Approaches to Research*, 3(2): 52–62.

Franzen S (2013) Engaging a specific, not general, public: The use of ethnographic film in public scholarship. *Qualitative Research*, 13(4): 414–27.

Franzke A, Bechmann A, Zimmer M, Charles E and the Association of Internet Researchers (2020) *Internet Research: Ethical Guidelines 3.0*. https://aoir.org/reports/ethics3.pdf (accessed 3 March 2021).

Frost N and Elichaoff F (2010) Feminist postmodernism, poststructuralism, and critical theory. In: Ryan-Flood R and Gill R (eds) *Secrecy and Silence in the Research Process: Feminist Reflections*. Abingdon: Routledge, pp. 42–72.

Furman R, Langer C, Davis C, Gallardo H and Kulkarni S (2007) Expressive, research and reflective poetry as qualitative inquiry: A study of adolescent identity. *Qualitative Research*, 7(3): 301–15.

Gabb J (2010) Home truths: Ethical issues in family research. *Qualitative Research*, 10(4): 461–78.

Gabriel Y and Connell N (2010) Co-creating stories: Collaborative experiments in storytelling. *Management Learning*, 41(5): 507–23.

Gagnon M (2011) Moving knowledge to action through dissemination and exchange. *Journal of Clinical Epidemiology*, 64: 25–31.

Galasiński D and Kozłowska O (2013) Interacting with a questionnaire: Respondents' constructions of questionnaire completion. *Quality & Quantity*, 47: 3509–20. doi: 10.1007/s11135-012-9733-0

Garcia B, Welford J and Smith B (2016) Using a smartphone app in qualitative research: The good, the bad and the ugly. *Qualitative Research*, 16(5): 508–25. doi:10.1177/1468794115593335

García R, Melgar P and Sordé T in conversation with Cortés L, Santiago C and Santiago S (2013) From refusal to getting involved in Romani research. In: Mertens D, Cram F and Chilisa B (eds) *Indigenous Pathways into Social Research: Voices of a New Generation*. Walnut Creek, CA: Left Coast Press, pp. 367–80.

Gaver B, Dunne T and Pacenti E (1999) Design: Cultural probes. *Interactions*, 6(1): 21–9.

Gerver M (2013) Exceptions to blanket anonymity for the publication of interviews with refugees: African refugees in Israel as a case study. *Research Ethics*, 9(3): 121–39. doi:10.1177/1747016113481176

Gillham B (2008a) *Developing a Questionnaire* (2nd edition). London: Bloomsbury.

REFERENCES

Gillham B (2008b) *Observation Techniques: Structured to Unstructured*. London: Bloomsbury.

Gilligan C and Eddy J (2017) Listening as a path to psychological discovery: An introduction to the Listening Guide. *Perspectives in Medical Education*, 6: 76–81. doi: 10.1007/s40037-017-0335-3

Goldsmith C (2015) *Living Lives, Building Futures: Refugee, Asylum Seeker and Migrant Needs Assessment*. London: Royal Borough of Kingston.

Grant R (1991) The resource-based theory of competitive advantage: Implications for strategy formulation. *California Management Review Spring*, 33(3): 114–35.

Grant A (2019) *Doing Excellent Social Research With Documents: Practical Examples and Guidance for Qualitative Researchers*. Abingdon: Routledge.

Grant M and Booth A (2009) A typology of reviews: An analysis of 14 review types and associated methodologies. *Health Information and Libraries Journal*, 26: 91–108.

Grinyer A (2009) The ethics of the secondary analysis and further use of qualitative data. *Social Research Update*, 56: 1–4. Summer 2009. University of Surrey.

Gu X, Abdel-Aty M, Xiang Q, Cai Q and Yuan J (2019) Utilising UAV video data for in-depth analysis of drivers' crash risk at interchange merging areas. *Accident Analysis and Prevention*, 123: 159–69. doi:10.1016/j.aap.2018.11.010

Gullion J (2018) *Diffractive Ethnography: Social Sciences and the Ontological Turn*. New York, NY: Routledge.

Hackney F, Saunders C, Willett J, Katie H and Griffin I (2020) Stitching a sensibility for sustainable clothing: Quiet activism, affect and community agency. *Journal of Arts & Communities*, 10(1): 35–52. doi:10.1386/jaac_00004_1

Halkier B (2010) Focus groups as social enactments: Integrating interaction and content in the analysis of focus group data. *Qualitative Research*, 10(1): 71–89.

Hamilton S (2009) Money. In: Wallcraft J, Schrank B and Amering M (eds) *Handbook of Service User Involvement in Mental Health Research*. Chichester: Wiley-Blackwell.

Hammersley M (2009) Challenging relativism: The problem of assessment criteria. *Qualitative Inquiry*, 15(1): 3–29.

Hammersley M (2010) Reproducing or constructing: Some questions about transcription in social research. *Qualitative Research*, 10(5): 553–69.

Hammersley M and Traianou A (2012) *Ethics in Qualitative Research: Controversies and Contexts*. London: SAGE.

Harris A (2016) The ethics of researching images found online. In: Warr D, Guillemin M, Cox S and Waycott J (eds) *Ethics and Visual Research Methods: Theory, Methodology and Practice*. New York, NY: Palgrave Macmillan, pp. 61–74.

Harris A and González C (2012) Introduction. In: Gutiérrez y Muhs G, Niemann Y, González G and Harris A (eds) *Presumed Incompetent: The Intersections of Race and Class for Women in Academia*. Boulder, CO: University Press of Colorado.

Harron P (2016) *The Equidistribution of Lattice Shapes of Rings of Integers of Cubic, Quartic, and Quintic Number Fields: An Artist's Rendering*. Ann Arbor, MI: ProQuest LLC.

Hart C (2018) *Doing a Literature Review: Releasing the Research Imagination* (2nd edition). London: SAGE.

Hawkins JE (2018a) The practical utility and suitability of email interviews in qualitative research. *The Qualitative Report*, 23(2): 493–501.

Hawkins JM (2018b) Textual analysis. In: Allen M (ed.) *The SAGE Encyclopedia of Communication Research Methods*. Thousand Oaks, CA: SAGE, pp. 1754–56.

Heath S, Chapman L and the Morgan Centre Sketchers (2018) Observational sketching as method. *International Journal of Social Research Methodology*, 21(6): 731–28. doi: 10.1080/13645579.2018.1484990

Henderson D and Taimina D (2001) Crocheting the hyperbolic plane. *The Mathematical Intelligencer*, 23(2): 17–28.

Henwood KL and Pidgeon NF (1992) Qualitative research and psychological theorizing. *British Journal of Psychology*, 83(1): 97–111.

Hoang JK, McCall J, Dixon AF, Fitzgerald RT and Gaillard F (2015) Using social media to share your radiology research: How effective is a blog post? *Journal of the American College of Radiology*, 12(7): 760–65. doi:10.1016/j.jacr.2015.03.048

Holroyd A and Shercliff E (2020) *Stitching Together: Good Practice Guidelines*. https://stitchingtogether.net/good-practice-guidelines/ (accessed 20 February 2021).

Hughes K and Tarrant A (2020a) An introduction to qualitative secondary analysis. In: Hughes K and Tarrant A (eds) *Qualitative Secondary Analysis*. London: SAGE, pp. 3–18.

Hughes K and Tarrant A (2020b) The ethics of qualitative secondary analysis. In: Hughes K and Tarrant A (eds) *Qualitative Secondary Analysis*. London: SAGE, pp. 37–58.

Inckle K (2015) Promises, promises: Lessons in research ethics from the Belfast project and 'The Rape Tape' case. *Sociological Research Online*, 20(1): 6. doi:10.5153/sro.3570

Irving DR and McCallum J (2020) The World of Cocos Malay music and dance: A documentary film on performing arts in the Cocos (keeling) Islands. *Journal of Music Research Online*, 11: 1–14.

Jackson A and Mazzei L (2012) *Thinking With Theory in Qualitative Research: Viewing Data Across Multiple Perspectives*. Abingdon: Routledge.

Jesson J, Matheson L and Lacey F (2011) *Doing Your Literature Review: Traditional and Systematic Techniques*. London: SAGE.

Jewitt C, Price S and Sedo A (2017) Conceptualising and researching the body in digital contexts: Towards new methodological conversations across the arts and social sciences. *Qualitative Research*, 17(1): 37–53. doi:10.1177/1468794116653036

Johnson J, Adkins D and Chauvin S (2020) Qualitative research in pharmacy education: A review of the quality indicators of rigor in qualitative research. *American Journal of Pharmaceutical Education*, 84(1): 138–46.

Jolivétte A (2015) (ed.) *Research Justice: Methodologies for Social Change*. Bristol: Policy Press.

Jones N, Pincock K, Hamad B, Malachowska A, Youssef S, Alheiwidi S and Odeh K (2020) Ensuring no voices are left behind: The use of digital storytelling and diary writing in times of crisis. In: Kara H and Khoo S (eds) *Researching in the Age of COVID-19*. Vol 2. *Care and Resilience*. Bristol: Policy Press.

Jones P and Osborne T (2020) Gaming and virtual reality in geographical research. In: von Benzon N, Holton M, Wilkinson C and Wilkinson S (eds) *Creative Methods for Human Geographers*. London: SAGE, pp. 285–96.

Joss S, Cook M and Dayot Y (2017) Smart cities: Towards a new citizenship regime? A discourse analysis of the British Smart City Standard. *Journal of Urban Technology*, 24(4): 29–49. doi:10.1080/10630732.2017.1336027

Kaboub F (2008) Positivist paradigm. *Encyclopaedia of Counselling*, 2(2): 343.

Kaniki A (2006) Doing an information search. In: Terre Blanche M, Durrheim K and Painter D (eds) *Research in Practice: Allied Methods for the Social Sciences*. Cape Town: University of Cape Town Press, pp. 18–32.

Kara H (2017) *Research and Evaluation for Busy Students and Practitioners: A Time-Saving Guide*. Bristol: Policy Press.

Kara H (2018) *Research Ethics in the Real World: Euro-Western and Indigenous Perspectives*. Bristol: Policy Press.

Kara H (2020) *Creative Research Methods: A Practical Guide* (2nd edition). Bristol: Policy Press.

Kara H, Lemon N, Mannay D and McPherson M (2021) *Creative Research Methods in Education: Principles and Practices*. Bristol: Policy Press.

Kaufman C (2010) Cross-disciplinary theoretical frameworks: Adding value to research analysis and dissemination. *International Journal of Arts and Sciences*, 3(8): 153–67.

Kende A (2016) Separating social research on activism from social science as activism. *Journal of Social Issues*, 72(2): 399–412. doi:10.1111/josi.12172

Kende A, Hadarics M, Bigazzi S, Boza M, Kunst JR, Lantos NA, Lášticová B, Minescu A, Pivetti M and Urbiola A (2020) The last acceptable prejudice in Europe? Anti-Gypsyism as the obstacle to Roma inclusion. *Group Processes & Intergroup Relations*, 24(3): 1–23. doi:10.1177/1368430220907701

Kenten C (2010) Narrating oneself: Reflections on the use of solicited diaries with diary interviews. *Forum: Qualitative Social Research*, 11(2): Art. 16.

Kingdon C (2005) Reflexivity: Not just a qualitative methodological tool. *British Journal of Midwifery*, 13(10): 622–27.

Kiyimba N and O'Reilly M (2016) The risk of secondary traumatic stress in the qualitative transcription process: A research note. *Qualitative Research*, 16(4): 468–76. doi: 10.1177/1468794115577013

Klassen A, Creswell J, Plano Clark V, Clegg Smith K and Meissner H (2012) Best practices in mixed methods for quality of life research. *Quality of Life Research*, 21(3): 377–80.

Kluge MA, Grant BC, Friend L and Glick L (2010) Seeing is believing: Telling the 'inside' story of a beginning masters athlete through film. *Qualitative Research in Sport and Exercise*, 2(2): 282–92.

Kouritzin S and Nakagawa S (2018) Toward a non-extractive research ethics for trans-cultural, translingual research: Perspectives from the coloniser and the colonised. *Journal of Multilingual and Multicultural Development*, 39(8): 675–87. doi:10.1080/1434632.2018.1427755

Kovach M (2009) *Indigenous Methodologies: Characteristics, Conversations, and Contexts*. Toronto, ON: University of Toronto Press.

Kozinets R (2010) *Netnography: Doing Ethnographic Research Online*. Thousand Oaks, CA: SAGE.

Kramer A, Guillory J and Hancock J (2014) Experimental evidence of massive-scale emotional contagion through social networks. *Psychological and Cognitive Sciences*, 111(24): 8788–90.

Kuntz A (2015) *The Responsible Methodologist: Inquiry, Truth-Telling, and Social Justice*. Walnut Creek, CA: Left Coast Press.

Lambert L (2014) *Research for Indigenous Survival: Indigenous Research Methodologies in the Behavioral Sciences*. Lincoln, NE: University of Nebraska Press.

Lancaster K (1965) The theory of qualitative linear systems. *Econometrica: Journal of the Econometric Society*: 395–408.

Lapadat J (2017) Ethics in autoethnography and collaborative autoethnography. *Qualitative Inquiry*, 23(8): 589–603. doi:10.1177/1077800417704462

Lapum J, Ruttonsha P, Church K, Yau T and David A (2012) Employing the arts in research as an analytical tool and dissemination method. *Qualitative Inquiry*, 18(1): 100–15.

Lazard L and McAvoy J (2020) Doing reflexivity in psychological research: What's the point? What's the practice? *Qualitative Research in Psychology*, 17(2): 159–77. doi:10.1080/14780887.2017.1400144

Leavy P (2009) *Method Meets Art: Arts-Based Research Practice*. New York, NY: Guilford Press.

Leavy P (2017) *Research Design: Quantitative, Qualitative, Mixed Methods, Arts-Based, and Community-Based Participatory Research Approaches*. New York, NY: The Guilford Press.

Leipold S, Feindt P, Winkel G and Keller R (2019) Discourse analysis of environmental policy revisited: Traditions, trends, perspectives. *Journal of Environmental Policy & Planning*, 21(5): 445–63. doi:10.1080/1523908X.2019.1660462

Lemon N and Salmons J (2020) *Reframing and Rethinking Collaboration in Higher Education and Beyond: A Practical Guide for Doctoral Students and Early Career Researchers*. Abingdon: Routledge.

Lenette C (2019) *Arts-Based Methods in Refugee Research: Creating Sanctuary*. Singapore: Springer Nature Singapore Pte Ltd.

Lenza M (2011) Autoethnography and ethnography in criminal justice research and policy development. In: Ekunwe I and Jones R (eds) *Global Perspectives on Re-Entry: Exploring the Challenges Facing Ex-Prisoners*. Finland: Tampere University Press, pp. 146–72.

Lewin K (1944) Constructs in psychology and psychological ecology. *University of Iowa Studies in Child Welfare*, 20: 23–27.

Livesey L (2014) An activist-academic's reflections. In: Wardrop A and Withers D (eds) *The Para-Academic Handbook: A Toolkit for Making, Learning, Creating, Acting*. Bristol: HammerOn Press, pp. 189–205.

Löfström E (2011) 'Does plagiarism mean anything? LOL.' Students' conceptions of writing and citing. *Journal of Academic Ethics*, 9: 257–75.

Lomborg S and Bechmann A (2014) Using APIs for data collection on social media. *The Information Society*, 30(4): 256–65. doi:10.1080/01972243.2014.915276

Luangaram P and Wongwachara W (2017) *More than Words: A Textual Analysis of Monetary Policy Communication*. Discussion Paper No. 54. Puey Ungphakorn Institute for Economic Research.

Lunde Å, Heggen K and Strand R (2013) Knowledge and power: Exploring unproductive interplay between quantitative and qualitative researchers. *Journal of Mixed Methods Research*, 7(2): 197–210. doi:10.1177/1558689812471087

Mackieson P, Shlonsky A and Connolly M (2018) Increasing rigor and reducing bias in qualitative research: A document analysis of parliamentary debates using applied thematic analysis. *Qualitative Social Work*, 18(6): 965–80. doi:10.1177/1473325018786996

Maguire M and Delahunt B (2017) Doing a thematic analysis: A practical, step-by-step guide for learning and teaching scholars. *All Ireland Journal of Higher Education*, 9(3): 3351–514 [sic].

Mainsah H and Proitz L (2019) Notes on technology devices in research: Negotiating field boundaries and relationships. *Qualitative Inquiry*, 25(3): 271–7. doi:10.1177/1077800418806597

Mandlis L (2009) Art installation as method: "fragements" of theory and tape. *Qualitative Inquiry*, 15(8): 1352–72.

Mannay D (2010) Making the familiar strange: Can visual research methods render the familiar setting more perceptible? *Qualitative Research*, 10(1): 91–111.

Markham A (2012) Fabrication as ethical practice: Qualitative inquiry in ambiguous internet contexts. *Information, Communication & Society*, 15(3): 334–53.

Martin G, Currie G and Lockett A (2011) Prospects for knowledge exchange in health policy and management: Institutional and epistemic boundaries. *Journal of Health Services Research and Policy*, 16(4): 211–17.

Martin W, Wharf Higgins J, Pauly B and MacDonald M (2017) "Layers of translation" – evidence literacy in public health practice: A qualitative secondary analysis. *BMC Public Health*, 17: 803. doi:10.1186/s12889-017-4837-z

Mason J (2016) *Qualitative Researching* (3rd edition). London: SAGE.

Matebeni Z (2014) My best participants' informed consent. In: Posel D and Ross F (eds) *Ethical Quandaries in Social Research*. Cape Town: HSRC Press, pp. 111–24.

Maxwell J (2016) Expanding the history and range of mixed methods research. *Journal of Mixed Methods Research*, 10(1): 12–27. doi:10.1177/1558689815571132

Mbuthia G, Olungah C and Ondicho T (2018) Health-seeking pathway and factors leading to delays in tuberculosis diagnosis in West Pokot County, Kenya: A grounded theory study. *PLoS ONE*, 13(11): e0207995. doi:10.1371/journal.pone.0207995

McCormack M, Adams A and Anderson E (2013) Taking to the streets: The benefits of spontaneous methodological innovation in participant recruitment. *Qualitative Research*, 13(2): 228–41.

Merton R (2012/1949) On sociological theories of the middle range. In: Calhoun C, Gerteis J, Moody J, Pfaff S and Virk I (eds) *Classical Sociological Theory*. Chichester: Wiley-Blackwell, pp. 531–43.

Mills C (1959) *The Sociological Imagination*. New York, NY: Oxford University Press.

Mizen P (2005) A little "light work"? Children's images of their labour. *Visual Studies*, 20(2): 124–39.

Moncur W (2013) The emotional wellbeing of researchers: Considerations for practice. Conference paper. Session: Ethics in HCI, at CHI 2013: Changing Perspectives, Paris, France.

Montgomery S (2017) *The Chicago Guide to Communicating Science*. Chicago, IL: University of Chicago Press.

Moodie S (2010) Power, rights, respect and data ownership in academic research with indigenous peoples. *Environmental Research*, 110(8): 818–20. doi:10.1016/j.envres.2010.08.009

Moon K and Blackman D (2014) A guide to understanding social science research for natural scientists. *Conservation Biology*, 28(5): 1167–77. doi:10.111/cobi.12326

Morris M (2008) *Evaluation Ethics for Best Practice: Cases and Commentaries*. New York, NY: The Guilford Press.

Mugumbate J and Chereni A (2019) Using African *Ubuntu* theory in social work with children in Zimbabwe. *African Journal of Social Work*, 9(1): 27–34.

Munté A, Serradell O and Sordé T (2011) From research to policy: Roma participation through communicative organization. *Qualitative Inquiry*, 17(3): 256–66.

Murray R (2011) *How to Write a Thesis* (3rd edition). Maidenhead: Open University Press.

Naik R, Zembe W, Adigun F, Jackson E, Tabana H, Jackson D, Feeley F and Doherty T (2018) What influences linkage to care after home-based HIV counseling and testing? *AIDS and Behavior*, 22(3): pp. 722–32. doi:10.1007/s10461-017-1830-6

Neale B (2013). Adding time into the mix: Stakeholder ethics in qualitative longitudinal research. *Methodological Innovations Online*, 8(2): 6–20.

Neçka E, Grohman M and Słabosz A (2006) *Creativity Studies in Poland*. Cambridge: Cambridge University Press.

New S (1997) The scope of supply chain management research. *Supply Chain Management*, 2(1): 15–22.

Newman W (2013) Mapping as applied research. In: Jarrett C, Kim K-H and Senske N (eds) The Visibility of Research: Proceedings of the 2013 ARCC Spring Research Conference. University of North Carolina at Charlotte, pp. 228–36.

Ngozwana N (2018) Ethical dilemmas in qualitative research methodology: Researcher's reflections. *International Journal of Educational Methodology*, 4(1): 19–28.

Nguyen H, Baldassar L, Wilding R and Krzyowski L (2021) Researching older Vietnam-born migrants at a distance: The role of digital kinning. In: Kara H and Khoo S (eds) *Qualitative and Digital Research Methods in Times of Crisis: Methods, Reflexivity and Ethics*. Bristol: Policy Press.

Noble S (2018) *Algorithms of Oppression: How Search Engines Reinforce Racism*. New York, NY: NYU Press.

Notermans C and Kommers H (2012) Researching religion: The iconographic elicitation method. *Qualitative Research*, 13(5): 608–25. doi:10.1177/1468794112459672

Nyumba T, Wilson K, Derrick C and Mukherjee N (2018) The use of focus group discussion methodology: Insights from two decades of application in conservation. *Methods in Ecology and Evolution*, 9: 20–32. doi:10.1111/2041-210X.12860

O'Brien B, Harris I, Beckman T, Reed D and Cook D (2014) Standards for reporting qualitative research: A synthesis of recommendations. Research report. *Academic Medicine*, 89: 1245–51. doi:10.1097/ACM.0000000000000388

O'Dell T and Willim R (2013) Transcription and the senses. *The Senses and Society*, 8(3): 314–34. doi:10.2752/174589313X13712175020550

Odena O (2013) Using software to tell a trustworthy, convincing and useful story. *International Journal of Social Research Methodology*, 16(5): 355–72.

Oliver M (2019) Activism and the academy: Losing the ideological and material battles. *Disability & Society*, 34 (7–8): 1028–33. doi:10.1080/09687599.2019.1612637

Omona W (2018) Combining grounded theory strategy with soft systems methodology in knowledge management research: An approach. *African Journal of Management Research*, 25: 12–28.

Owton H (2013) Integrating multiple representations: Fighting asthma. *Qualitative Inquiry*, 19(8): 600–3.

Paget D (1987) Verbatim theatre: Oral history and documentary techniques. *New Theatre Quarterly*, 3(12): 317–36.

Pasquinelli C and Trunfio M (2020) Overtouristified cities: An online news media narrative analysis. *Journal of Sustainable Tourism*, 28(11): 1805–24. doi:10.1080/09669582.2020.1760871

Patrick LD (2016) Found poetry: Creating space for imaginative arts-based literacy research writing. *Literacy Research*, 65(1): 384–403.

Patton M (2008) *Utilization-Focused Evaluation*. Thousand Oaks, CA: SAGE.

Pawson R and Tilley N (1998) *Realistic Evaluation*. London: SAGE.

Perry K (2011) Ethics, vulnerability, and speakers of other languages: How university IRBs (do not) speak to research involving refugee participants. *Qualitative Inquiry*, 17(10): 899–912.

Perez C (2019) *Invisible Women: Exposing Data Bias in a World Designed for Men*. London: Vintage.

Petros S (2012) Use of a mixed methods approach to investigate the support needs of older caregivers to family members affected by HIV and AIDS in South Africa. *Journal of Mixed Methods Research*, 6(4): 275–93.

Phillippi J and Lauderdale J (2018) A guide to field notes for qualitative research: Context and conversation. *Qualitative Health Research*, 28(3): 381–8. doi:10.1177/1049732317697102

Phillips L and Bunda T (2018) *Research Through, With and as Storying*. Abingdon: Routledge.

Phillips R and Kara H (2021) *Creative Writing for Social Research: A Practical Guide*. Bristol: Policy Press.

Pickering L and Kara H (2017) Presenting and representing others: Towards an ethics of engagement. *International Journal of Social Research Methodology*, 20(3): 299–309.

Pickler R (2018) Theory use and usefulness in scientific advancement. *Nursing Research*, 67(2): 61–2. doi:10.1097/NNR.0000000000000267

Piper H and Sikes P (2010) All teachers are vulnerable but especially gay teachers: Using composite fictions to protect research participants in pupil–teacher sex-related research. *Qualitative Inquiry*, 16(7): 566–74.

Plant B (2012). Philosophical diversity and disagreement. *Metaphilosophy*, 43(5): 567–591.

Pope C (2010) Talking T-shirts: A visual exploration of youth material culture. *Qualitative Research in Sport and Exercise*, 2(2): 133–52. doi:10.1080/19398441.2010.488023

Portschy J (2020) Times of power, knowledge and critique in the work of Foucault. *Time & Society*, 29(2): 392–419. doi:10.1177/0961463X20911786

Poth C (2021) *Little Quick Fix: Research Ethics*. London: SAGE.

Powell K (2010) Making sense of place: Mapping as a multisensory research method. *Qualitative Inquiry*, 16(7): 539–55.

Prendergast M (2015) Poetic inquiry, 2007–2012: A surrender and catch found poem. *Qualitative Inquiry*, 21(8): 678–85.

Qwul'sih'yah'maht (Robina Anne T) (2015) Honouring the oral traditions of the Ta't Mustimuxw (Ancestors) through storytelling. In: Strega S and Brown L (eds) *Research as Resistance: Revisiting Critical, Indigenous, and Anti-Oppressive Approaches* (2nd edition). Toronto, ON: Canadian Scholars' Press Inc, pp. 177–98.

REFERENCES

Radicchi A, Henckel D and Memmel M (2017) Citizens as smart, active sensors for a quiet and just city. The case of the "open source soundscapes" approach to identify, assess and plan "everyday quiet areas" in cities. *Noise Mapping*, 4: 104–123. doi: 10.1515/noise-2017-0008

Rainford J (2019) *Equal Practices? A Comparative Study of Widening Participation Practices in Pre- and Post-92 Higher Education Institutions.* Doctoral dissertation. Staffordshire University.

Ralph N, Birks M and Chapman Y (2015) The methodological dynamism of grounded theory. *International Journal of Qualitative Methods*, 14(4): 1–6. doi:10.1177/1609406915611576

Ramlo S (2016) Mixed method lessons learned from 80 years of Q methodology. *Journal of Mixed Methods Research*, 10(1): 28–45. doi:10.1177/1558689815610998

Rapport F (2004) Introduction: Shifting sands in qualitative methodology. In: Rapport F (ed.) *New Qualitative Methodologies in Health and Social Care Research*. London: Routledge, pp. 1–17.

Read R, Cooper A, Edelstein H, Sohn J and Levin B (2013) Knowledge mobilisation and utilisation. In: Levin B, Qi J, Edelstein H and Sohn J (eds) *The Impact of Research in Education: An International Perspective*. Bristol: Policy Press, pp. 23–39.

Rhodes C (2009) After reflexivity: Ethics, freedom and the writing of organization studies. *Organization Studies*, 30(6): 653–72. doi:10.1177/0170840609104804

Richardson MJ (2015) Theatre as safe space? Performing intergenerational narratives with men of Irish descent. *Social & Cultural Geography*, 16(6): 615–33.

Ritchie J and Ormston R (2014) The applications of qualitative methods to social research. In: Ritchie J, Lewis J, McNaughton Nicholls C and Ormston R (eds) *Qualitative Research Practice: A Guide for Social Science Students and Researchers* (2nd edition). London: SAGE, pp. 27–46.

Rix E, Wilson S, Sheehan N and Tujague N (2018) Indigenist and decolonizing research methodology. In: Liamputtong P (ed.) *Handbook of Research Methods in Health Social Sciences*. (online pre-print). Singapore: Springer.

Robinson A, Emden C, Croft T, Vosper G, Elder J, Stirling C and Vickers J (2011) Mixed methods data collection in dementia research: A "progressive engagement" approach. *Journal of Mixed Methods Research*, 5(4): 330–44. doi:10/1177/1558689811416940

Robinson S and Mendelson A (2012) A qualitative experiment: Research on mediated meaning construction using a hybrid approach. *Journal of Mixed Methods Research*, 6: 332. doi:10.1177/1558689812444789

Robson C and McCartan K (2016) *Real World Research* (4th edition). Chichester: John Wiley & Sons.

Rodriguez K and Lahman M (2011) Las Comadres: Rendering research as performative. *Qualitative Inquiry*, 17(7): 602–12.

Rooke B (2013) Four pillars of internet research ethics with Web 2.0. *Journal of Academic Ethics*, 11: 265–8.

Rose D, Fleischmann P, Wykes T and Bindman J (2002) *Review of Consumers' Perspectives on Electro Convulsive Therapy*. London: SURE.

Ross K and Call-Cummings M (2020) Reflections on failure: Teaching research methodology. *International Journal of Research & Method in Education*, 43(5): 498–511. doi: 10.1080/1743727X.2020.1719060

Rowsell J (2011) Carrying my family with me: Artifacts as emic perspectives. *Qualitative Research*, 11(3): 331–46. doi:10.1177/1468794111399841

Saldaña J (2015) *Thinking Qualitatively: Methods of Mind*. Thousand Oaks, CA: SAGE.

Saldaña J and Omasta M (2018) *Qualitative Research: Analyzing Life*. Thousand Oaks, CA: SAGE.

Salmons J (2016) *Doing Qualitative Research Online*. Thousand Oaks, CA: SAGE.

SCIE (2007) *Collection of Examples of Service User and Carer Participation in Systematic Reviews*. London: SCIE.

Salmons J and Kara H (2020) *Publishing From Your Doctoral Research: Create and Use a Publication Strategy*. Abingdon: Routledge.

Samuel G, Ahmed W, Kara H, Jessop C, Quinton S and Sanger S (2018) Is it time to re-evaluate the ethics governance of social media research? *Journal of Empirical Research on Human Research Ethics*, 13(4): 452–54. doi:10.1177/1556264618793773

Schembri S and Latimer L (2016) Online brand communities: Constructing and co-constructing brand culture. *Journal of Marketing Management*, 32(7–8): 628–51. doi: 10.1080/0267257X.2015.1117518

Schoneboom A (2010) Project Skive: Can a multimedia art exhibit function as an ethnography of workplace resistance? *Creative Approaches to Research*, 3(1): 3–15.

Schrooten M (2012) Moving ethnography online: Researching Brazilian migrants' online togetherness. *Ethnic and Racial Studies*, 35(10): 1794–809. doi:10.1080/0149870.2012.659271

Scott C (2018) *Elucidating Perceptions of Ageing Through Participatory Drawing: A Phenomenographic Approach*. Doctoral dissertation. University of Brighton.

Seligman M and Csikzentmihalyi M (2000) Positive psychology: An introduction. *American Psychologist*, 55(1): 5–14.

Sen A (1979) *Equality of What? The Tanner Lecture on Human Values*. Stanford University, 22 May 1979.

Seuren L, Wherton J, Greenhalgh T, Cameron D, A'Court C and Shaw S (2020) Physical examinations via video for patients with heart failure: Qualitative study using conversation analysis. *Journal of Medical Internet Research*, 22(2). https://www.jmir.org/2020/2/e16694/ (accessed 12 February 2021).

Shah S and Greer S (2018) Polio monologues: Translating ethnographic text into verbatim theatre. *Qualitative Research*, 18(1): 53–69.

Shanahan M-C (2011) Science blogs as boundary layers: Creating and understanding new writer and reader interactions through science blogging. *Journalism*, 12(7): 903–19.

Shercliff E and Holroyd A (2020) Stitching together: Participatory textile making as an emerging methodological approach to research. *Journal of Arts and Communities*, 10(1): 5–18. doi:10.1386/jaac_00002_1

Sherwood J (2013) An aboriginal health worker's research story. In: Mertens D, Cram F and Chilisa B (eds) *Indigenous Pathways into Social Research: Voices of a New Generation*. Walnut Creek, CA: Left Coast Press, pp. 203–17.

Shimp C (2007) Quantitative behavior analysis and human values. *Behavioural Processes*, 75: 146–55.

Silver C and Lewins A (2014) *Using Software in Qualitative Research: A Step-by-Step Guide* (2nd edition). London: SAGE.

Silverman D (2020) *Interpreting Qualitative Data* (6th edition). London: SAGE.

Simpson A and Smith A (2014) Introduction. In: Simpson A and Smith A (eds) *Theorizing Native Studies*. Durham: Duke University Press.

Simpson P (2016) Stories. In: Broussine M (ed.) *Creative Methods in Organisational Research*. London: SAGE, pp. 92–107.

Sousanis N (2015) *Unflattening*. Cambridge, MA: Harvard University Press.

Smith L (2012) *Decolonizing Methodologies*. London: Zed Books.

Smith E, Gidlow B and Steel G (2012) Engaging adolescent participants in academic research: The use of photo-elicitation interviews to evaluate school based outdoor education programmes. *Qualitative Research*, 12(4): 367–87.

Snyder H (2019) Literature review as a research methodology: An overview and guidelines. *Journal of Business Research*, 104: 333–9. doi:10.1016/j.busres.2019.07.039

Soane J (2019) Out of practice: Theoretical speculations in and out of the business of architecture. *Architectural Design*, 89(3): 48–53.

Sørensen H (2016) "The end of proof"? The integration of different mathematical cultures as experimental mathematics comes of age. In: Larvor B (ed.) *Mathematical Cultures: Trends in the History of Science*. Cham. Springer. doi:10.1007/978-3-319-28582-5_9

Sou G and Cei Douglas J (2019) *After Maria: Everyday Recovery from Disaster*. Manchester: The University of Manchester https://www.hcri.manchester.ac.uk/research/projects/after-maria/

Sou G and Hall S (2021) Communicating crisis research with comics: Representation, process and pedagogy. In: Kara H and Khoo S (eds) *Qualitative and Digital Research Methods in Times of Crisis: Methods, Reflexivity and Ethics*. Bristol: Policy Press.

Stame N (2013) A European evaluation theory tree. In: Alkin M (ed.) *Evaluation Roots: A Wider Perspective of Theorists' Views and Influences* (2nd edition). Thousand Oaks, CA: SAGE, pp. 355–70.

Stark L (2012) *Behind Closed Doors: IRBs and the Making of Ethical Research*. Chicago, IL: The University of Chicago Press.

Stein S (1998) *Solutions for Writers: Practical Craft Techniques for Fiction and Non-fiction*. London: Souvenir Press.

Sternberg R (2006) Introduction. In: Kaufman J and Sternberg R (eds) *The International Handbook of Creativity*. Cambridge: Cambridge University Press, pp. 1–9.

Stockburger I (2015) Stancetaking and the joint construction of zine producer identities in a research interview. *Journal of Sociolinguistics*, 19(2): 222–40.

Stol K-J, Ralph P and Fitzgerald B (2016) Grounded theory in software engineering research: A critical review and guidelines. In: Proceedings of the 38th International Conference on Software Engineering, pp. 120–131.

Storr W (2020) *The Science of Storytelling*. London: William Collins.

Suri H (2011) Purposeful sampling in qualitative research synthesis. *Qualitative research journal*, 11(2): 63–74.

Sutherland L-A (2020) Finding 'hobby' farmers: A 'parish study' methodology for qualitative research. *Sociologia Ruralis*, 60(1): 129–50. doi:10.1111/soru.12262

Sutton B (2011) Playful cards, serious talk: A qualitative research technique to elicit women's embodied experiences. *Qualitative Research*, 11(2): 177–96. doi:10.1177/1468794110394070

Szajnfarber Z and Gralla E (2017) Qualitative methods for engineering systems: Why we need them and how to use them. *System Engineering*, 20: 497–511. doi:10.1002/sys.21412

TCPS2 (2018) *Tri-Council Policy Statement: Ethical Conduct for Research Involving Humans*. Canadian Institutes of Health Research, Natural Sciences and Engineering Research Council of Canada, Social Sciences and Humanities Research Council of Canada.

Thanem T and Knights D (2019) *Embodied Research Methods*. London: SAGE.

Thomas A (2013) The process that led me to become an Indigenous researcher. In: Mertens D, Cram F and Chilisa B (eds) *Indigenous Pathways into Social Research: Voices of a New Generation*. Walnut Creek, CA: Left Coast Press, pp. 41–57.

Thomas G (2016) *How to Do Your Case Study* (2nd edition). London: SAGE.

Thomson L (2018) The guided tour: A research technique for the study of situated, embodied information. *Library Trends*, 66(4): 511–34. doi:10.1353/lib.2018.0015

Thomson P and Kamler B (2016) *Detox Your Writing: Strategies For Doctoral Researchers*. Abingdon: Routledge.

Thornicroft G and Tansella M (2005) Growing recognition of the importance of service user involvement in mental health service planning and evaluation. *Epidemiologia e Psichiatria Sociale*, 14(1): 1–3.

Tie Y, Birks M and Francis K (2019) Grounded theory research: A design framework for novice researchers. *SAGE Open Medicine*, 7: 1–8. doi:10.1177/2052312118822927

Tierney W and Hallett R (2010) In treatment: Writing beneath the surface. *Qualitative Inquiry*, 16(8): 674–84.

REFERENCES

Tight M (2019) *Documentary Research in the Social Sciences*. London: SAGE.

Timmermans S and Tavory I (2012) Theory construction in qualitative research: From grounded theory to abductive analysis. *Sociological Theory*, 30(3): 167–86. doi: 10.1177/0735275112457914

Towers N, Abushaikha I, Ritchie J and Holter A (2020) The impact of phenomenological methodology development in supply chain management research. *Supply Chain Management: An International Journal*, 25(4): 443–56. doi:10.1108/SCM-04-2019-0153

Tracy SJ (2010) Qualitative quality: Eight "big-tent" criteria for excellent qualitative research. *Qualitative Inquiry*, 16(10): 837–51.

Tuck E and Guishard M (2013) Uncollapsing ethics: Racialized sciencism, settler coloniality, and an ethical framework of decolonial participatory action research. In: Kress T, Malott C and Porfilio B (eds) *Challenging Status Quo Retrenchment: New Directions in Critical Research*. Charlotte, NC: Information Age Publishing, pp. 3–27.

Turner D and Price M (2020) 'Resilient when it comes to death': Exploring the significance of bereavement for the well-being of social work students. *Qualitative Social Work*: 1–17. doi:10.1177/14733250020967737

Uprichard E and Dawney L (2019) Data diffraction: Challenging data integration in mixed methods research. *Journal of Mixed Methods Research*, 13(1): 19–32. doi: 10.1177/1558689816674650

van Wyk I (2014) The ethics of dislike in the field. In: Posel D and Ross F (eds) *Ethical Quandaries in Social Research*. Cape Town: HSRC Press, pp. 199–213.

Vaughn ., Jacoby S, Williams T, Guerra T, Thomas N and Richmond T (2012) Digital animation as a method to disseminate research findings to the community using a community-based participatory approach. *American Journal of Community Psychology*, 51(1–2): 30–42.

Velardo S and Elliott S (2018) Prioritising doctoral students' wellbeing in qualitative research. *The Qualitative Report*, 23(2): 311–18.

Walker P (2013) Research in relationship with humans, the spirit world, and the natural world. In: Mertens D, Cram F and Chilisa B (eds) *Indigenous Pathways into Social Research: Voices of a New Generation*. Walnut Creek, CA: Left Coast Press, pp. 299–316.

Walter M and Andersen C (2013) *Indigenous Statistics: A Quantitative Research Methodology*. Routledge: Left Coast Press/Abingdon.

Walter M and Andersen C (2016) *Indigenous Statistics: A Quantitative Research Methodology*. Abingdon: Routledge.

Warren J (2014) *Music and Ethical Responsibility*. Cambridge: Cambridge University Press.

Watson C (2011) Staking a small claim for fictional narratives in social and educational research. *Qualitative Research*, 11(4): 395–408. doi:10.1177/1468794111404317

Weeks S (2014) Insider, outsider: Marriage proposals, advocacy and other ethical quandaries in law and society research. In: Posel D and Ross F (eds) *Ethical Quandaries in Social Research*. Cape Town: HSRC Press, pp. 140–52.

Whitney D and Trosten-Bloom A (2010) *The Power of Appreciative Inquiry: A Practical Guide to Positive Change* (2nd edition). Oakland, CA: Berrett-Koehler Publishers, Inc.

Wibeck V, Hansson A, Anshelm J, Asayama S, Dilling L, Feetham P, Hauser R, Ishii A and Sugiyama M (2017) Making sense of climate engineering: A focus group study of lay publics in four countries. *Climatic Change*, 145: 1–14. doi:10.1007/sl0584-017-2067-0

Willis R (2019) The use of composite narratives to present interview findings. *Qualitative Research*, 19(4): 471–80. doi:10.1177/1468794118787711

Willox A, Harper S and Edge V (2013) Storytelling in a digital age: Digital storytelling as an emerging narrative method for preserving and promoting indigenous oral wisdom. *Qualitative Research*, 13(2): 127–47. doi:10.1177/1468794112446105

Wilson S (2008) *Research is Ceremony: Indigenous Research Methods*. Halifax and Winnipeg: Fernwood Publishing.

Woodyatt C, Finneran C and Stephenson R (2016) In-person versus online focus group discussions: A comparative analysis of data quality. *Qualitative Health Research*, 26(6): 741–49. doi:10.1177/1049732316631510

Wright N and Larsen V (2012) Every brick tells a story: Study abroad as an extraordinary experience. *Marketing Education Review*, 22(2): 121–42. doi:10.2753/MER1052-8008220203

Xie N, Kalia K, Strudwick G and Lau F (2019) Understanding mental health nurses' perceptions of barcode medication administration: A qualitative descriptive study. *Issues in Mental Health Nursing*, 40(4): 326–34. doi:10.1080/01612840.2018.1528321

Yin R (2018) *Case Study Research and Applications: Design and Methods* (6th edition). London: SAGE.

Zarhin D (2018) Conducting joint interviews with couples: Ethical and methodological challenges. *Qualitative Health Research*, 28(5): 844–54. doi:10.1177/1049732317749196

INDEX